DAVE BARRY'S

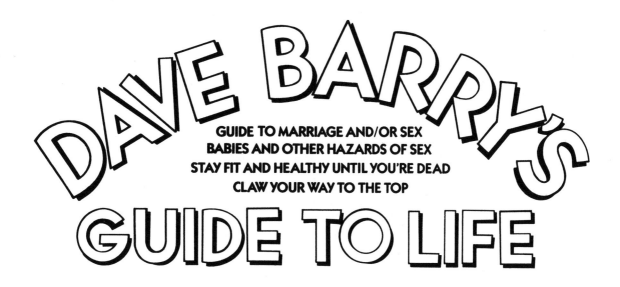

GUIDE TO MARRIAGE AND/OR SEX
BABIES AND OTHER HAZARDS OF SEX
STAY FIT AND HEALTHY UNTIL YOU'RE DEAD
CLAW YOUR WAY TO THE TOP

GUIDE TO LIFE

by Dave Barry

Illustrated by Jerry O'Brien

WINGS BOOKS

NEW YORK • AVENEL, NEW JERSEY

This edition is published by Wings Books,
distributed by Random House Value Publishing, Inc.,
40 Engelhard Avenue, Avenel, New Jersey 07001,
by arrangement with Rodale Press, Inc.

Random House
New York • Toronto • London • Sydney • Auckland

Printed and bound in the United States of America

Library of Congress Cataloging-in-Publication Data
Barry, Dave.
Dave Barry's guide to life.
p.   cm.
Contains the complete and unabridged texts of: Dave Barry's guide
to marriage and/or sex, Babies and other hazards of sex, Stay fit
and healthy until you're dead, and Claw your way to the top.
ISBN 0-517-06486-3
1. Life—Humor.   2. American wit and humor.   I. Title.
PN6231.L48B3 1991   91-16577
818'.5402—dc20   CIP
ISBN 0-517-06486-3

15 14 13 12 11 10 9

Dave Barry's Guide to
MARRIAGE
AND/OR SEX

Contents

Introduction... page **ix**

Chapter 1 **How to Find Somebody to Go on Dates with and Eventually Get Married to Who Is Not a Total Jerk** .... page **1**

Chapter 2 **Living in Sin** .... page **13**

Chapter 3 **A Frank, Mature, Sensitive, and Caring Discussion of Human Sexuality with Dirty Pictures** .... page **21**

Chapter 4 **Breaking Up or Getting Engaged** .... page **32**

Chapter 5 **Important Prenuptial Chapter** .... page **39**

Chapter 6 **How to Have a Perfect Wedding No Matter What** ... page **42**

Chapter 7 **Newlywed Finances** .... page **59**

Chapter 8 **How to Argue Like a Veteran Married Couple** .... page **65**

Chapter 9 **Children: Big Mistake, or Bad Idea?** .... page **69**

Chapter 10 **How to Have an Affair** .... page **76**

Chapter 11 **How to Put New Life into Your Marriage or Else Get a Divorce** .... page **80**

Index .... page **88**

MAKE SURE YOUR MARRIAGE PROPOSAL IS DONE WITH CREATIVITY

HOWEVER, MAKE SURE THAT YOU KNOW YOUR SWEETHEART REAL GOOD

Introduction

Marriage is a wonderful thing. Everybody should get married unless he or she has a good reason not to, such as that he or she is the Pope. I personally have been married two times that I know of, and you don't hear me complaining.

What's the secret of a happy marriage? Call me a romantic if you want, but for me, the answer is the same simple, beautiful idea that has been making relationships work for thousands of years: separate bathrooms. You give two people room to spread out their toiletry articles, and you have the basis of a long-term relationship. But you make them perform their personal hygiene activities in the same small enclosed space, year in and year out, constantly finding the other person's bodily hairs stuck on their deodorant sticks, and I don't care how loving they were when they started out. I don't care if they were Ozzie and Harriet. They'll be slipping strychnine into each other's non-dairy creamer.

Of course even an ideal marriage, even a marriage where the bathrooms are 75 feet apart, is going to have a certain amount of conflict. This is because marriages generally involve males and females, which are not called "opposite sexes" for nothing.

Why Men and Women Have Trouble Getting Along

At the risk of generalizing, I would say that the basic problem can be summarized as follows:

WHAT WOMEN WANT: To be loved, to be listened to, to be desired, to be respected, to be needed, to be trusted, and sometimes, just to be held.

WHAT MEN WANT: Tickets for the World Series.

So we can see that men and women do not have exactly the same objectives in mind. Which is why, as a rule, the only time you see two people of the opposite sex who have achieved true long-term stability in a marriage is when at least one of them is in a coma.

This is strange, when you think about it. I mean, look around at the other species. Most of them are much stupider than humans are, not counting humans who pay to watch automobile races, yet they have their male-female relationships all worked out. Take squids. Squids may have tiny little brains, but they know exactly how to have relationships. The female squid goes into heat at exactly the right time, and all the male squids come around and wave their tentacles in exactly the most attractive way, and she picks out the one with the biggest suckers, or whatever and they mate. And they know exactly *how* to mate, the same way that squids have been mating for 46 million years, without any kind of formal instruction whatsoever.

Wouldn't that be great? I don't mean having sex with a squid. I don't recommend that unless you get truly desperate (see "The Singles Scene," in Chapter 1). I mean having everything all worked out between the sexes; having a *procedure,* where everybody knew what to do and what to expect, and nobody ever felt guilty or inadequate.

Yet here *we* are, humans, the most sophisticated species on Earth, having evolved over the course of millions of years to the point where many of us have satellite dishes on our lawns, and we have less savvy, in terms of our relationships, than invertebrates.

People say: "Well, if you want a marriage to succeed, you have to work at it." And I say: *Why?* It isn't fair! The other species don't have to work at it! They don't even have to *think* about it! Can you imagine a female snake agoniz-

TRUE LOVE

ing about why a male snake never pays attention to her? Or a male cockroach nervously asking a female, after sex, if it was Good for her? Of course you can't! Cockroaches can't talk! But you know what I mean. I mean we have a problem here.

To date, the efforts to solve this problem have consisted mainly of articles in women's magazines, the ones that always have the following general lineup of articles:

21 Fun Drapery Possibilities
5 Common Mascara Blunders
10 Quick and Easy
        Mayonnaise-Based Entrees
14 Ways to Tell If Your Child
        Is Shooting Up
11 Exciting Pudding Concepts
6 New and Extremely Dense
        Chocolate Desserts
147 Weight-Loss Ideas

Somewhere in there they always have an article with a title like "12 Tips for Getting Some Quantity of Romance Back into Your Marriage," featuring advice such as: "TIP NUMBER THREE: Try not to blow your nose during sex."

These articles are fine, except for one thing: Men don't read them. Men read the sports section, or action adventure novels where the main characters are males who relate to each other primarily via automatic weapons. True, sometimes there are women in these novels, but only for the purpose of having firm breasts.

Clearly what is needed is some kind of book that women *and* men would want to read, a book that could bring the sexes together and help them reach some common ground by means of a straight-forward, common-sense discussion of all aspects of finding the right mate, falling in love with this person, getting married, and living happily ever after. This was exactly my goal, when I set out to write this book. Unfortunately, as you'll see, I failed completely, but what the hell— you already bought the book, so you might as well read it.

A Thoughtful Word of Advice Before You Get Started

You cannot have a successful relationship just by reading this book. For a relationship to succeed, both parties must be willing to work. Work, work, work, that's the key. Endless, constant, extremely difficult, unpaid work. More work than is involved in the construction of major bridges and tunnels. I am getting very tired just thinking about it.

Also there will be hard times along the way. Awful times. Terrible, horrible times. That is why this book includes helpful advice such as in Chapter 3, where we talk about adding zip to your sex life via Saran Wrap and other common household products, and also how to recognize the warning signs that your spouse is having an affair, and what kind of gun you should buy.

But we're getting ahead of ourselves. First you have to meet somebody.

CHAPTER 1

How to Find Somebody to Go on Dates with and Eventually Get Married to Who Is Not a Total Jerk

In getting into the field of marriage, one very important decision you must make is who, exactly, will be your spouse. I am not saying this is the *most* important decision. It is certainly not as important as selecting the right wedding caterer (see Chapter 6, "How to Have a Perfect Wedding No Matter What"). But you should definitely give it some thought.

To know where to look for a marriage partner, you need to know what kind of person you want. For example, if you want to meet a person who likes to bowl, you would go to a bowling alley; whereas if you want to meet a person who is rich, sensitive, attractive, and intelligent, you would not. So your first step is to scientifically develop a "psychological profile" of your Ideal Mate.

How to Develop A Psychological Profile of Your Ideal Mate

Choose the phrase that you feel best completes the sentences below:

Wealth

The person I wish to have for a mate should be able to afford:

1. Scotland.
2. Occasional dinners out.
3. Underwear.

Sensitivity

The person I wish to have for a mate should be sensitive enough to:

1. Instantly be aware of my every mood.
2. Swerve to avoid driving over pedestrians.
3. Not deliberately back up and run over pedestrians a second time.

Personal Appearance

The person I wish to have for a mate should be attractive enough to:

1. Be a movie star.
2. Be a movie star's accountant.
3. Be a movie star's accountant's intestinal parasite.

Intelligence

The person I wish to have for a mate should be smart enough to:

1. Discuss great works of literature.
2. Hold great works of literature right side up.
3. Differentiate between great works of literature and food.

HOW TO SCORE: Add up the numbers corresponding to your answers, then check the chart below.

IF YOUR ANSWERS TOTAL . . .	YOU'RE MOST LIKELY TO FIND YOUR IDEAL MATE . . .
1 through 8	Married to somebody else.
9 through 15	Engaged to somebody else.
16	In prison.

Okay! Now that you have a good idea of what you're looking for, it's time to get out and join . . .

The Singles Scene

The Singles Scene is located in bars that are so dark and loud it's impossible to see or hear anybody else. You can meet, fall in love, and get engaged without ever getting a clear view of the other person, which can lead to a situation where you arrive at your wedding, with all your friends and relatives, and you discover that you are betrothed to a cigarette machine. (Which actually may not seem like such a total disaster, once you find out what else is available on the Singles Scene.)

To avoid this kind of embarrassment, you should do what other smart singles do: Before you sit down, go around the room discreetly shining a police flashlight into the other singles' faces. Once you have selected a likely looking one, you should sit down near this person and get into a spontaneous conversation.

How to Get into
A Spontaneous Conversation

In the old days, the way people got into conversations was the woman would take a cigarette out of her purse and pretend to look for a match, which was the signal for six or seven available lurking men to lunge toward her, Zippos flaming, sometimes causing severe burns.

Smoking, however, has pretty much lost its glamor, to the point where trying to get a strange male to light your cigarette in public would be viewed as comparable to trying to get him to pick your nose. Which is a shame, really, because men are deprived of the chance to feel bold and masculine and necessary in the hostile bar environment. It would be nice if we had a modern bar-meeting ritual. Like maybe the woman could come in with a jar of relish, and she could sit there pretending she couldn't get the lid off, and the man could come along and offer to help, and soon they would be engrossed in a fascinating conversation. ("Are you fond of relish? Huh! I am fond of relish myself!")

But for now, we are stuck with the system where one party has to boldly walk right up to the other party and, with no real excuse, attempt to start a conversation. At one time this was strictly the man's responsibility, but now, what with Women's Liberation, it is still strictly the man's responsibility.

Men, this is nothing to be nervous about. After all, why do you think the woman came to a singles bar, if not to

KNOW YOUR SINGLES BARS!

WHICH DIMLY LIT, CROWDED SINGLES BAR WOULD BE YOUR BEST BET TO FIND A DATE IN?

ANSWER: BAR "A" IS YOUR BEST BET, UNLESS YOU ALREADY HAVE A VENEREAL DISEASE

WHAT YOU HOPE TO FIND IN A SINGLES BAR

GREAT LOOKING GUYS

GREAT LOOKING GIRLS

WHAT IS ACTUALLY AVAILABLE

meet a guy like you, only smarter and more attractive? So go to it!

The trick is to know some good "opening lines" that are guaranteed to get a woman's attention and make her realize you are a caring and sharing kind of guy who has things on his mind such as international politics and great literature, and who doesn't just want to grope her body.

Some Good Opening Lines

• "How about those problems in the Middle East?"
• "How about those Brothers Karamazov?"
• "I don't just want to grope your body. I mean, not here in the bar."

What the Woman Should Do If She Is Not Interested

She should attempt to fend the male off via one of the following gently tactful yet firm statements:
• "Haha HA HA HA (cough cough cough) (spit)."
• "I'm sorry, but I just washed my hair."
• "I'm sorry, but unfortunately you hold no more physical attraction for

me than those photographs you sometimes see of a cold virus magnified several million times."

If subtlety doesn't work, if the man turns out to be the type who views himself as such an extreme Stud Muffin that he cannot imagine a woman who would not want to conceive a child via him, then the woman should take a more direct approach, such as Mace.

Meeting People through Personal Ads

These are those little paid advertisements that people take out in magazines or newspapers. A lot of people laugh at these ads, but in fact this is the way top stars such as Johnny Carson and Joan Collins get most of their spouses.

If you want your ad to be effective, however, it must have certain characteristics:

1. *It should say you are profoundly attractive.* Nobody in the personal ads, nobody, is ever "average-looking." If, for example, you had Elephant Man's Disease, you would describe yourself as "rugged."

2. *It should be extremely specific.* For example, if you're a man, you don't just say you're looking for "a nice

SWM – RUGGED NON-SMOKER, NON-DRINKER, NON-SWEARER, 30-YEAR-OLD CHRISTIAN WITH A WONDERFUL SENSE OF HUMOR SEEKS A SWF, SBF, SHF, OR SINGLE FEMALE OF ANY RACE OR SPECIES FOR LOVE, COMPANIONSHIP, AND ROMANTIC STROLLS IN THE MOONLIGHT ALONG THE BEACH. ALSO MUST ENJOY THE FINER THINGS IN LIFE: BOWLING, GOLF, POLKAS, BINGO, AND LOTS OF RAW UNINHIBITED SEX. NO ACCOUNTANTS OR TEXANS, PLEASE.

RESPOND TO NO. 147A

147A

woman." You say you're looking for "a 5′8″ 23-year-old blonde Capricorn woman of Croatian ancestry weighing 109 pounds and having a degree in cultural anthropology from Duke University." This lets everybody know you are in a position to pick and choose, and not some semi-desperate schlump who has to advertise for dates.

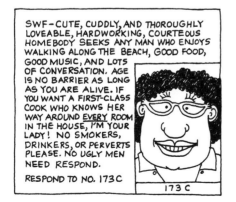

SWF – CUTE, CUDDLY, AND THOROUGHLY LOVEABLE, HARDWORKING, COURTEOUS HOMEBODY SEEKS ANY MAN WHO ENJOYS WALKING ALONG THE BEACH, GOOD FOOD, GOOD MUSIC, AND LOTS OF CONVERSATION. AGE IS NO BARRIER AS LONG AS YOU ARE ALIVE. IF YOU WANT A FIRST-CLASS COOK WHO KNOWS HER WAY AROUND <u>EVERY</u> ROOM IN THE HOUSE, I'M YOUR LADY! NO SMOKERS, DRINKERS, OR PERVERTS PLEASE. NO UGLY MEN NEED RESPOND.

RESPOND TO NO. 173C

173 C

3. *It should say you like "candlelight dinners and long walks on the beach."* All personal classified ads contain this phrase, not because anybody really *wants* to take long walks on the beach, but because people want to prove they're Romantic and Sensitive. The beaches of America are teeming with couples who met because of personal ads, staggering along, sweating, and picking sea-urchin spines out of their feet, each person afraid to reveal to the other that he or she would rather be watching a rental movie.

Meeting People through Clubs and Organizations

Often it seems that the happiest marriages are the ones where the man and the woman share an interest in a hobby, like bass fishing. Because of this shared interest, such couples can pass countless intimate hours together, talking bait, plus they can use their vacation time to go on long fishing trips to secluded wilderness areas where they will find time to just be alone together, hour after hour, day after day, on some scum-encrusted, mosquito-infested lake, totally

FISHIN'

alone, until finally one of them disembowels the other with a scaling knife.

To get into a relationship like this, you need to develop an interest, preferably one that does not involve sharp implements, and go hang out with other people who have the same interest. Let's say, for example, that you have an interest in cats. Now I, personally, cannot imagine having any interest in cats other than to find out what happens when you submerge them for various lengths of time in roofing cement, but I am sure there are lots of formal pro-cat organizations in your area, which you could locate by asking a police officer. Go to their meetings and survey the crowd until you find a likely prospect to strike up a conversation with ("Hi! I see we share an interest in cats! Perhaps we should get married!").

If this doesn't work, you might try stamp collectors, or one of your major churches.

Meeting People at the Office

If you get an office job, you'll be involved in a serious relationship within a matter of days. This is the good news. The bad news is, this relationship will probably involve a person who is technically already married to somebody else. This is because, to a married person, the office is a highly romantic environment, where everybody wears nice clothes and discusses important issues such as the Three-Month Sales Forecast, in stark contrast to the home environment, where people tend to wear bathrobes with jelly stains on them and get into vicious day-long arguments over who put the ice tray back in the refrigerator with a dead roach in it (see Chapter 8, "How to Argue Like a Veteran Married Couple"). So the office becomes essentially a large, carpeted pit of illicit passion, where at least two-thirds of the activity is related to motel arrangements.

Whatever method you use to meet somebody, your next step is to go on a number (174) of dates so you can get to know what this person is really like.

Tips for Gals: 13 Common First-Date Warning Signs That a Guy Might Be a Jerk

1. He brings his mom.
2. He smells bad.
3. He smells a little too good.
4. He proudly carries the American Express Platinum Card.
5. He periodically blows his nose elaborately into a handkerchief, then folds it up carefully and puts it back into his pocket as though it was some kind of valuable artifact.
6. He wants to take you to a hockey game.
7. He wants to know if you know how to clean fish.
8. He always calls the waitress "Sweets."
9. He manages to let you know how much money he makes by some contrivance such as pulling a piece of paper out of his pocket and saying: "I'll be darned! Here's my W-2 form!"
10. He wears wing-tip shoes when he doesn't have to.
11. He has pictures of his car.
12. He has a personalized license plate on his car.
13. He has motivational cassette tapes in his car.

Dating

"Dating" simply means "going out with a potential mate and doing a lot of fun things that the two of you will never do again if you actually get married." Dating is a very important part of the mate-selection process throughout all of nature. Some sectors of nature, such as insects, date for only a few seconds; birds, on the other hand, perform an elaborate Dating Dance. In fact, dancing is all that

WHICH GUY IS THE JERK? WHICH GUY IS THE ACCOUNTANT? WHICH GUY IS THE MILLIONAIRE?

ANSWER: MR. B IS ALL THREE: A MILLIONAIRE ACCOUNTANT JERK. THE OTHER THREE ARE SLIME.

birds *can* do, because in order to make it possible for them to fly, they cannot have sexual organs, which is why we have to import flocks of new birds from Canada every year.

Human beings dated as far back as ancient times, as is shown by the biblical quotation: "And Balzubio DID taketh Parasheeba to a restaurant, and they DID eateth potato skins." The next recorded date was between Romeo and Juliet, a young Italian couple who went out despite their parents' objections, and just about everybody involved ended up either stabbed or poisoned.

After this tragedy, there was very little dating for several centuries. During this time, marriages were arranged by the parents, based on such things as how much cattle the bride and the groom would each bring to the union. Often the young couple wouldn't even *meet* until the wedding, and sometimes they were not strongly attracted to each other. Sometimes, quite frankly, they preferred the cattle. So now we feel that dating is probably a better system.

Who Should Ask Whom for the Date

As we noted earlier, these are free and liberated and nonstereotypical times we live in, by which I mean it is the responsibility of the man to ask for the date, and the responsibility of the woman to think up excuses that get progressively more obvious until the man figures out that the woman would rather chew on a rat pancreas.

FAMOUS COUPLES THROUGHOUT HISTORY

THE WIZARD OF OZ AND DOROTHY

SAMSON AND DELILAH

TARZAN AND CHEETAH

ROMEO AND JULIET

Four Fun Things to Do on a Date

1. Go to a restaurant and have something to eat.

2. Go to a restaurant and have a completely different thing to eat.

3. Go to a completely different restaurant.

4. Go to visit interesting places such as New York and Europe and see if they have any restaurants.

Things You Can Talk About on a Date

1. Your various entrees.

Falling in Love

When two people have been on enough dates, they generally fall in love. You can tell you're in love by the way you feel: your head becomes light, your heart leaps within you, you feel like you're walking on air, and the whole world seems like a wonderful and happy place. Unfortunately these are also the four warning signs of colon disease, so it's always a good idea to check with your doctor.

But if it turns out to be love, it's time to think about taking the next major step in a relationship: French-kissing.

Ha ha! Just kidding. The next major step is to live in Sin, which we will

THE WORLD RECORD FOR MOST DATES IN ONE YEAR IS HELD BY NORMA LEE JOHNSON OF LAS VEGAS, NEVADA. IN 1986 SHE DATED 7,413 MEN.

cover in the next chapter. Of course if you belong to a religious sect that believes that a couple should get married first, you should skip the next chapter and go straight to the one about sex, unless it is a very strict religious sect, in which case you should burn this book immediately.

CHAPTER 2

Living in Sin

For many years, it was generally considered to be wrong to live in Sin. Now, however, thanks to the Sexual Revolution (May 6, 1967), living together is considered a normal and in fact very useful phase in a relationship, a phase that is accepted and even endorsed by virtually all sectors of society except of course your parents. Your parents hate it. It doesn't matter how nice or respectable the person is you're living with. You could be living with Abraham Lincoln, and your parents would still hate it. Especially if you are a guy.

But, hey, it's your life to live, and if you really want to move in with somebody, your feelings have to take precedence over your parents'. The best thing to do is confront their concerns head-on, by sitting down with them, face to face, and lying.

"Mom and Dad," you should say,

"Bill and I are *not* living together. He came over to my apartment this morning to help me kill a spider and by mistake he left his toothbrush and all his clothes and furniture."

Your parents will pretend they believe you, because the truth is they really don't want to even think about the idea of you and S-E-X. All parents are like this. No matter how old you get, in their minds you will always have the wisdom and emotional maturity of Beaver Cleaver.

Moving in Together

Moving in together is an exciting and romantic adventure for both of you, a time of caring and sharing the joys of little discoveries such as what another person's used dental floss looks like. But this is also a time when you must try to be practical. You must bear in mind that no matter how much you love each other now, somewhere down the road you will inevitably have traditional "lovers' quarrels" wherein one of you will hurl all of the other one's possessions out the window and possibly kill an innocent pedestrian. This is why most experts recommend that you get a ground-floor apartment furnished mainly with lightweight, easy-to-hurl Tupperware.

The Most Serious Issue Likely to Come between a Man and a Woman Living Together

(WARNING: Those of you who detest blatant and unfair but nonetheless generally true sexual stereotypes should leave the room at this time.)

Okay. The major issue facing a man and a woman who decide to live together is: Dirt. I am serious. Men and women do not feel the same way about dirt at all. Men and women don't even *see* dirt the same way. Women, for some hormonal reason, can see individual dirt molecules, whereas men tend not to notice them until they join together into clumps large enough to support commercial agriculture. There are exceptions, but over 85 percent of all males are legally classifiable as Cleaning Impaired.

This can lead to serious problems in a relationship. Let's say a couple has decided to divide up the housework absolutely even-steven. Now when it's the woman's turn to clean, say, the bathroom, she will go in there and actually clean it. The man, on the other hand, when it's his turn, will look around, and, because he is incapable of seeing the dirt, will figure nothing major is called for, so

LIVING TOGETHER DEMANDS SOME PREPLANNING

he'll maybe flush the toilet and let it go at that. Then the woman will say: "Why didn't you clean the bathroom? It's *filthy!*" And the man, whose concept of "filthy" comes from the men's rooms in bars, where you frequently see bacteria the size of cocker spaniels frisking around, will have no idea what she's talking about.

So what happens in most relationships is, the man learns to go through the motions of cleaning. Ask him to clean a room, and he'll squirt Windex around seemingly at random, then run the vacuum cleaner over the carpet, totally oblivious to the question of whether or not it's picking up any dirt.

I have a writer friend, Clint Collins, who once proposed that, as a quick "touch-up" measure, you could cut a piece of two-by-four the same width as the vacuum cleaner and drag it across the carpet to produce those little parallel tracks, which as far as Clint could tell were the major result of vacuuming. (Clint was also unaware for the first 10 or 15 years of his marriage that vacuum cleaners had little bags in them; he speculated that the dirt went through the electrical cord and into the wall.)

What this means is that, if your live-together relationship is going to work, both of you must be sensitive to the special needs of the Cleaning Impaired. Unfortunately for you women, this means you must spend many hours patiently going over basic cleaning concepts that may seem simple and obvious to you, but will be baffling mysteries to the Cleaning Impaired person, such as:

1. Where clean dishes actually come from.

2. What you can do with used pizza boxes besides stack them in the corner of the living room for upwards of two years.

3. How some people do more in the way of cleaning the bedroom than simply spray a few blasts of Right Guard deodorant on the two-foot-high mound of unlaundered jockey shorts.

And so on. The best way to avoid conflict is if you make up lists that state clearly what cleaning chores each of you will be responsible for. At first, the Cleaning Impaired person's list should be fairly modest:

NORMAL PERSON'S WEEKLY CHORE LIST	CLEANING IMPAIRED PERSON'S WEEKLY CHORE LIST
1. Clean kitchen. 2. Clean bathroom. 3. Clean entire rest of domicile.	1. Don't get peanut butter on sheets.

Speaking of peanut butter, another area where a first-time live-together couple can run into trouble is the kitchen. Here again we need to confront the depressing fact that, despite all the progress that has been made in other areas, such as coeducational softball, when it comes to sharing equally in food-preparation responsibilities, many men are still basically scumballs. I know I am. This was driven home to me on a recent Thanksgiving day, when my family had dinner at the home of friends named Arlene and Gene.

Picture a typical Thanksgiving scene: on the floor, three small children and a dog who long ago had her brain eaten by fleas are running as fast as they can directly into things, trying to injure themselves. On the television, the Detroit Lions are doing pretty much the same thing. In the kitchen, Arlene, a prosecuting attorney responsible for a large staff, is doing something to a turkey. Surrounding Arlene are thousands of steaming cooking containers. I would no more enter that kitchen than I would attempt to park a nuclear aircraft carrier, but my wife, who runs her own business, glides in very casually and picks up exactly the right kitchen implement and starts doing exactly the right thing without receiving any instructions whatsoever. She quickly becomes enshrouded in steam.

So Gene and I, feeling guilty, finally bumble over and ask what we can do to help, and from behind the steam comes Arlene's patient voice asking us to please keep an eye on the children. Which we try to do. But there is a famous law of physics that goes, "You cannot watch small children and the Detroit Lions at the same time, and let's face it, the Detroit Lions are more interesting." So we would start out watching the children, and then one of us would sneak a peek at the TV and say, "Hey! Look at this tackle!" And then we'd have to watch the Instant Replay to find out whether the tackled person was dead or just permanently disabled. By then the children would have succeeded in injuring themselves or the dog, and this voice from behind the kitchen steam would call, very patiently, "Gene, *please* watch the children."

I realize this is awful. I realize this sounds just like Ozzie and Harriet. I also realize that there are some males out there, with hyphenated last names, who have evolved much further than Gene and I have, who are not afraid to stay home full-time and get coated with baby vomit while their wives work as test pilots, and who go into the kitchen on a daily basis to prepare food for other people, as opposed to going in there primarily for beer. But I think Gene and I are more typical. I think most males rarely prepare food for others, and when

GENE AND DAVE WATCH TRANSFIXED WHILE FIDO DANCES FOR THE KIDS

they do, they have their one specialty dish (spaghetti, in my case) that they prepare maybe twice a year in a very elaborate production number, for which they expect to be praised as if they had developed, right there in the kitchen, a cure for heart disease.

What Men Have to Do about This

It's very simple, men. If you want to have a decent and fair live-together relationship, you have to start cooking whole entire meals all by yourself on a regular basis. And by "meals," men, I do not mean "Kraft Cheez Whiz eaten directly from the jar with a spoon." I mean meals that somebody *else* would eat. That even your *mom* would eat.

This is not as hard as you think, men. All you need to do is learn some "recipes."

Recipes for Guys

Recipe Number One: Food Heated Up

This dish has long been a specialty of women and the great chefs of Europe, who have learned that, with a few exceptions, such as grape soda, almost all food tastes better when you heat it up. In fact some foods, such as baked potatoes, are very hard to eat any other way.

TO PREPARE: Get enough units of food to feed yourself and the person you are living with. Now select a pot that you feel is the correct size. Now put this pot back and select another one, because the one you selected first was wrong. (Trust me here, guys. In 15 years, I have never once selected an initial pot that my wife did not feel, based on her vastly superior experience and hormonal instinct, was the wrong size.)

Okay. Now try to put the food unit inside the pot. (CULINARY HINT: For extra elegance, try removing the food unit from its can or wrapper first!) If it fits, cook it on top of the stove on "medium" heat until just before it overflows the top and wrecks the stove. If it doesn't fit into the pot, it's probably a turkey, a roast, or a ham, which you can tell by counting the number of legs and referring to this convenient chart:

FOOD TYPE	NUMBER OF LEGS	COOKING TEMPERATURE
Turkey	2	medium
Roast	0	medium
Ham	0	medium

These larger foods should be placed inside the little room under the stove (the "oven") and cooked on "medium" heat until just before they fill the entire dwelling area with dense acrid smoke.

IMPORTANT NOTE: If the food unit is, in fact, a turkey, be sure to check inside and remove the traditional Surprise Packet of yuckola blobs that is always found in the interiors of deceased frozen turkeys for reasons that nobody can really explain. One theory is that it is placed there as a protest by dissatisfied workers at the turkey manufacturing plant. A more plausible theory is that the blobs are actually dormant baby turkeys. Most savvy chefs immediately throw them into the garbage or flush them down the toilet, which incidentally is how there came to be giant albino turkeys in the New York City sewer system whose only natural enemies are the alligators.

Recipe Number Two: Two Kinds of Food in the Same Meal

Yes! This really is possible! In fact, your extremely advanced chefs will sometimes serve as many as *three* kinds of food, although I do not recommend that you attempt this yourself.

TO PREPARE: Follow the recipe for Food Heated Up, except use *two* food units, *two* pots, *two* stoves, etc. The trick is to select foods that "complement" each other, as illustrated by the following chart:

Okay. We've covered the two biggest potential problem areas involved in living together, namely dirt and food. This leaves sex, which in the interest of decency we will put in a separate chapter.

TYPE OF FOOD	COMPLEMENTS	DOES NOT COMPLEMENT
Meat	Ketchup, beer	Meat
Foods from cans (beets, ravioli, etc.)	Foods from bags, beer	Cool Whip (usually)
Other	Beer	Jerky°

°Consult with physician

CHAPTER 3

A Frank, Mature, Sensitive, and Caring Discussion of Human Sexuality with Dirty Pictures

NOTE: THE MATERIAL PRESENTED IN THIS CHAPTER WAS REVIEWED AND APPROVED BY THE OMAHA BOARD OF CENSORS. PICTURED ABOVE ARE MEMBERS: THE REVEREND FATHER JAMES J. FITZGERALD, CHAIRMAN; MRS. ELSIE MOYER; CAPT. ELROY FENTON, OMAHA P.D.; ESTHER BLATT; AND VERNON EPP.

Special Advance Warning to Decent People

I'm afraid that, in this chapter, we must talk about sex in a very explicit manner, because we want to expand the Frontiers of Human Understanding and also we want to sell as many books as possible to adolescent boys. This means we are going to have to use certain highly clinical sexual terms, such as "puberty" and "mollusk," which can lead to arousal in some instances. So if you have a shred of decency in you, you'll want to stop reading and go make fudge or something until this chapter is over. You'd better leave right now, because the heavy pornography starts almost immediately after these asterisks.

✿   ✿   ✿

Still with us, eh? Ha Ha! Don't feel ashamed. You'd be surprised at some of the readers we get in this chapter.

Okay. Now that we've cleared out the religious fanatics, let's take a look (so to speak) at . . .

The Major Male Sexual Organs

The major male sexual organs are the testaments, the nomads, the doubloons, the inner tubules, the vasal constrictors, the reversion unit, and of course the Main Organ, or "wiener."

Men are very protective of these organs. This is because Mother Nature decided, apparently as a prank, to place them on the *outside* of the male body, where they are most likely to get hit by baseballs, or punched by small children, or even—this makes me cringe, just thinking about it—attacked by crazed birds. And what is worse, Mother Nature made these organs extremely sensitive.

You know how women are always talking about the Pain of Childbirth, and how awful it is, and how men will never really understand it? Well, we men don't wish to make a big deal about this, but if you women really want to experience *pain*, you ought to try being male and taking a line drive to the privates. Yes sir. When this happens in a professional baseball game, and the player is down on the ground, writhing in agony, obviously clutching his private parts, the color commentator always says to the announcer: "Looks like he had the wind knocked out of him, Ted." But the male spectators know better, and if you look around you'll notice that they're all hunched over protectively, thousands of them, as if a sudden epidemic of Bad Posture Disease has swept through the crowd.

What this means is that, as they are growing up, males develop an attitude about their sexual organs very similar to the one that overprotective, doting parents have about their children. This is not a problem when the organs are young and innocent and basically dormant. But things change drastically when we reach puberty.

"IT'S A LINE DRIVE UP THE MIDDLE!"

Puberty generally occurs in males about two years late. By this I mean it occurs about two years after it occurs in females, which is somewhere around sixth grade. I remember at the end of my fifth-grade year, when we left for summer vacation, and the boys and girls were all just about even in the race for adulthood. But when we got back the next fall, the girls suddenly, out of the clear blue sky, were all a foot taller and had somehow acquired bosoms and God only

FEMALES USUALLY EXPERIENCE THE ONSET OF PUBERTY BY THE SIXTH GRADE

MALES USUALLY EXPERIENCE THE ONSET OF PUBERTY BY THE EIGHTH GRADE

knew what else. It was as though they had all attended Summer Bosom Camp.

This gives the girls an unfair head start. They get two whole years in which to get used to having sexually advanced bodily parts, and the result is they develop a certain maturity about it, a coolness of judgment, a savoir faire, that they retain for the rest of their lives.

Boys, meanwhile, are condemned to two years of wandering around the corridors of the junior high school, their eyes cruelly positioned by Mother Nature at just about bosom level, and consequently they develop this tremendous

yearning to catch up. When puberty finally strikes them, this pent-up desire has become so powerful that they develop erections that last for an average of slightly over three years. You men out there know what I'm talking about. The main reason adolescent males carry school books is they need something to hold in front of them.

Okay, then. To summarize what we have, in the typical healthy young male: We have a creature who tends to be highly indulgent toward his sexual organs, and we have organs that are semi-out-of-control much of the time, and almost always Ready to Party. Now let us contrast this with the sexual development of the typical female, starting with a discreet and sensitive examination of . . .

The Major Female Sexual Organs

I don't know what the major female sexual organs are. I get extremely confused just looking at the diagrams. Frankly, I don't think *anyone* really has a handle on the entire female reproductive system, because the organs are located inside the female body, where you can't see them. The only way a woman can have even a vague idea of what's going on in there is to have a gynecologist root around with primitive implements, and perhaps even call in an associate for consultation ("Hey Bob! Come in here! What do you make of *this?!*").

So in contrast to men, who are always touching themselves and giving themselves little nicknames, women develop an attitude of almost clinical detachment about their reproductive systems.

Furthermore, where men's organs seem to be carefree and impulsive, women's are serious and hard-working, with a single-minded devotion to the idea of having a baby. No matter what the woman is doing on the outside—having a

THE SEXUAL ORGANS ARE EASY TO LOCATE ON THE HUMAN BODY. TRACE A LINE WITH YOUR FINGER FROM YOUR NAVEL TO YOUR KNEES. SOMEWHERE ALONG THIS LINE YOU WILL FEEL SOMETHING. IF YOU FEEL A BUMP, CHANCES ARE YOU'RE A MALE. IF YOU FEEL A DIP, THEN YOU'RE PROBABLY A FEMALE. IF YOU FEEL BOTH A BUMP AND A DIP, THEN YOU'RE A LITTLE BIT OF BOTH BUT NOT ENOUGH OF EITHER.

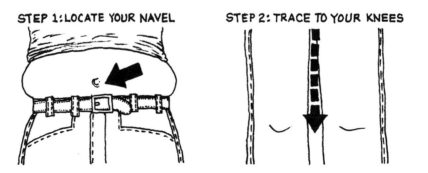

STEP 1: LOCATE YOUR NAVEL   STEP 2: TRACE TO YOUR KNEES

career, writing a novel, bowling—her organs are busy on the inside, gathering food for the baby, fixing up the baby's room, etc. At the end of each month they sigh, throw everything away and start all over again, thus sending the woman the friendly biological reminder: "Okay. Fine. Go ahead and have your fun out there. Don't mind us in here, slaving away, trying to ensure the very survival of the human race."

In summary, then, we see that, because of the location and nature of their respective organs, women tend to have a more serious, thoughtful, and responsible attitude toward relationships than men do. I realize this is an absurd generalization, but my feeling is that if we can't have absurd generalizations, we might as well not even bother to write books.

Answers to Common Sexual Questions

Q. How long should sexual intercourse last?

A. This is an area of some disagreement between the sexes. As a rule, women would like to devote as much time to foreplay and the sex act as men would like to devote to foreplay, the sex act, and building a garage. This tends to lead to dissatisfaction on the part of the woman, who is often just beginning to feel pleasantly sensuous when the man is off rooting around in the refrigerator to see if there's any Jell-O left.

Q. Well, isn't there some sensitive and caring and loving technique that a couple can use to slow the man down?

A. Yes. When the woman senses that the man is nearing climax, she can whisper: "The Internal Revenue Service called again today, but don't worry, I hung up on them."

Q. I am a good-looking woman, as you can see from the enclosed glossy color photographs of me naked.

A. Yes. Thank you.

Q. Although I have an otherwise wonderful marriage, my husband seems to be losing interest in me sexually. It's the little things: he hardly ever smiles at me; he often works late; and he comes home with as many as four naked women. So I thought, to rekindle the old flame, I'd surprise him, using a method suggested by Marabel Morgan in her book *The Total Woman*, namely greeting him at the door wearing only Saran Wrap. However, we were out of Saran Wrap, so I used Tupperware, which I feel is a better product anyway, but this unfortunately failed to produce the desired result, in the sense that when my husband saw me, he suffered some kind of seizure, and I had to drive him to the hospital while attempting to cover my private parts with two quart canisters and a Deviled Egg Transporter. My question is: Can we deduct this mileage on our income tax?

A. That depends on your individual situation.

Q. Listen, I, ummm, I have this kind of weird sexual hangup, which is that I, ummmm . . . this is *very* embarrassing . . .

A. Go ahead! Say it! Don't be ashamed! That's what we're here for! To help!

Q. Okay, but I want to whisper it. (whisper whisper whisper)

A. My God! Really?

Q. Um, yes.

A. The Joint Chiefs of Staff?!

Q. Well, yes.

A. How do you get the hamsters into the accordion?

Necking Tips for Guys

The big problem with necking is figuring out whether or not your date wants to Do It. On the Planet of the Ideal Women, your date would just come right out and tell you. She'd say: "What do you say we lie down on the couch and neck like crazy?" Or: "Although I like you as a friend, I frankly would not neck with you even if the alternative were death by leeches."

But here on the planet Earth, she won't say anything. Sometimes this means she isn't interested. But sometimes it doesn't. Generally the way a guy finds out specifically what his date is thinking is at some point he lunges at her, lips puckered, and she responds by either puckering back, or quickly turning her head sideways, in which case the guy winds up sort of licking her hair, looking like a world-class dork. There is no face-saving way for a guy to get out of this situation, other than to have an instantaneously fatal seizure.

Assuming your date is responsive, your next move is to attempt "French-kissing," which is when you stick your tongue into her mouth, and she sticks her tongue into your mouth, and so there the two of you are, with your tongues in each other's mouths. This is a really sexy thing to do, according to French people, although you should bear in mind that they also like to eat snails.

HOW TO FRENCH-KISS

STEP 1: OPEN YOUR MOUTH AND STICK OUT YOUR TONGUE

STEP 2: STICK YOUR TONGUE IN YOUR FRIEND'S MOUTH, AND THEY STICK THEIR TONGUE IN YOUR MOUTH.

STEP 3: DON'T FORGET ABOUT THOSE HANDS!

STEP 4: GET IN THE CAR, WAVE GOODBYE TO THE PARENTS, AND GO OUT ON YOUR DATE!

Anyway, assuming your date seems to be responding positively to you, in the sense that she has not yet kneed you in the groin, and also assuming that you really and truly respect her as a human being and love her and plan to marry her, it's time to move on to . . .

Heavy Petting

The big problem here is the bra strap. You cannot casually unhook a bra strap. The bra-strap industry sees to this. Scientists over at the Bra Strap Research Center in Amarillo, Texas, work night and day with volunteer males and lifelike female dummies (see illustration) coming up with newer and more complicated fastening devices, devices where the first hook actually re-hooks itself after you go on to the second one, such that nobody can get these bras off, especially not a lust-crazed male in a dark room. Many priceless jewelry collections are now protected solely by bra straps.

If you get through the bra strap, your next challenge is the undergarments, which you will probably have to ask your date for assistance with, because they can be complex beyond human imagining, but I strongly advise that before the two of you tackle them, you should leave the restaurant.

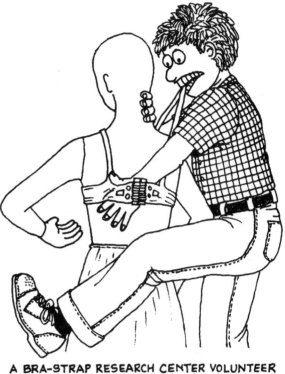

A BRA-STRAP RESEARCH CENTER VOLUNTEER TACKLES THE LATEST DESIGN

Solid Advice about Condoms

Guys, you should definitely use a condom. All major health authorities agree on this. The whole nation has become violently pro-condom, not just for guys having sex, but also for guys

95% OF THE WORLD'S CONDOM SUPPLY COMES FROM COLOMBIA, WHERE THE CONDOM BUSH, *CITCALYHPORP REBBUR*, IS GROWN

mean—the cover always is a picture of a handsome and of course brooding man embracing a woman with green eyes and a bosom that is clearly heaving, sometimes most of the way out of her dress. The title is always something fairly humid, like *Loins of Passion*.

You sexually inexperienced couples should get hold of one of these books, because inside you will find a number of passages that are chock-full of explicit, down-to-earth, practical "straight talk" about the sexual act:

"As Sabrina gazed upward at Baron LeGume, whose dark, brooding

puttering around the yard, domestic animals, most vegetables, and all major war monuments. Better safe than sorry!

Where to Get Additional Explicit Helpful Information on Sex

The best source of reliable information is romance novels, which you can find in better bookstores and supermarkets everywhere. You know the books I

DIAGRAM OF A TYPICAL ROMANCE NOVEL COVER

SEXY SCRIPT TITLE

OBVIOUSLY FAKE AUTHOR'S NAME

SEXY YOUNG VIRILE MAN, IN NEED

SEXY YOUNG WOMAN, IN NEED

FLOWERS, AND INVITING WOODS IN THE BACKGROUND

eyeballs were turgid with passion, she felt the tormented tenseness of his throbbing, pulsating malehood, and she knew, with a knowledge borne of knowing, that she could no longer hold back the surging waves of passion that washed over her, like waves of something, as his brooding throbbing pulsating highly engorged lips sought hers, not that she wanted to hold them back, we're talking about the waves of passion here, although she knew that somehow, somewhere, perhaps deep within the shuddering throes of year-ninghood that even now gripped the very core of her womanhood, if you get what we mean, that she must find a way, through the hazy mists of desire, to end this sentence, although she sensed somehow that . . ."

And so on. You young couples should study these helpful and realistic passages thoroughly, so you can use them for guidance when you are attempting sex ("You mean to tell me *that's* the tormented tenseness of your malehood?").

CHAPTER 4

Breaking Up or Getting Engaged

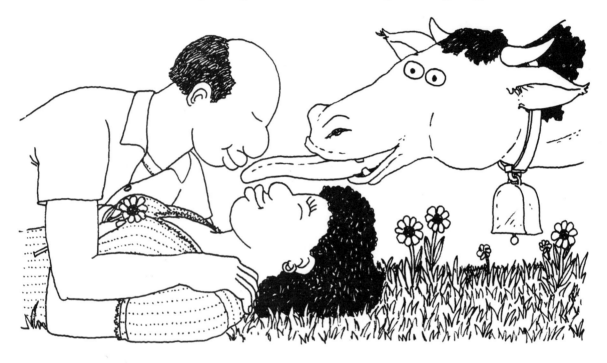

After a while, the sparkle tends to go out of a relationship. I don't care how passionate you are. I don't care if you're like those couples in romantic movies who, in the scene where they finally realize they're in love, lunge into each other's arms and fall to the ground, wherever they are, even if it is a pasture, and roll around amongst the cow doots in a sexual frenzy. You don't think those couples keep that kind of thing up, do you? Throughout life? Of course not. What would their clothes smell like?

The point being, a relationship can survive on pure romance for only so long. Sooner or later, Mundane Reality starts to seep in, and you need to make a decision:

• Do you break up with this person and look around for another one in hopes of once again experiencing the searing surge of unbridled passion, ideally in a carpeted environment? Or,

• Do you accept that your relationship can move to a more-mature stage, a stage based not so much upon impulse and romance and physical attraction as upon liking the same television shows? In short, do you get married?

How to Tell
If You Are Compatible
with Somebody

One way to find out if another person is "right" for you is to spend a lot of time with this person, talking and sharing experiences, so that you really get to know him or her as a human being. This is what we call the old-fashioned, or "stupid" way. The modern way is to take a Compatibility Quiz.

The Compatibility Quiz is a concept that was developed by top research scientists at *Cosmopolitan* magazine, a highly informative publication whose cover always has a picture of a glamorous woman, wearing an extremely low-cut outfit, whose breasts appear to be pointing straight up. In fact, they are pointing *down: Cosmopolitan* suspends these women by their feet from the ceiling. That is the price you have to pay, if you truly wish to be glamorous.

Anyway, if you want to know whether your relationship will work out, you need to sit down and answer these questions:

Money

Who do you feel should be the "breadwinner" in a family?
  A. The man.
  B. The woman.
  C. H. Ross Perot.

Children

Which of the following statements best describes your feelings toward children?
  A. "Put that down this instant!"
  B. "I said *put that down!*"
  C. "*Never* put your finger in that part of the doggy!!"

Housework

In a modern marriage, who do you feel should be responsible for the housework?
  A. Nobody.
  B. Leona Helmsley.
  C. It should be divided up fairly and equally among the servants.

Recreation

Your idea of a pleasant romantic evening is:
A. Sipping a glass of wine and watching a roaring fire.
B. Drinking a few martinis and roaring at the fire.
C. Drinking a bottle of gin and setting things on fire.

Sex

The kind of sex you enjoy most is:
A. With another person.
B. With several other persons, but no animals.
C. At least not invertebrates.
D. Unless they are fairly tame.

Religion

How would you describe your attitude toward religion?
A. About your height, only thinner.
B. I am not especially big on religion, but I have watched it on television.
C. I am religious to the point of human sacrifice.

Family Crises

Bill and Denise are a young married working couple with no children. One day they set out from Reno, Nevada, on foot at exactly 4:30 P.M. Bill walks three miles per hour and rests for ten minutes each hour, while Denise walks at exactly two miles per hour without stopping. After a couple of days they are both dead from scorpions. Which of the following statements most closely matches your feelings regarding this?
A. It serves them right.
B. I hear Reno is quite nice.
C. I myself prefer a moister climate.

Current Events

The capital of Vermont is:
A. Where they keep the governor.
B. Very cold.
C. Probably in New England.

HOW TO SCORE: Give yourself one point for each answer. No, what the heck, give yourself *two* points for each answer. Now add up your points and compare your total with the total for the person you're trying to be compatible with. If both of your totals are numbers, odds are you two will hit it off pretty well. At least until you get married. Or maybe not. How the hell should I know?

Your total:	Your potential mate's total:

Alternative Method for Stupid People

Another excellent way to decide whether another person is compatible with you is to use astrology. The word "astrology" comes from the Greek or possibly Latin words "astro" and "ology," so right away we can see that it is very scientific. In fact, astrology rests on a proven principle, namely that if you know the exact positions where the moon and the various planets were when a person was born, you can get this person to give you money. The way you do this is by making up random, semi-unintelligible pieces of advice, such as "attend to future considerations."

To use astrology for your own personal benefit, simply locate your astrological "sign" on the following chart, then look up your horoscope in any

YOUR BIRTHDAY		YOUR ASTROLOGICAL SIGN
Jan. 15–Feb. 13		VIRGIL
Feb. 14–Mar. 18		AQUARIUM
Mar. 19		NEPTUNE
July 20–July 3		LEON
Labor Day		PSORIASIS
June 6 at around 2:30		BOB L. HOCKMUNSTER, JR.
Giants° 6–Dodgers 3		SNEEZY

°Clinched playoff berth

reputable newspaper and govern your entire life accordingly:

Most people believe that breaking up is easier than working at a relationship. Hahahahaha.

How to Break Up

The ideal way to break up is the one featured in the famous best-selling book, *Love Story*, where the beautiful heroine, sensing that the relationship is getting maybe a little stale, contracts a fatal disease. In real life, however, it's never that easy. You never have a really good excuse for breaking up with the other person, so you feel guilty, and you put off confronting the problem. I have a friend who found it so difficult to tell his girlfriend he no longer loved her that he just kept going along with the program, until finally, one day, they actually got married. They had a big wedding, and she was up there, in front of all her friends and family, thinking this was the happiest day of her life, and he was standing there in a rental tuxedo, thinking: "Should I tell her now? Nah. Better wait till after we cut the cake." This kind of thing happens all the time.

So if you're going to break up, you have to overcome your guilt and break up *now*. Otherwise you'll never find the person you really want, the person with whom you can achieve your goal of Lifelong Happiness. You should follow the example of famous former ravishing beauty Elizabeth Taylor, who sheds husbands like used Kleenex and has consequently achieved Lifelong Happiness dozens of times.

Of course your major concern, in breaking up, is how to do it in such a way that the other person doesn't get so upset that he or she stabs himself or herself. Or yourself. I recommend that you take the honest approach. Come right out with the truth. That is always best, in the end. To build up your courage, practice holding imaginary conversations with your lover, wherein you set forth, calmly and rationally, the reasons why you feel the breakup is necessary, then try to imagine, and sensitively respond to, the various objections your lover might have:

YOU: Listen, I, um, I, uhh . . .

YOUR LOVER: Yes? Is there something you wish to tell me?

YOU: Um.

YOUR LOVER: Are you trying to tell me that, although you care for me deeply, and you will cherish always the times that we have had together, you

FOUR POPULAR METHODS OF BREAKING UP

really feel that we both need more space to grow and enrich our lives as separate individuals? For my sake as well as yours?

    YOU: Well.

    YOUR LOVER: Then perhaps it would be best if we broke up, with no hard feelings or remorse on either side.

    YOU: Okay by me.

    After you've mentally rehearsed this dialogue enough times, you simply go through it again, out loud, but this time in the presence of your lover. You'll be surprised at how smoothly it goes:

    YOU: Listen, I, um, I, uhh . . .

    YOUR LOVER: If you break up with me, I'm going to kill myself.

    YOU: I was thinking we should get married.

    There! See how easy that was? I am so very happy for the both of you! Onward to our "Important Prenuptial Chapter."

CHAPTER 5

Important Prenuptial Chapter

Should you and your spouse-to-be have a prenuptial agreement? We put this question to five of the country's leading attorneys, and they sent us bills totalling $63,500. This should give you an idea of how important it is to try to avoid those pesky legal squabbles that could crop up down the road. So just in case, we have prepared the following Low-Cost But Fair Prenuptial Agreement for you. Of course, as is the case with any binding legal document, we strongly suggest that, before you sign it, you place it on a flat surface.

Low-Cost but Fair Prenuptial Agreement

BE IT HEREBY AGREED that since (*name of bride*), hereinafter referred to as The Bride, and (*name of groom*), hereinafter known as The Groom, have decided that they love each other with a deep and undying passion, at least for the time being, and consequently want to get married,

THEREFORE they do hereby agree that, in case later on for some reason God forbid they decide to get a divorce, they will both adhere to the following Deal:

1. MONEY. If there is any money, it shall be divided up equally and fairly between The Bride's and The Groom's attorneys.

2. DISHES. The Bride and The Groom shall equally divide up such dishes as have not been reduced to microscopic shards in the Traditional Pre-Divorce Violent Shrieking Kitchen Argument.

3. WEDDING-GIFT FONDUE SETS STILL IN THE ORIGINAL UNOPENED BOXES. The Bride and The Groom shall each keep eight fondue sets, and the rest shall be given to charity.

4. OTHER POSSESSIONS. The Bride shall get to keep whatever she picked out, including the living room, dining room, and bedroom furniture as well as any major appliances, carpets, lamps, paintings, etc. The Groom shall get to keep the Rolling Stones album *Get Yer Ya Yas Out* and the NHL Power Play table hockey game, including both pucks.

5. FRIENDS. Friends shall be divided up by sex and distributed accordingly.

6. RELATIVES. The Bride and The Groom shall each keep whatever relatives they had at the time of the original marriage. If there is any question about this, such as Uncle Bob, whom nobody can remember which family he belongs to, then he shall be allowed to visit either The Bride or The Groom, at his discretion, with the provision that he leaves after a couple of weeks.

7. DOG. The dog shall be the property of whichever party was supportive of it and cleaned up after it the time it was throwing up what looked like raccoon parts on the bed.

Tips for the New Bride

HOW TO GET ALONG WITH YOUR MOTHER-IN-LAW: Your best bet is drugs.

DEALING WITH YOUR HUSBAND'S OLD BUDDIES: Odds are your

IT'S NOT EASY TO CHOOSE BETWEEN YOUR WIFE AND YOUR BUDDIES!

husband will have old buddies from college or reform school with whom he has shared many important Male Bonding Experiences such as fighting and burping and taking turns driving cars into the lobbies of major hotels.

After you are married, you should not try to cut him off from these friends. They are a very important part of his life. They are able to discuss with him, as you cannot, a lot of important questions that guys are concerned about, such as: Who was pitching for the Yankees when Bill Mazeroski hit the bottom-of-the-ninth home run that won the 1960 World Series for the Pirates? Now you are continuing to read this paragraph, but believe me, your husband stopped at the end of the last sentence and is now staring at the ceiling and saying: "Whitey Ford? Nah.

Louis Arroyo? Nah." This is why he needs his buddies. To resolve questions like this.°

So you should make a special effort to make your husband's buddies feel welcome in your home. Invite them over for dinner. Invite them on your honeymoon. Don't make a big scene if they leave beer cans in the aquarium. And above all, don't force your husband to choose between them and you. I am not suggesting here that your husband would leave the woman he has pledged to spend the rest of his life with just so he could hang around with a bunch of guys talking sports and drinking beer. I am saying they would probably also order some pizza.

°It was Ralph Terry.

CHAPTER 6

How to Have a Perfect Wedding No Matter What

I am going to assume, in this chapter, that you're getting married for the first time and consequently you want to do it in the most traditional and ludicrously elaborate way possible. Those of you who are getting married for the second or third time will probably want a low-key, informal wedding. I know this was the case when my wife and I married

each other. It was the second wedding for both of us, and the most formal and organized part of it (I am being serious here) came when the wedding party played Capture the Flag.

Similarly, some friends of mine named Hannah and Paddy had their second-time-around wedding in a bar, amidst a dense haze of cigarette smoke and much loud drinking, such that the actual ceremony, performed by a judge, was barely noticeable. The judge kept trying to get people's attention by pounding on the bar and shouting, "Quiet down! We have to marry Hannah and Paddy!"

But first-time marriers usually prefer to have a traditional wedding, defined by experts as "a wedding where the flowers alone cost more than Versailles." One advantage of this kind of wedding is that, over the years, the various responsibilities have clearly been divided up between the bride's family and the groom's family:

RESPONSIBILITIES OF THE BRIDE'S FAMILY: The announcement; the church; the invitations; the clergyman; the rehearsal; the bridesmaids' luncheon; the flowers; the dresses; the reception; the food; the liquor; the photographer; the limousines; lodging and transportation for out-of-town guests; gratuities; the honeymoon; the national defense; a nice thoughtful present for the newlyweds such as a house.

RESPONSIBILITIES OF THE GROOM'S FAMILY: Not throwing up on the other guests.

Of course there is one other major responsibility of the groom, which is to buy the engagement ring. Guys, I know it can be intimidating to walk into a jewelry store and try to handle a slick salesman, but you'll do fine if you know a few basic technical facts about diamonds.

Diamond Formation

Millions of years ago, lumps of carbon fell down on the ground and got covered up by dirt and mountains, after which they were subjected to intense pressure by lobbying groups such as the National Rifle Association. Over the years, these lumps were buried deeper and deeper beneath the Earth's surface, so that today we don't even know where the hell they are. Nor care.

Meanwhile, shopping centers began to form, and inevitably they developed jewelry stores. This is where we stand today.

How Diamonds Are Measured

The standard unit of measurement for diamonds is called the "carat," which basically measures how much you love your fiancee. A guy who is only

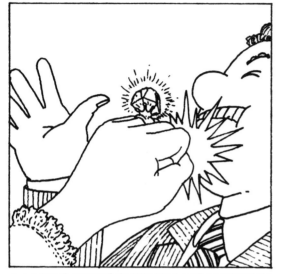

A LARGE STONE CARRIES A LOT OF WEIGHT

perfect or you are going to kill yourself with a cyanide capsule, which it is the responsibility of the maid or matron of honor to provide.

Actually, planning a wedding is not all that difficult, provided you do almost nothing else for the better part of a year. Naturally, this will be a very busy and exciting time for you. But as you go through it, you must make sure, amid all the excitement and hustle and bustle, that you don't lose sight of the whole point of the wedding—its deeper meaning and the central reason for its entire existence. Your gown.

Your Wedding Gown

Listen up, brides. You get only one shot in your life at a real wedding gown, and you better not blow it. Because a wedding gown is more than just a dress. It's a dress that costs a whole ton of money. It's a dress that you'll cherish for several decades in a box in a remote closet, perhaps to be taken out one day by your daughter when she's looking for (sniff) a wedding gown of her own. She'll wisely reject yours, of course, because by that time it will have served as the home environment for 60,000 generations of insects. The last thing she wants, when she's up at the altar on her

mildly attracted to his fiancee will buy her a ring with only a few carats, whereas a guy who really loves his fiancee will buy her a stone so large that she can never again swim in ponds for fear she will become embedded up to her shoulder in bottom muck.

That takes care of the groom's responsibilities; everything else is up to you brides-to-be. You're going to be very, very busy planning your wedding, because naturally you want everything to be perfect. Remember at all times, brides-to-be, *this is your own very special day, and it damned well better be*

A WEDDING DRESS SHOULD NOT BE THAT "SOMETHING OLD"

YOU: What kinds of gowns do you have for under $2,000?

COUTURIER: Well, we have this one right here.

YOU: This is a group of used Handi-Wipes sewn together.

COUTURIER: Yes. By preschool children.

With this kind of guidance, you'll be able to select a truly memorable gown, one that will cause your parents to remark in admiration: *"How much?!* That's more than we spent on our first *house!"* If they don't make this remark, your gown is not memorable enough, and you should take it right back to the couturier to have some more pearls glued on.

After you've selected your gown, it's time to get on with planning the rest of the wedding. This task will be easier if you use this convenient Wedding Planner Checklist:

Bride's Wedding Planner Checklist
Six Months before the Wedding

This is the time to choose your wedding site. It should be extremely traditional. Ideally, you want St. Paul's

own Very Special Day, is for a millipede to come strolling out of her bodice.

Nevertheless you must have a wonderful gown. This is where you need the expert help of a qualified bridal couturier, who can answer your technical questions:

Cathedral, in London, England. This is where Princess Diana got married to Prince Charles in a ceremony that lasted longer than a number of major wars. Also it required more horses. This is the kind of memorable wedding you definitely want to shoot for.

If St. Paul's is not available, look for a large traditional religious building, such as a church or synagogue, closer to home. In many cases, these buildings are affiliated with major religions, which may require that you hold specific religious beliefs before you can get married there. This is a good thing to check out beforehand, by calling up the person in charge:

YOU: Hi. I was thinking of getting married in your church or synagogue, and I was wondering if I had to hold any specific religious views.

RELIGIOUS PERSON: Why yes, you do.

YOU: How many?

RELIGIOUS PERSON: Let's see, here . . . five, six . . . looks like eight in all.

YOU: Fine, fine. Could you please mail me a set?

If the building is really right for you, with adequate parking and every-thing, you should go ahead and agree to hold the beliefs, even if they involve animal sacrifice. This is your wedding, after all.

The other major things that must be accomplished six months before the wedding are:

• The bride should select a caterer and a nice country club for the reception, and her parents should with-draw their life's savings so they can put down a deposit.

• The mother of the bride and the mother of the groom, if they do not already know each other, should have a luncheon wherein they get along about as well as Iran gets along with Iraq.

Five Months before the Wedding

Now is the time to select your bridesmaids. This is a very large honor, which you bestow only upon people who meet the following criteria:

1. They should be female.

2. They should be willing to wear bridesmaids' dresses.

This second criterion is the most important, because the whole point of the bridesmaid's dress is to render the person wearing it so profoundly unat-tractive that she cannot possibly outshine you, the bride. In fact, one of the really fun things a bride gets to do is go to the bridal salon with her mother, and the two of them get drunk and howl with laughter as they consider various comical outfits that they might encase the bridesmaids in. Some of them go so far as to select actual clown suits, but most prefer the traditional look, which is:

• Long frilly dresses in bright pastel colors reminiscent of Bazooka bubble gum or some experimental and ulti-mately unsuccessful ice cream flavor with a name like "Pumpkin Surprise."

• "Puffed" sleeves that make any woman who is larger than Audrey Hepburn look like a Green Bay Packer.

• Large "fun" floppy hats that obscure the bridemaid's face so thoroughly that you could use men if you really had to.

You need not feel restricted to this look, however. This is your Very Special Day, and you can make the bridesmaids

ALTERNATE BRIDESMAIDS' OUTFITS

FOR UGLY PEOPLE'S WEDDINGS   FOR BIKERS' WEDDINGS   FOR APPALACHIAN WEDDINGS

wear anything you want. Veils, fur stoles, whalebone corsets, hats with waxed fruit, kneepads, anything. Remember: they have to pay for it.

Four Months before the Wedding

This is a good time to select a silver pattern and a groom. (see Chapter 1, "How to Find Somebody to Go on Dates With"). In fact, your smart modern bride will often select several grooms, so as to guarantee that in case one or two of them get "cold feet," she'll still be able to have her Very Special Day.

You must be much more careful in selecting your silver pattern. It should have a name similar to the ones developers give to shoddy new apartment complexes, such as "Coventry Downe Manor"; and each place setting should consist of a regular fork, a dinner fork, a breakfast fork, a snack fork, a soup fork, a holiday fork, an emergency fork, a Care Bear fork, a Pez dispenser, and the equivalent knives, spoons, ladles, scone handlers, beet prongs, tuffet churners, prawn smelters, and clam goaders. Remember: Your silver is your first major family heirloom, to be cherished and stored in the same closet where you cherish your wedding dress until such time as one of you files for divorce.

Three Months before the Wedding

This is the time for the formal announcement of your engagement to appear in your local newspaper. Your local newspaper should have a name like *The Morning, Afternoon & Evening Chronic Spokesperson-Fabricator*, and the wording of the announcement should be as follows:

"(*Your parents' names*) are extremely relieved to announce the engagement of (*your name*) to (*your fiance's name*), who is not really good enough, son of (*your fiance's parents' names*), who are quite frankly dreadful, but (*your parents' names*) will settle for just about anything at this point because suitors are not exactly knocking down (*your name*)'s door despite all the money (*your parents' names*) spent on her teeth. An elaborate wedding is planned."

This is also when you send out your invitations. You are naturally going to want to invite me and a number of my friends, because we are a lot of fun at any kind of affair where there is free liquor, plus if the band is really lame, which it will be (see page 50), we are not afraid to express our displeasure by hurling segments of the prime rib entree, which by the way may be served buffet-style for informal afternoon weddings. Others you might consider inviting include your family and any member of the groom's family who can produce a receipt proving he or she has purchased at least one full place setting.

The wedding invitation should be worded as follows:

The invitation should be on a little card, which you mail to your invitees along with a little matching R.S.V.P. card and a return envelope that says POSTAL SERVICE WILL NOT DELIVER WITHOUT STAMP.

Mr. and Mrs. Bob A. Doomus
Request the Honour and the Favour
of You Showing Up at the Marriage of
Their Daughtour

Salina Fennel
to
Mr. Dwayne R. LePoon, Jr.
or
Mr. Bill V. "Scooter" Fencemender
Depending On If Dwayne Can Get Off Work

at Our Lady of Recurring Lower Back Pain Religious Church
Saturday, the Twenty-fifth of June
at 1:30 o'clock P.M. Fahrenheit
Bring a Gift

R.S.V.P.   No tank tops

We Already Got a Fondue Set

Two Months before the Wedding

This is when the mother of the groom should go out and buy a dress to wear to the wedding that is fancy enough so that the mother of the bride will be convinced that the groom's mother is trying to upstage the bride, and consequently the bride's mother will think about virtually nothing else for the rest of her life.

This is also when you should hire a band. It makes no difference which one. All wedding bands are the same. They're all cloned from living cells that were taken from the original wedding band, "Victor Esplanade and his Sounds of Compunction," and preserved in a saline solution in Secaucus, New Jersey (which, incidentally, is also the home of the first native American Formica trees). They'll show up in stained tuxedos, and no matter what kind of music you ask them to play, they'll play it in such a way that it sounds like "New York, New

VICTOR ESPLANADE AND HIS SOUNDS OF COMPUNCTION

York." Really. If you feel like dancing to some rock 'n' roll, and you ask them if they maybe know "Honky Tonk Woman," they'll say, "Oh sure, we know that one," and they'll play "New York, New York." They can't help it. We're talking genetics.

One Month before the Wedding

Now is the time for you and the groom to get your blood tests. If your groom's blood fails, get another groom. If your blood fails, get some new blood. We are much too far into the planning process to turn back now.

By now you should also have lined up a photographer. You'll want to have lots of photographs of your wedding to show to your family and friends, who will have been unable to see the actual ceremony because the photographer was always in the way.

Often you can save money by having your pictures taken by a friend or relative who is familiar with photography in the sense of owning a camera and knowing where a Fotomat is. I have some good friends named Rob and Helene who took this approach, and the pictures came out really swell except that for some technical reason there is no light in any of them. Just these vaguely human-oid shapes. We all love to get these pictures out and look at them. "Look!" we say. "There's Helene! Or Rob! Or the cake!"

Two Weeks before the Wedding

By now your advance wedding gifts should have started to arrive, including at least 14 attractive and functional fondue sets. Also by this time the bride should start to notice a scratchy feeling at the back of her throat, indicating that she is just starting to come down with a case of Mongolian Death Flu.

One Week before the Wedding

This is where the groom starts to get actively involved in the wedding preparations, by having a "bachelor's party" where he gets together with his "chums" for one last "fling" and wakes up several days later in an unexplored region of New Zealand. Meanwhile you, the bride, are bustling about, looking after the hundreds of last-minute details, having the time of your life despite the intermittent paralysis in your right leg.

The highlight of this week, of course, is the Rehearsal Dinner, when the wedding principals, especially the immediate families, take time out from the hectic pace of preparations to share in an

A TYPICAL BACHELOR'S PARTY

evening of warmth and conviviality, culminating when the mother of the bride and the mother of the groom go after each other with dessert forks.

The Wedding Day

This is it! The biggest day of your life, and there's no way that any dumb old 108-degree fever is going to put a damper on it!

A good idea is to put your wedding gown on early, so the sweat stains can expand from your armpit areas and cover the entire gown, and thus be less noticeable. And now it's on to the wedding site!

As the guests arrive, the ushers (What do you mean, you forgot the ushers?! Get some!!) should ask the guests whether they want smoking or nonsmoking, and seat them accordingly (except the mother of the bride and the mother of the groom, who should be seated in separate states). Then, at the appointed time, the organist should start playing a traditional song, such as "Here Comes the Bride" or "Happy Birthday to You," and the wedding procession should come down the aisle, in the following order:

1. A cute little nephew, who will carry the ring and announce, at the most dramatic part of the ceremony, that he has to make poopy. If you have no cute little nephew, rent one.

2. The groom (if available).

3. The bridesmaids, walking sideways to minimize the risk that they will injure a member of the audience in the eye with their puffed shoulders.

4. You, the bride, the Center of Everything, smiling radiantly, your eyes sparkling like the most beautiful stars in the sky until, as you reach the altar, they swell shut in reaction to the antibiotics.

From that point on, it will all be a happy blur to you—the ceremony, the reception, dancing with your new husband to your Special Song ("New York, New York"). Enjoy it all, for you'll never have a wedding like this again, even if you do recover fully.

IT'S ALL SMILES FOR THE PHOTO SESSION!

THE TRADITIONAL "CUTTING OF THE CAKE"

THE MODERN "CUTTING OF THE CAKE"

(WHO GETS TO SLICE THE FIRST PIECE SHOULD BE DECIDED IN ADVANCE)

But the best part of all will come later, on your Wedding Night, just the two of you, alone at last—you in your filmy, lacy, highly provocative peignoir, and your groom on his back in the shower snoring and dribbling saliva on his rental tuxedo. My advice to you is: relax, have a glass of wine, and check his pulse every 15 minutes. Don't be alarmed if he has none. This is normal, for grooms.

Pranks

It is the responsibility of the best man and the ushers to play fun and comical pranks on the Happy Couple, such as—this is a good one!—just before they come rushing out of the reception, ready to leave on their honeymoon, you take their car and—get this, guys!—you sell it and keep the money. Ha ha! The Happy Couple will sure talk about *that* for a number of years!

The Honeymoon

Most couples prefer to take their honeymoons away from the familiar and the ordinary, to go to an exotic, different, and foreign place, such as Epcot Center. I am not kidding here. A lot of couples really do honeymoon at Disney World. Of course they don't admit this. They say they're "honeymooning in Florida," because they don't want people to know that the highlight of the whole wild lustful romantic adventure was shaking hands with Goofy.

Of course there are plenty of other possibilities for your honeymoon. Your friendly travel agent will give you

THE NEWLYWEDS HAVING A WONDERFUL HONEYMOON

mounds of brochures from all kinds of resorts desperate to obtain your honeymoon dollar:

For A Honeymoon Memory That Will Long Remain Lodged in the Esophagus of Your Mind...

Sea Cucumber Island

"Your Personal Little Wad of Paradise"

Nestled in the aromatic waters of the Houston Ship Channel, situated within easy traveling distance of such popular attractions as Houston, Texas; Interstate 10; and Paris, France,* Sea Cucumber Island offers everything you need to make your "dream honeymoon" become extremely real:

• A complimentary glass of Manischewitz Extra Dense Cream de Grape Champagne Wine** upon your arrival to "toast" the happy couple.

• Fully flushing toilets*** in many rooms "Sanitized for Your Protection."

• Food.****

• Ping-Pong.*****

ENJOY SWIMMING IN OUR WARM, PLACID WATERS

ENJOY TOURS OF THE BAY OF CUCUMBERS

PRICES START AS LOW AS $299******

Sea Cucumber Island

°Via jet airplane. Not included.

°°We get to drink it.

°°°In some cases.

°°°°If the Vend-o-Matic man came. Not included.

°°°°°You supply paddles and balls. And table. Also net.

°°°°°°Does not include anything.

Thank-You Notes

Thank-you notes are your last major responsibility as a bride, and the rules of etiquette require that you try to get them all done before the marriage legally dissolves.

The proper wording depends on whether or not you remember what the people gave you. If you do remember, your note should say specific nice things about the gift:

Dear Mr. and Mrs. Sternum:

Thank you ever so much for the very thoughtful fondue set. Mark and I feel that, of all the fondue sets we received, the one you gave us is definitely one of the nicer ones, in that particular color.

Sincerely,
Elaine and Mark

If you don't remember what gift they gave you, you'll have to compensate by sounding very grateful for it:

Dear Mr. and Mrs. Sternum:

We just don't know how we can ever thank you for the extremely wonderful gift you gave us. It has become the focal point of our entire lives! We think about it all the time. We are seriously thinking about quitting our jobs and forming a religious cult that just sits around all day worshipping this gift.

With Extreme Sincerity,
Elaine and Mark

CHAPTER 7

Newlywed Finances

HOUSEHOLD MONEY MANAGEMENT

It's sad but true that money causes a great many unnecessarily fatal squabbles among newlyweds. Very often this is because of a difference in priorities. For example, you want to buy food, while your spouse wants to buy a thoroughbred racehorse. It's important, in these situations, for both of you to be willing to sit down together and try to achieve a work-able compromise. In this case, you could buy a thoroughbred racehorse and eat it.

Often, however, the solutions are not that simple. This is why it's so important that right now, while you're just starting out, you draw up a realistic household budget. I can help you here. I have lived in a realistic household for many years, and I would say, based on experience, that your typical weekly expenses should run pretty close to the following:

REALISTIC WEEKLY HOUSEHOLD BUDGET FOR TWO PEOPLE	
Food that you buy and eventually eat	$30.00
Food that you buy and store in the back of the refrigerator until you have to throw it out because it looks like the thing that burst out of that unfortunate man's chest and started eating the spaceship crew in the movie *Alien*	55.00
Pennies that you get as change and put in a jar, intending to someday put them in those wrappers and take them to the bank, when in fact you will die well before you ever get around to this	117.48
Rent, clothing, car payments, insurance, gas, electricity, telephone, magazines	829.12
Miscellaneous	2,747.61

As you can see, there are a lot of expenses associated with running a household, and to meet them, you will need Financial Discipline. Each week, when you get your paychecks, you must set aside $3,779.21 right off the bat, to cover your weekly household budget. If your combined weekly paychecks total less than this amount, perhaps you should go back and marry a rich person (see Chapter 1). Your other option is . . .

Credit Cards

Credit cards are an excellent source of money. The way they work is, people you don't even know mail them to you, and then stores, for some reason, let you use them to actually *buy* things. (No, I can't figure it out either!)

The thing is, you have to be responsible about how you use your credit cards. You can't just rush out and charge every single item in the store. Think ahead! How would you fit it all into your car?

So I strongly recommend that you be cautious with credit, following the wise Borrowing Rule of Thumb employed by the federal government, which is: "Never borrow any amount of money larger than you can comfortably pronounce."

HOW TO MAKE YOUR OWN CREDIT CARD

STEP 1

CUT A 3 3/8-INCH STRIP OFF OF A SHEET OF THIN WHITE PLASTIC.

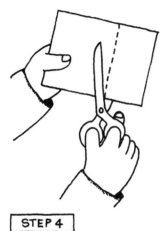

STEP 2

CUT A 2 1/8-INCH STRIP FROM THE 3 3/8-INCH STRIP, CROSSWISE.

YOU SHOULD END UP WITH A 2 1/8-BY-3 3/8-INCH CARD.

STEP 3

USING A LAUNDRY MARKER, WRITE THE WORDS "MAJOR CREDIT CARD" ON ONE SIDE IN OFFICIAL-LOOKING LETTERS. ADD SOME STARS, WORDS, EAGLES, OR OTHER NEAT STUFF TO PERK THINGS UP.

STEP 4

USING A FRIEND'S MAJOR CREDIT CARD, SANDWICH YOUR "MAJOR CREDIT CARD" AND YOUR FRIEND'S CARD TOGETHER ON A COOKIE TIN AND BAKE FOR 15 MINUTES AT 500 DEGREES.

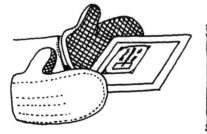

STEP 5

AFTER CARDS HAVE COOLED, PEEL THEM APART. YOUR CARD SHOULD HAVE YOUR FRIEND'S NAME AND NUMBER NEATLY INDENTED IN IT. THEN FILE THE CORNERS TO A ROUNDED APPEARANCE.

FILE OFF CORNERS

STEP 6

ON THE REVERSE SIDE OF THE CARD, POSITION A 5/16-INCH STRIP OF BLACK TAPE ABOVE A 5/16-INCH STRIP OF WHITE TAPE. SIGN YOUR FRIEND'S NAME. YOUR CARD IS NOW READY TO USE.

BLACK TAPE   WHITE TAPE

Your Checking Account

This is another potential source of money, although it's usually impossible to tell how much money is in it. The important thing is to try to keep your checkbook "balanced." Here's how.

1. Each month the bank will send you an envelope containing a bunch of used checks, which, for tax purposes, you should place in a two-ply grocery bag and eventually misplace. Also in the envelope will be:

• A little note entitled "TO OUR CUSTOMERS!" that will feature a cheerful and totally unintelligible message like this: "Good News! First Fiduciary Commonwealth National Savings & Loan & Bank & Trust is now offering 3.439087654% Growth Bonds of Matu-

rity yielding 2.694968382857% Compound Annualized Rate of Secretion!" You should try to save this note, for tax purposes.

• A piece of paper covered with numbers (your "statement").

2. Okay. Now open up your checkbook and take a look at the kind of checks you have. If you have the kind with little nature scenes printed on them, or, God help us, little "Ziggy" cartoons, you're much too stupid to balance your own checking account, and you should definitely go back and marry a rich person (see Chapter 1).

3. Now examine your check "register" (the part of your checkbook that you sometimes write on). It should look like this:

4. Now compare and see if any recognizable numbers on the "register" are the same as any numbers the bank has printed on the "statement." If you find any, you should put a little happy face next to them, like this: ☺

5. If your total number of happy faces is five or more, then your account is what professional accountants call "in balance," and you can go on ahead and watch TV. If you score lower than five, you should get on the phone immediately and explain to your bank that they have made some kind of error.

Your Home: Buying vs. Renting

Aside from Madonna and Sean Penn, most newlyweds rent their first home. This can actually be a pleasant experience, as you discover the Fun Side

THERE ARE STILL MANY INTERESTING HOUSES AVAILABLE FOR NEWLYWEDS

of apartment life: getting to know your new neighbors; listening to what kind of music your new neighbors like to play very early in the morning on their 150,000-watt sound system; having your new neighbors' legs come through your ceiling when water from their leaking toilet rots their floor, etc.

But sooner or later, despite this recurring joy of these communal experiences, you're going to want to have a place of your very own. Step one is to figure out how expensive a house you can afford. This depends on your combined annual incomes, as is shown by the following chart:

YOUR COMBINED ANNUAL INCOME	PRICE OF HOME YOU CAN AFFORD
Up to $20,000 $20,000–$40,000 $40,000–$80,000 $80,000–$100,000	Don't be an idiot. There are no homes that you can afford.

But don't despair, young couples! You can still realize the dream of owning a home of your own, provided you're willing to do what generations of newlyweds have done before you: roll up your sleeves, do the hard work, and make the tough sacrifices involved in nagging your parents for a down payment. They probably have some money left, even after your wedding, and your job is to whine and wheedle and look pathetic until they give it to you. Make sure you leave them something for food:

COST OF YOUR NEW HOME	AMOUNT YOUR PARENTS SHOULD HAVE LEFT FOR FOOD AFTER LENDING YOU THE DOWN PAYMENT
Up to $50,000 $50,000–$100,000 Over $100,000	$150 $75 Various canned goods.

CHAPTER 8

How to Argue Like
a Veteran Married Couple

Most young couples begin married life knowing very little about how to argue with each other, and are forced to learn through trial and error. Sadly, some of them never do learn, a good example being that couple on "The Waltons" who never fought about anything, and consequently wound up with three or four hundred children.

There is no need for this kind of tragedy. We veteran married couples have, over the years, especially on long car trips, developed certain time-tested techniques that even an inexperienced person can use to turn any issue, no matter how minor, into the kind of vicious, drawn-out argument where you both spend a lot of time deliberately going through doors you don't really need to go through, just so you can slam them viciously.

When you get involved in marital arguing, the role model you want to bear in mind is World War I, which got started when some obscure nobleperson, Archduke Somebody, got assassinated way the hell over in the Balkans, and the next thing you know people in places as far away as Cheyenne, Wyoming, were rushing off to war. These were people who wouldn't have known a Balkan if they woke up in bed with one, but they were willing to get shot at because of what happened there. It's the same with a good marriage argument. If you really

ARCHDUKE SOMEBODY

do it right, you should reach the point where neither of you has the vaguest recollection what the original disagreement was, but both of you are willing to get divorced over it. This is the kind of veteran marital relationship you young couples can develop, if you follow these proven techniques.

The most important technique is: *Always be on the lookout for conversational openings that can lead to arguments!* To illustrate this, let's look at a typical marital conversation:

MARY: Honey, could you please try not to leave your socks on the coffee table?

JOHN: Why of course, dear. I'm sorry.

Pretty pathetic, right, married couples? Mary has created the perfect opening for a good argument, and John has *totally* dropped the ball, by admitting he was wrong. *Never admit you're wrong, young married persons!*

Now you're saying, "But what if John's socks are right there, on the coffee table? How can he argue about *that?*"

The answer is: He can't. So what he has to do is, he has to somehow get the argument, or at least his end of it, focused on a *completely different topic*, ideally a *strident accusation* that he has *dredged up out of his memory* and that is *totally unrelated to the issue at hand.* This is very important, young married persons: You must always maintain a supply of retaliative, irrelevant accusations in your mind, so that you can dredge them up when you need them.

Let's say, in this case, that John once thought Mary was flirting with her old flame Bill at a party. This is a good thing to accuse her of in the current argument, as it is totally unrelated to the coffee table. However, John must be careful how he brings it up; if he does it *too* abruptly, Mary could become confused, and the argument could end right there:

MARY: Honey, could you please try not to leave your socks on the coffee table?

JOHN: Oh *yeah?* Well what about your old flame, Bill?

MARY (confused): Huh?

So what John needs to do—this is the essential skill of marital arguing—is to come up with a smooth way to get from *Mary's* topic to *his* topic. This technique is called a "segue," (pronounced "segue"), and if you do it right, it will usually lead to a whole new series of mutant topics you can argue about. Let's see how it works:

MARY: Honey, could you please try not to leave your socks on the coffee table? ← OPENING TOPIC

JOHN: Why do you always do that? ← SEGUE

MARY: Always do what?

JOHN: Always look for things to criticize.

MARY: I *don't* always look for things to criticize. I just don't like finding your damn . . .

JOHN: Fine. Great. Curse at me. I didn't see you cursing at *Bill,* at the Johnsons' party. ← INTRODUCTION OF COUNTERTOPIC

MARY: What is *that* supposed to mean?

JOHN: Oh, come on. You were flirting with him.

MARY: I was flirting? And I suppose you weren't *all over* Jennifer? ← FIRST MUTANT TOPIC

JOHN: I don't see how you could have known what I was doing, after all you had to drink. ← SECOND MUTANT TOPIC

See how effectively this veteran married couple handled the situation? In just a few quick sentences, they have

CREATIVE ARGUING IS THE KEY TO
A LONG-LASTING MARRIAGE

gone from a seemingly unpromising top-ic, socks, to a whole treasure trove of issues that they can debate and dredge up again for years to come. I'm not saying you young couples will get this kind of results your first time out of the gate, but with a little practice, you'll get the hang of it, and it can lead to the discovery of a whole new facet of your relationship (see Chapter 11, "How to Put New Life into Your Marriage or Else Get a Divorce").

CHAPTER 9

Children: Big Mistake, or Bad Idea?

FAMILY PORTRAIT

In this chapter, we're going to talk about how children affect your marriage. We're *not* going to talk about how you actually produce the children in the first place. We covered that topic thoroughly in an earlier book, *Babies and Other Hazards of Sex*, which explores the whole area of childbirth in great detail and reaches the following scientific breakthrough conclusions:

1. It is very painful.
(If you'd like additional facts on this topic, you can read the book, although it doesn't contain any.)

For now, however, we're going to talk about how your married life will change *after* you have children, so that you'll be able to carefully and rationally weigh the pros and cons of parenthood, then barge right ahead and have children without any understanding of what you're really getting into, just like everybody else.

What It Really Means to Be a Parent

What it really means to be a parent—note this carefully, because it's the essence of the whole thing—is: You will spend an enormous portion of your time lurking outside public-toilet stalls.

For reasons that modern medical science has been unable to explain, children almost never have to go to the bathroom when they are within eight or nine miles of their own home toilets. It does no good to try to make them. Tell a child to go to the bathroom before you leave home, and the child will insist that not only does he or she not have to go *now*, but he or she will probably never have to go to the bathroom *ever again*.

And of course when you get where you're going, let's say a restaurant, the child will wait until your entrees are about to emerge from the kitchen, then announce that he or she has to go. Children are incredibly sensitive to approaching entrees.

So you will take the child to the bathroom, and, if it is an especially loath-

some bathroom, a bathroom that has clearly not been cleaned since the fall of Rome, a bathroom where the floor is littered with the skeletons of Board of Health employees who died attempting to inspect it, if it is *this* kind of bathroom, the child will immediately announce that he or she has to do Number Two.

And of course you must stay there with the child. The child will want you to stand *right outside* the toilet stall, while the child goes in there, and ... and nobody really knows. It's a real mystery, what young children do in public-toilet stalls. Whatever it is, it takes them longer than it took you, the parents, to produce them in the first place.

What I hate about this is that restaurant men's rooms are often fairly small and intimate places, and while I'm standing there, waiting for my son, strangers are constantly coming in to pee, and there I am, inches away from them, lurking there with no apparent purpose, like some kind of sex pervert who *likes* being in disgusting men's rooms. So, to show that this is not the case, I try to keep a conversation going with my son. Except the only thing I can think of to talk to him about is how the old Number Two is going. I mean, you'd feel like an idiot in that situation, talking about the Strategic Defense Initiative. So we have these ludicrous exchanges:

ME (brightly): So! Robert! How's it going in there?!
ROBERT (irritated): You just *asked* me that.
ME (grinning like a madman at the peeing stranger so as to reassure him that everything is okay): Ha ha!

Eventually, the child will emerge from the stall, when he or she is abso-

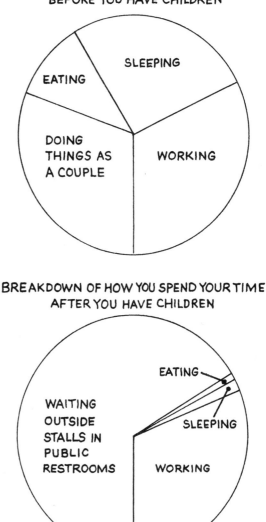

BREAKDOWN OF HOW YOU SPEND YOUR TIME
BEFORE YOU HAVE CHILDREN

BREAKDOWN OF HOW YOU SPEND YOUR TIME
AFTER YOU HAVE CHILDREN

lutely sure that the entrees are stone frozen cold. The child doesn't care about the food, because children don't go to restaurants to eat. They go to restaurants to go to the bathroom and play loud shrieking games under the table, so that you, the parents, are constantly ducking your heads under and hissing, *"Stop that!"* like some deranged species of duck. The child never actually touches the food, which is why many modern restaurants are saving money by serving reusable children's entrees made entirely out of plastic.

Where Can I Find Decent, Affordable Child Care?

Hahahahahaha.

Forgive me for laughing in a bitter and cynical fashion, but you happen to have hit upon the most serious problem facing the Free World today: the international child-care crisis.

In the old days, of course, the Free World had an excellent system of high-quality, low-cost child care in this country, namely your mother. Unfortunately, however, your mother is no longer interested in caring for children. She is interested in spending what little is left of her life among furniture that does not have Hawaiian Punch stains all over it. And you, of course, can't engage in child care, because you need to get out and have a Rewarding Career so you can have a chance to earn enough money to pay for child care.

Except there is hardly any available. You go around checking out pre-school facilities, and you keep finding yourself in dank basements where the staff is missing a large percentage of its teeth and the educational materials consist of four crayons—all burnt sienna—and a GI Joe doll with most of the limbs pulled off. The result is that people are desperate. People who work in New Jersey are dropping their children off each morning at child-care centers in Utah.

Fortunately there is some hope. A new company recently opened for business, called the Exactly What You Are Looking For Child Care Company. It has spacious, clean, modern, well-equipped facilities within walking distance of your home or office; it's open from 5 A.M. until as late as you want; and it's staffed by middle-aged British women who love children and attend church regularly and are all licensed pediatricians. The cost is $3.50 per child per day. If you're interested in enrolling your child in this excellent program, all you have to do is kill the Wicked Witch of the West.

BE SURE TO SELECT A CHILD-CARE CENTER STAFFED BY PEOPLE WHO ENJOY PLAYING WITH KIDS

How Children Affect Your Sex Life

Children are Nature's very own form of birth control. To illustrate how they perform this vital function, let's take a look at a minute-by-minute schedule, showing how my wife and I put our six-year-old son, Robert, to bed on a typical evening. To make sure we have some time to ourselves, we try to have him in bed by 8 P.M., which means we start the procedure a full hour earlier:

7 P.M.—We announce to Robert that it's time to get ready for bed.

7:04, 7:09, 7:12, 7:14, 7:17, 7:18, 7:22, 7:24, 7:25, 7:26 & 7:27—We announce to Robert that he really has to start getting ready for bed Right Now and we are Not Kidding.

7:28—Robert goes to his room and actually starts getting ready for bed.

7:29—Robert notices that his rubber Godzilla doll is missing. *How* he notices this, in a room containing roughly 78,500 toys, nobody can explain, but he does notice it, and of course all other activities must cease until we can resolve this matter because God forbid that a child should be required to go to bed without his rubber Godzilla doll.

7:43—We locate Godzilla and Robert begins getting ready for bed again. He is supposed to take off his clothes and put on his pajamas. He can do this All By Himself.

9:27—So far, All By Himself, Robert has removed his shirt and, if he is really on a roll, one of his shoes. I go in to help him along.

9:30—Now in his pajamas, Robert has his teeth brushed, which is the signal for him to announce that he is hungry. We tell him that this is his own fault, because he did not finish supper, and he absolutely cannot have any more food, no sir, forget it, not a chance, it's time he learned his lesson, etc.

9:57—Robert finishes a bowl of Zoo-Roni and submits to having teeth brushed again.

10:02—We read a bedtime story, *Horton Hatches the Egg*, by Dr. Seuss, which takes us quite a while because we must study every page very, very carefully in case there is some tiny detail we might have possibly missed when we read it on each of the previous 267 consecutive nights.

10:43—We announce that it's time to go to bed.

10:45, 10:47, 10:51, 10:54, 10:56 & 10:59—We announce that it really is time to go to bed Right Now and we are Not Kidding.

11:03—Robert actually gets into his bed. We tuck him in, kiss him good night, and creep silently out of the room, alone at last.

11:17—Robert falls asleep and is immediately awakened by a terrible nightmare caused by being in bed with his face six inches from a rubber Godzilla doll. We remove it.

11:28—We kiss Robert good night and creep silently out of the room, alone at last.

11:32—Hearing noise from Robert's room, we return to find him sobbing loudly. So upset that he is barely able to choke out the words, he explains that he has just realized that the mother bird in *Horton Hatches the Egg* loses her baby in the end, and even though she was terribly mean, she is probably very sorry by now, and very lonely. We try to explain that this is not at *all* the point that Dr. Seuss was trying to make, but Robert is inconsolable. Finally we agree to let him climb into bed with us, but "just for one minute."

2:47 A.M.—We return Robert to bed, kiss him good night, and creep silently from the room, alone at last.

3:14, 3:58, 4:26, 5:11 & 5:43—The household goes on Red Alert status as various routine nightmares occur, each one causing us to stagger, half-asleep, down the hallway, like actors in a scene from *Night of the Living Dead Parents*.

6:12—Dawn breaks.

Whenever I read newspaper stories about people who have, say, nine children, I never ask myself: "How do they manage to take care of them all?" I ask myself: "Where did they find the time to *conceive* them all?"

I don't mean to suggest, by what I've said in this chapter, that children are bad for a relationship. Because in the end, the negative aspects of being a parent—the loss of intimacy, the expense, the total lack of free time, the incredible burden of responsibility, the constant nagging fear of having done the wrong thing, etc.—are more than outweighed by the positive aspects, such as never again lacking for primitive drawings to attach to your refrigerator with magnets.

KIDS SURE CAN MAKE PESTS OF THEMSELVES

CHAPTER 10

How to Have an Affair

My first piece of advice is that if you're planning to have an affair, you should read this chapter in a safe place, such as the linen closet. You don't want to be sitting around the living room, in plain view of your spouse, reading a chapter entitled, in great big letters, "How to Have an Affair." I recommend that you hide this book under your garments and

say to your spouse: "Well, I guess I'll go sit in the linen closet with a flashlight for a while!" Your spouse will never suspect a thing. Unless you don't have a linen closet. That would be a dead giveaway.

Another dead giveaway is acting guilty. Let's take a typical person—we'll call him "Ed"°—who is having an affair with a woman at his office. If Ed has a

° Although his name is actually "Steve."

guilty conscience, he may accidentally reveal this in casual conversation with his wife:

ED'S WIFE: Would you like another corn muffin, dear?

ED: I'm having an affair with a woman in my office!

Even if Ed's wife is not a trained psychologist, she might conceivably gather, from certain subtle verbal "clues" Ed is subconsciously dropping, that something "fishy" is going on. Ed must make more of an effort to watch his words:

ED'S WIFE: Would you like another corn muffin, dear?

ED: I'm *not* having an affair with a woman in my office!

Most affairs occur at the office, of course, which leads us to another important rule of affair-having: *Never be discreet at the office.* To illustrate why this is important, let's consider two people, Ellen and Chuck, who have worked together in a large corporate office for several years, and have recently started having an affair.

Up to this point, Ellen and Chuck have probably been behaving the way men and women always behave in offices, which is to say: constantly winking and leering and engaging in loud and fun suggestive sexual banter. Behaving like lust-crazed fools has been a major form of entertainment in offices for as long as anybody can remember; in terms of total American corporation employee hours consumed, suggestive banter ranks well ahead of work, and only slightly behind making Xerox copies of personal documents.

But like so many couples, Chuck and Ellen, now that they are engaging in *real*, as opposed to pretend, sexual activity, suddenly decide they have to be discreet. They never banter. They never eat lunch together any more. They walk past each other without even looking at each other. When they are forced, by circumstances, to be together, they display the same kind of warmth and closeness toward each other as the Vice-president of the United States displays toward deceased heads of state. They are formal and cool.

They are also morons. The other employees, who, if they have been in the corporate world more than six weeks, have already witnessed hundreds of other major office affairs, will immediately recognize the cause of this sudden change in behavior. Ellen and Chuck might just as well go around wearing convention-style nametags that say:

Within days everybody in the office will know what's going on. The affair will be discussed extensively in staff meetings. It could well appear in the annual report to the stockholders.

What this means, of course, is that if you want your affair to go unnoticed by your co-workers, you have to be blatantly obvious about it. Chuck should wait until the office is extremely quiet, then stand up at his desk and shout across 47 desks to Ellen: "HEY ELLEN! WHAT DO YOU SAY WE MEET AT THE OUT O' TOWN MOTOR LODGE AFTER WORK TODAY AND HAVE SEXUAL INTERCOURSE!" And Ellen should shout back: "HECK YES!! I HAVE MY DIAPHRAGM RIGHT HERE IN MY PURSE!"

Chuck's and Ellen's co-workers would never suspect a thing. "What a couple of kidders Chuck and Ellen are!" the co-workers would chuckle.

How You Can Tell If Your Spouse Is Having an Affair

You can always tell. No matter how careful your spouse is, he or she is going to make a mistake somewhere, and you'll catch it, if you know the Major Warning Signs, which are:

1. Your spouse acts strange.
2. Your spouse, trying to trick you, acts normal.

If you notice either of these Warning Signs, you should wait until your spouse is in a vulnerable position, such as reclining in a dental chair, and then you should point-blank ask the following gently probing question (if your spouse is male): "*Well?* Who is she?"

Now listen closely to the answer. If it's something specific like: "You mean the person I'm having an affair with? She is Dorina Mae Swiggins," that means your suspicions are probably justified. But if it's something evasive like: "What are you talking about?" or "Who is *Who?*", then you quite frankly have to ask yourself how come your spouse is refusing to answer a simple direct question. Either way, this would be a good time to read the next chapter.

CHAPTER 11

How to Put New Life into Your Marriage or Else Get a Divorce

Time takes its toll on every marriage. The sense of romance and adventure that you feel as you take your wedding vows on that bright Saturday afternoon in June inevitably gives way to familiarity and even boredom, often as early as 8:30 that evening. Yet some couples seem to go on happily forever, a good example being Ferdinand and Imelda Marcos, former owners of the Philippines. Long ago, they discovered a secret that has worked its magic for many successful couples: thoughtfulness. Ferdinand and Imelda were always showing each other, in little ways, that they cared. For example, when Imelda would get depressed because of the hassle and strain of everyday life, plus the fact that she was bloating up like an inflatable life raft, Ferdinand would say to her: "Buttercup, you look depressed. Why not take the national treasury and purchase every luxury consumer object in France?" This thoughtful gesture never failed to perk her up.

Of course you may not be in a position to demonstrate quite that level of care, but there are things you can do to show your commitment to each other—little, thoughtful, romantic gestures that say you still think the other person is "somebody special." For example, you can:

1. Try to remember (you guys, especially) to flush the toilet.

2. Remember your spouse's birthday. "Hey!" you can say. "Wasn't your birthday last month?"

3. Go dancing, or even . . .

4. Go dancing with your spouse.

5. On your anniversary, give your spouse an appropriate traditional gift for whatever year it is, as shown on the accompanying chart:

A NIGHT OF DANCING WITH YOUR SPOUSE CAN BRING YOU CLOSER, OR AT LEAST ALLOW YOU TO RUB BELLIES FOR A WHILE

NUMBER OF ANNIVERSARY	TRADITIONAL GIFT
1st	Ore
5th	McNuggets
10th	Veg-o-Matic
15th	Oil change
20th	"Slim" Whitman album
30th	TV tray or assault rifle
40th	Frankincense
50th	Ointment
60th	Suppository
70th	Indonesian Fighting Snake

DR. EVA C. TUBBY PERFORMS DAVE'S SECOND WEDDING

6. Consider renewing your wedding vows. The best place to do this is Las Vegas, where "wedding chapels" are a major industry, along with divorce, gambling, and scorpion paperweights. My wife and I renewed our vows in Vegas a little while back, on a Friday the 13th, in the very same chapel (everything I am telling you here is the truth) where Joan Collins got married her third or fourth time. The whole thing took less than four minutes and cost only $50, plus a tip for the minister, who was named (I swear) Dr. Eva C. Tubby.

7. Go on a Getaway Vacation Fling. Just the two of you. One day, when the pressure gets to be too much, you should just say to your spouse, out of the

WHY NOT SNEAK OFF TO FLORIDA FOR A WEEK?

blue: "Let's go!" Then you should impulsively throw a few items into a suitcase, jump into a cab, race to the airport, and hop on the next plane to Hawaii, or the Caribbean, or Europe, or wherever you want to go. Why not?

You'll be glad you did it. Once you're up in the air, settled back in your seats, sipping champagne (Why not?), the two of you can hold hands, close your eyes, and just let your minds drift away to . . .

THE CHILDREN!! MY GOD, YOU FORGOT THE CHILDREN!!! TURN THE PLANE BACK RIGHT NOW!!!

Sometimes, however, even thoughtful and romantic gestures such as these don't do the trick. Sometimes you find that the two of you, no matter how much you may once have cared for each other, are starting to drift apart. It's the little things that give you away: you hardly ever talk any more; you no longer kiss each other when you come home; you live in different states; etc. Maybe it's time to face up to the fact that you're just not right for each other any more. Hey, it happens. People change. They get older, they get larger, and sometimes they start to smell bad. Maybe the time has come to think about—let's come right out and say it:

Divorce

The most important thing is to get yourself a lawyer. Oh, I realize you probably think you and your spouse can work this thing out amicably without any third parties. But what if suddenly your *spouse* gets a lawyer, and you end up stone broke on the street wearing only a Hefty trash bag? You can't afford to take this chance. You need a lawyer, too, so you and your spouse can *both* end up wearing Hefty trash bags. I recommend the ones with the patented "Cinch Sak" drawstring top.

How to Select a Lawyer

The best way to select a lawyer is to watch late-night television, which is where your top legal minds advertise. You're looking for one who can demonstrate:

• *Integrity*, in the form of wearing a dark suit;

• *A sound knowledge of the law*, in the form of standing in front of a shelf with a lot of books on it; and

• *A sincere personal interest in you*, in the form of making the following speech: "Hello. I'm Leonard Packmonger, of Leonard Packmonger Legal Attorneys of the Law Associates. Does

your back hurt sometimes? Do you ever use consumer products? If so, I would say that, based upon my many, many weeks of experience in handling cases just like yours, you definitely have good grounds for a major lawsuit. Come on in and let's talk about it and sign some binding documents. Just for stopping by, we'll give you a free, no-obligation neck brace."

Grounds for Divorce

At one time it was difficult to get out of a marriage unless there was some kind of very serious problem with it, such as that one or more of the people involved had become deceased.

Today, fortunately, it is easier to get divorced in most states than to get a transmission repaired properly. The only requirement is that you have a legal reason, which is technically known as "grounds." If you have no grounds of your own, you can probably get some from your lawyer, who will have an ample supply left over from previous cases; or you can select some from this convenient list of grounds, all of which are 100 percent legally valid in every state in the union. Or at least they should be.

- Wearing shorts and black knee socks at the same time.
- Calling you "Sweetie Beancakes" in front of strangers.
- Forgetting to buy beer.
- Repeatedly putting the ice-cube tray back in the refrigerator with two or fewer ice cubes in it.
- Bringing the car home with just enough gas in it so that, if you shut the engine off and coast on the downhill slopes, you can get as far as the end of the driveway.
- Any cigar-related activity.
- Standing next to you with a sour facial expression at a party while you tell a really terrific joke and then loudly announcing the punchline three-tenths of a second before you get to it and then saying: "Isn't that AWFUL?" (NOTE: In some states this is grounds not only for divorce, but also for murder.)

- Golf.
- One day, with no warning, bringing home:
    1. a cat, or
    2. an Amway representative.
- Leaving his or her toenails in a prominent location as though they were decorative art objects.
- Using the word "frankly" a lot and not meaning it as a joke.
- Operating a loud household appliance during the Super Bowl.
- Secretly liking Geraldo Rivera.

The Divorce Proceedings

You want to keep them as quiet as possible. You don't want them to be highly publicized, like the divorce a few years back in Palm Beach, Florida, involving wealthy socialites Peter and Roxanne Pulitzer, in which Peter claimed that Roxanne had slept with a three-foot trumpet. Naturally the national news media found this to be far more interesting than anything that has ever happened in the Middle East, so now *everybody* has heard about it. Roxanne Pulitzer could visit a remote and primitive Amazon jungle tribe, and the tribespeople would all gather around her and make trumpet sounds.

YOU SHOULD BE PREPARED FOR ANYTHING DURING YOUR DIVORCE PROCEEDING - EVEN THE TRUTH!

So you want to avoid letting your intimate secrets out. Not that I am suggesting for one second that you have ever slept with a trumpet. You are more the bassoon type.

Starting Over after the Divorce

Eventually the divorce will become final, and you can start picking up the broken pieces of your life and selling them to pay off your legal bills. But also you must think about the future, and, yes, meeting someone new. You must not be afraid. Oh, sure, you got burned and you got hurt. But that is no reason to give up. You must not be afraid. You must show the same kind of gumption as the cowboy, who, if he gets thrown off a horse, climbs right back on, and if he gets thrown off again, climbs right back on again, and so on, until virtually all of his brain cells are dead.

Back to Chapter 1.

Index

Bazooka bubble gum, 47
Bra Strap Research Center, 29

Clam goaders, 48
Cleaver, Beaver, 14

Deviled Egg Transporter, 27

Elephant Man's Disease, 6
Esplanade, Victor, 50

Flag, Capture the, 42

Giant albino turkeys, 19
Godzilla, 73, 74
Guard, Right, 16

Harriet, Ozzie and, 17
Helmsley, Leona, 33

Indonesian Fighting Snake, 82

Jell-O, 26

Karamazov, Brothers, 6

LeGume, Baron, 30
LePoon, Dwayne R., Jr., 49
Lodge, Out o' Town Motor, 78
Loins of Passion, 30

Marcos, Ferdinand and Imelda, 80–81
Mayonnaise, xi
Mongolian Death Flu, 51
Mutant argument topics, 67

National Rifle Association, 43
Nature, Mother, 22

Pancreas, rat, 10
Perot, H. Ross, 33

Pez, 48
Planet of the Ideal Women, 27
Pope, the, ix
Princess Diana, having a wedding as nice as, 46
"Pumpkin Surprise," 47

Roni, Zoo-, 74

Sea Cucumber Island Resort, 56–57
Secretion, Compound Annualized Rate of, 62
Service, Internal Revenue, 26
Seuss, Dr., 74
Sin, living in, 13–14
Somebody, Archduke, 66
Squid, having sex with, x
Staff, Joint Chiefs of, 27
Strategic Defense Initiative, 71
Strychnine, ix
Summer Bosom Camp, 24

Taylor, Elizabeth, 36
Trumpets, having sex with, 85, 87
Tupperware, hurling, 14
Tupperware, role in sex act, 27

Urchins, sea, 7

Whip, Cool, 20
Whitman, "Slim," 82
Wipes, Handi-, 45
World Series, ix

Ziggy, 62
Zippos, 3

BABIES
& OTHER
HAZARDS OF SEX

**How to make a tiny
person in only 9 months,
with tools you probably
have around the home**

Contents

Chapter 1 **Should You Have a Baby? Should Anybody?** .... page **93**

Chapter 2 **Pregnancy** .... page **103**

Chapter 3 **Getting Ready for Baby** .... page **110**

Chapter 4 **Preparing for Birth** .... page **116**

Chapter 5 **The Actual Blessed Event** .... page **122**

Chapter 6 **The Hospital Stay** .... page **128**

Chapter 7 **Maintenance of a New Baby** .... page **132**

Chapter 8 **The First Six Months** .... page **142**

Chapter 9 **Six Months to a Year** .... page **151**

Chapter 10 **The Second Year** .... page **159**

Chapter 11 **The Third Year** .... page **170**

Epilogue: Should You Have Another? .... page **179**

Index .... page **181**

Author's Qualifications to Write a Book about Babies

Dave Barry, 36, has a son, Robert, who began as a baby and successfully reached the age of 3 without becoming an ax murderer or anything, as far as anybody knows.

In addition, Mr. Barry has spent a number of hours thinking about babies, and has observed them in other people's cars at traffic lights. He also owns a dog, and at the age of 15 completed much of the course required to obtain a Red Cross Senior Life-saving Badge.

Chapter 1

Should You Have a Baby? Should Anybody?

UNPREGNANT WOMAN
(PROBABLY WILL REMAIN
UNPREGNANT, TOO)

PREGNANT WOMAN

Some Important Pompous Advice to Couples about to Get Pregnant

Getting pregnant is an extremely major thing to do, especially for the woman, because she has to become huge and bloated and wear garments the size of café awnings. This is the woman's job, and it is a tradition dating back thousands of years to a time when men were not available for having babies because they had to stand outside the cave night and day to fend off mastodons.

Of course, there is very little mastodon-fending to be done these days, but men still manage to keep themselves busy, what with buying tires and all. So it is still pretty much the traditional role of the woman to get pregnant and go through labor and have the baby and feed it and nurture it up until it is

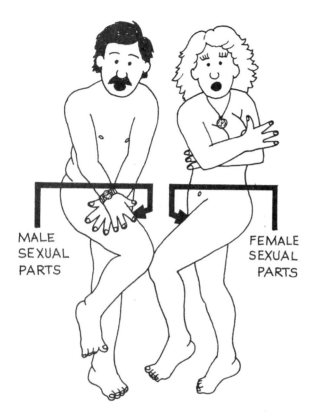

MALE
SEXUAL
PARTS

FEMALE
SEXUAL
PARTS

old enough to throw a football with reasonable accuracy.

In recent years, however, men have become more involved in childbirth and childrearing as part of a federally mandated national trend. Under the terms of this trend, men are beginning to see that they can free themselves from the restrictions of their self-made macho prisons and allow

themselves to show their emotions openly—to laugh, to cry, to love, to just generally behave like certified wimps. What this means to you males is that if you get a female pregnant, you are now expected to behave in an extremely sensitive manner and watch the baby come out. I will explain how to do this later.

My point here, young couples, is that baby-having is extremely serious business, and you probably don't have the vaguest idea what you're doing, as is evidenced by the fact that you're reading a very sloppy and poorly researched book. So I think you should start off with the quiz on the opposite page to test your knowledge of important baby facts.

Male Birth Control

To understand the problems involved in birth control, let's look at this quotation from the excellent 1962 medical reference work *Where Do Babies Come From?*, which I purchased from a nurse at a yard sale:

"The way the rooster gets his sperm inside the hen, to fertilize her egg, is very strange to us."

The problem with this quotation, of course, is that it suggests we have given a great deal of thought to the question of how to get sperm inside a chicken. But it does

Quiz for Young Couples Who Want to Have a Baby and Who Clearly Have No Idea What They're Getting Into

1. HOW MANY TIMES DO YOU ESTIMATE THAT A BABY'S DIAPER MUST BE CHANGED BEFORE THE BABY BECOMES TOILET TRAINED?

a. One million billion jillion.

b. One skillion hillion drillion gazillion.

c. Many babies never become toilet trained.

2. WHAT IS THE MOST DISGUSTING THING YOU CAN IMAGINE THAT A BABY MIGHT DELIBERATELY PUT INTO ITS MOUTH?

a. A slime-covered slug.

b. A slime-covered slug that has just thrown up all over itself.

c. A slime-covered slug that has just thrown up all over itself because it has fallen into a vat of toxic sewage.

3. WHEN IS THE BEST TIME TO TAKE A BABY TO A NICE RESTAURANT?

a. During a fire.

b. On Easygoing Deaf People's Night.

c. After the baby has graduated from medical school.

4. WHAT DO YOU DO IF YOUR TWO-MONTH-OLD BABY IS SCREAMING IN AN AIRPLANE AND REFUSES TO SHUT UP AND IS CLEARLY DISTURBING THE OTHER PASSENGERS?

a. Summon the stewardess and say: "Stewardess, whose baby is this?"

b. Summon the stewardess and say: "Stewardess, this baby is very interested in aviation. Please take it up and show it around the cockpit for the duration of the flight."

c. Summon the stewardess and say: "Stewardess, please inform the captain that this infant has just handed me a note in which it threatens to continue crying unless it is taken to Havana immediately."

HOW TO SCORE   Give yourself one point for each question you answered. If you scored three or higher, you are very serious about this, and you might as well go ahead and have a baby. If you scored two or lower, you either aren't really interested in having a baby, or you have the I.Q. of a tree stump. In either case, you should read the section on birth control.

Those of you who are going to have babies should skip the sections on birth control, because they contain many sexually explicit terms, such as "rooster." You can go directly to the section, "How Much Does It Cost to Have a Baby?"

bring up the basic issue in birth control, which is to avoid fertilization you somehow have to keep the male sperm away from the female egg. This is not easy, because men contain absurd quantities of sperm, produced by the same hormone that causes them to take league softball seriously.

The most effective method of birth control for males is the one where, just when the male and the female are about to engage in sex, the friends of the male burst out of the bushes and yell and jump up and down on the bumper and spray shaving cream all over the car. The problem is that this

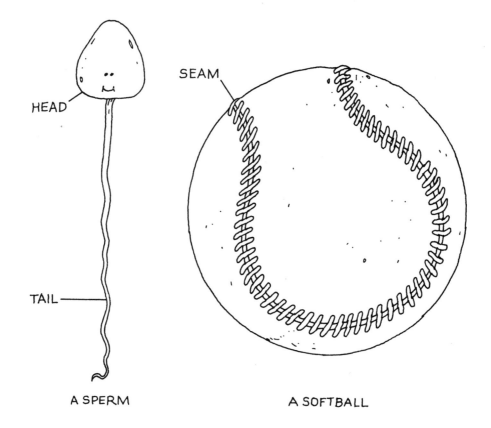

HEAD

TAIL

A SPERM

SEAM

A SOFTBALL

method is pretty much limited to teenage males. Another popular form of teenage birth control is the condom, which the male uses by placing it in his wallet and carrying it around for four years and pulling it out to show his friends in the Dairy Queen parking lot.

THE CONDOM LADY

STANDARD CONDOM

MEXICAN CONDOM

When I was a teenage male, it was very difficult to obtain condoms, because you had to buy them at the drugstore from the Condom Lady, who was about 65 and looked like your grandmother only more moral. She had a photographic memory so she knew exactly who you were, and as soon as you left the store, she would dial a special number that would connect her with a gigantic loud-

THE AFTERMATH OF A TYPICAL VASECTOMY

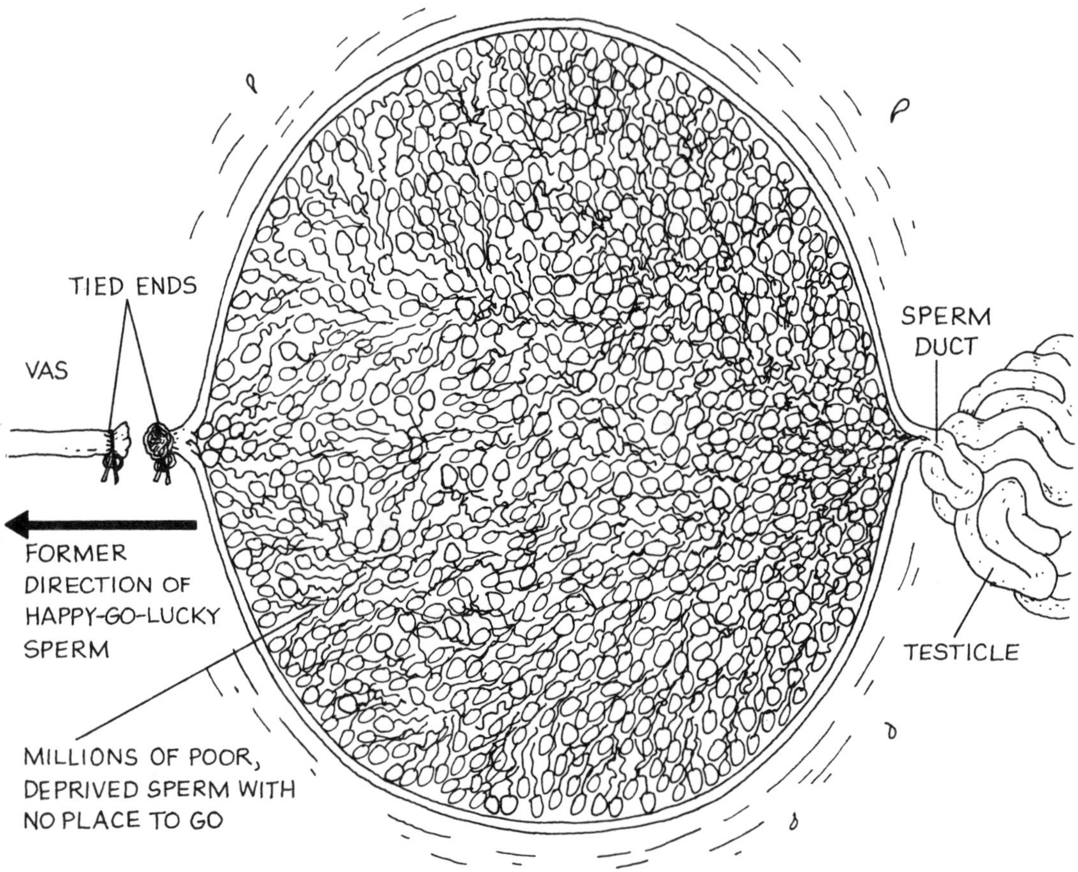

TIED ENDS

VAS

SPERM
DUCT

FORMER
DIRECTION OF
HAPPY-GO-LUCKY
SPERM

TESTICLE

MILLIONS OF POOR,
DEPRIVED SPERM WITH
NO PLACE TO GO

speaker system so she could announce to your parents and your teachers and everybody in your church or synagogue and people on the street that you had just bought condoms. Now they sell condoms right out in the open on display racks, just like breath mints or something, and the Condom Lady has switched over to selling *Penthouse* magazine to middle-aged businessmen at the airport.

For older males, the most effective form of birth control is the vasectomy, which is a simple surgical procedure that can be done right in your doctor's office. Notice I say *your* doctor's office. I myself would insist on having it done at the Mayo Clinic surrounded by a team of several dozen crackerjack surgeons and leaders of all the world's major religious groups. I don't take any chances with so-called minor surgical procedures, because the last one I had was when the dentist took my wisdom teeth out, and subsequently I almost bled to death in the carpet department at Sears.

The way I understand it, what happens in a vasectomy is they tie some kind of medical knot in the male conduit so the sperm can't get through. Of course, this leads to the obvious question, which is: Won't the sperm back up? Will these poor pathetic males someday explode like water balloons, spewing sperm all over and possibly ruining an important sales presentation? I say the American Medical Association ought to get the hell off the golf course and answer this question before the public becomes needlessly alarmed.

Female Birth Control

Female birth control is much more complicated, because once sperm are safely inside a female, they become very aggressive. They barge up and down the various feminine tubes and canals, hooting and whistling, until they locate the egg. Then they strike up a conversation, feigning great interest in the egg's personality, but actually looking for the first opportunity to penetrate.

There is no absolutely foolproof way to stop this fertilization process. The old wives'

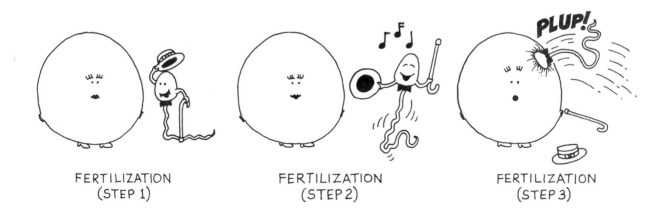

FERTILIZATION
(STEP 1)

FERTILIZATION
(STEP 2)

FERTILIZATION
(STEP 3)

tale, of course, is that a female could avoid getting pregnant by not having sex, but this was disproved by a recent experiment in which Harvard University biologists placed 50 old wives in a locked condominium for two years, and 35 percent of them got pregnant anyway merely by looking at pictures of Raymond Burr.

But there are things that a woman can do. She can insert one of the many feminine insertion devices shaped like alien space vehicles, which are designed to scare the sperm into stampeding right back out the

A TYPICAL IUD

vestibule. Or she can take the pill, which messes with her hormones in such a way that her body gets fooled into thinking it is already pregnant. The egg gets all bloated and starts to feel weepy and nauseous in the morning, and when it comes clomping down the fallopian tubes, the sperm all go stampeding right back out the vestibule.

What the public is eagerly awaiting, of course, is a birth-control pill for males. If you ever see members of the public gathering in eager little knots, that's what they're waiting for. The male medical establishment has been assuring us for years that such a pill is right around the corner. "Believe us," they say, "there's nothing we'd rather do than come up with a pill that messes with our hormones, so we can take this burden from the women, who have been unfairly forced to bear it for far too long. In fact, we'd probably finish developing the male birth-control pill tonight, but we have to play league softball."

How Much Does It Cost to Have a Baby?

In primitive times, having a baby was very inexpensive. When women were ready to give birth, they simply went off and squat-

PRIMITIVE BIRTHING

charge you much more. It is a good idea to "shop around" before you settle on a doctor. Ask about the condition of his Mercedes. Ask about the competence of his mechanic. Don't be shy! After all, you're paying for it.

The Cost of Everything after the Baby Is Born Right Up until It Goes to College or, God Help You, Graduate School

Again, it is very hard to be specific here, largely because I haven't done any research. In my own case, I estimate that the cost of raising our son, Robert, to age three, which is where he is at the moment, breaks down as follows:

> Little metal cars—$13,000
> Everything else—$4,000

If we extrapolate this out for the next 18 years, assuming that inflation continues, and that we don't have a nuclear war, which would pretty much render the point moot, we can conclude that in the long term a child can cost just scads of money. Maybe you should go back and read the section on birth control.

ted in a field; this cost nothing except for a nominal field-rental charge. Today, of course, the medical profession prefers that you have your baby in a hospital, because only there can doctors, thanks to the many advances in medical equipment and techniques, receive large sums of money.

It is difficult to predict exactly what the doctor's bill for your pregnancy will be, because every situation is different. If your doctor's Mercedes-Benz is running well, he may charge you as little as $2,000; if there are complications, such as that he has been hearing a little ticking sound in the transmission lately, then he may be forced to

Should the Woman Quit Her Job to Have a Baby?

The advantage of quitting your job is that if you want to, you can make a really nasty speech to your boss, right in front of everybody, where you tell him he's incompetent and has the worst case of bodily odor in the annals of medicine. The disadvantage is that you'll lose your income, which means for the next eight or nine years the only new article of clothing you will be able to afford for yourself will be dress shields.

The advantage of keeping your job is that you will be able to stand around the Xerox machine for a couple of months showing pictures of your child to your co-workers, who will ooh and ahh even though very young infants tend to look like unwashed fruit.

What about Insurance?

Don't worry. Your insurance needs will automatically be taken care of by squadrons of insurance salesmen, who can detect a pregnant woman up to 11 miles away on a calm day, and who will show up at your house carrying sleeping bags and enough freeze-dried food to enable them to stay for weeks if necessary.

The Intangible Benefits

Of course, you can't reduce children to mere dollars and cents. There are many intangible benefits, by which I mean benefits that, when coupled with 50 cents, will buy you a cup of coffee.

For example, I know a person named Michael who, although he does not personally own any children, once got a major benefit from his five-year-old nephew. What happened was they were at this big open-air concert in Boston to celebrate the Bicentennial, and when it was over the crowd was enormous and it looked as though they'd never get out. So Michael held his nephew aloft and yelled, "Sick child! Sick child! Make way!" loud enough so nobody could hear the nephew saying, "I'm not sick, Uncle Mike." And the crowd made way, which meant Mike got home hours sooner than he would have otherwise.

So there is an example of a person getting a large intangible benefit from a child, and it wasn't even technically his child. Also, you can get terrific tax deductions for children. Of course, the same can be said for insulation, but you'd look like an idiot, waving insulation aloft at an outdoor concert.

Chapter 2

Pregnancy

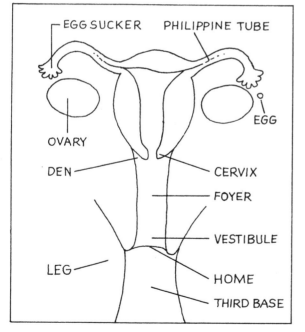

EGG SUCKER   PHILIPPINE TUBE

EGG

OVARY

DEN

CERVIX

FOYER

VESTIBULE

LEG

HOME

THIRD BASE

W hat on earth is going on inside pregnant women that makes them become so large and weepy? This is the fascinating biological topic we will explore in this chapter, at least until we start to feel nauseous.

The Female Reproductive System

The female reproductive system is extremely complicated, because females contain a great many organs, with new ones being discovered every day. Connecting these organs is an elaborate network of over seven statute miles of tubes and canals (see diagram). Nobody really understands this system. Burly male doctors called "gynecologists" are always groping around in there with rubber gloves, trying to figure out what's going on. Or so they claim.

Fertilization

The fertilization process starts in the ovaries, which each month produce an egg. After a hearty breakfast, this egg treks down the fallopian tubes, where it is propositioned by millions of sperm, which are extremely small, totally insincere one-celled animals. Often, to attract the egg, the sperm will engage in ritual behavior, such as ruf-

fling their neck feathers. No wait, I'm thinking of birds.

Anyway, the egg, a fat and globular kind of cell with very little self-esteem, finds itself in this dimly lit fallopian tube surrounded by all these sleek, well-traveled sperm, and sooner or later one of them manages to penetrate. Then the sperm all saunter off, winking and nudging each other toward the bile duct, while the fertilized egg slinks down to the uterus, an organ shaped like Webster Groves, Missouri. The egg attaches itself to the uterine wall, and thus begins an incredibly subtle and complex chain of hormonal secretions that signal to the woman's body that it is time to start shopping around for fluffy little baby garments. Pregnancy has begun.

The Stages of Development of the Fetus

WEEK 5:   The fetus is only 6.7 liters in circumference yet has already developed the ability to shriek in airplanes.

WEEK 10:   The fetus is almost 12 millipedes in longitude and has a prehensile tail and wings. It will probably lose these things before it is born.

WEEK 20:   The fetus measures 4 on the Richter scale and is perusing mail-order catalogs from the Fisher-Price company.

WEEKS 30–40:   The fetus is on vacation.

WEEK 50:   The fetus can run the 100-meter dash in 10.23 seconds and has developed an interest in pottery.

Pregnancy and Diet

You must remember that when you are pregnant, you are eating for two. But you must also remember that the other one of you is about the size of a golf ball, so let's not go overboard with it. I mean, a lot of pregnant women eat as though the other person they're eating for is Orson Welles. The instant they find out they're pregnant they rush right out and buy a case of Mallomars, and within days they've expanded to the size of barrage balloons.

Answers to Common Questions about Pregnancy

Q. WHAT WILL HAPPEN TO MY BODY DURING PREGNANCY BE-SIDES THAT I WILL BECOME HUGE AND TIRED AND THROW UP A LOT AND BE CONSTIPATED AND DE-VELOP HEMORRHOIDS AND HAVE TO URINATE ALL THE TIME AND HAVE LEG CRAMPS AND VARICOSE VEINS?

A. Many women also have lower back pain.

Q. IS IT SAFE TO GAMBLE AND CURSE DURING PREGNANCY?

A. Yes, but during the first trimester you should avoid gaudy jewelry.

Q. HOW LONG WILL I BE PREG-NANT?

A. Most of us learn in health class that the human gestation period is nine months. Like most things we learn in health class, this is a lie. The only people who still believe it are doctors, who make a big fuss out of giving you a "due date" nine months from when they think you were fertilized, as if it takes some kind of elabo-rate medical training to operate a calen-dar.

I have done exhaustive research on this question in the form of talking to my friends and listening in on other people's conversations in the supermarket checkout line, and I have concluded that no woman has ever given birth on her "due date." About a quarter of all pregnant women give birth "prematurely," which means during the doctor's vacation that immediately pre-cedes the "due date." All other women— and ask them if you don't believe me— remain pregnant for at least 14 months, and sometimes much longer if the weather has been unusually hot.

Q. CAN I HAVE SEX WITH MY HUSBAND WHILE I'M PREGNANT?

A. No.

Q. WELL, CAN I HAVE SEX WITH SOMEONE ELSE'S HUSBAND?

A. I don't see why not.

Keep in mind that it's a *baby* you're eating for. If you're going to eat for it, don't eat like an adult; eat like a *baby*. This doesn't mean you can't have Mallomars; it means you must hold them in your hands until the chocolate melts and then rub it into your hair and the sofa. If you eat at a restaurant, feel free to order that steak you crave, but have the waiter cut it into 650,000 tiny pieces and then refuse to touch them, preferring instead to chew and swallow the cocktail napkin and then throw up a little bit on your dress.

Important Advice for Husbands

The key here is to be sensitive. You must not let your wife think you find her unattractive just because she's getting tremendously fat. Go out of you way to reassure her on this point. From time to time, say to her: "I certainly don't find you unattractive just because you're getting tremendously fat." If you go to a party where every woman in the room is slinky and lithe except your wife, who is wearing a maternity outfit that makes her look like a convertible sofa, be sure to remark from time to time, in a strident voice, that you can't judge a book by its cover. Your wife is bound to remember this sensitive gesture.

During her pregnancy your wife will have many emotional moods caused by the fact that there are gallons of hormones racing around inside her. The two of you will be sitting in your living room, watching the evening news on television, when all of a sudden she'll run into the bedroom in tears because of a report about a monsoon wiping out a distant Asian village. Follow her. Comfort her. Tell her: "They're just distant Asians, for God's sake."

Teaching Your Child in the Uterus

Can you teach your child while it's still in the uterus? The answer is yes, at least according to this couple I saw on the "Phil Donahue Show" once, and I don't see why they would lie about it. Their kids all came out of the womb with a deep appreciation for classical music. Frankly, I don't understand why parents think this is so important, because as I recall my youth, children who appreciated classical music were infinitely more likely to get beat up on the playground. The smart move, if you want your child to have the respect and admiration of its peers, would be to teach it how to spit convincingly or lead cheers.

But never mind what you teach the child while it's in the uterus; the important thing

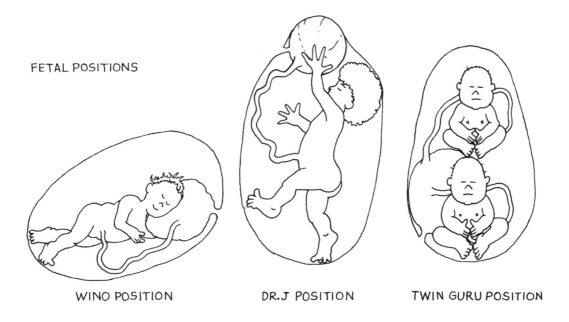

FETAL POSITIONS

WINO POSITION   DR.J POSITION   TWIN GURU POSITION

is that you *can* teach it, and you'd better, if you want it to get into Harvard Medical School. Of course, the teaching method has to be very simple. I mean, you can't go in there with slide projectors or anything. Where would you plug them in? So you'll pretty much have to content yourself with yelling at the stomach. This is the man's job, because let's face it, the woman would look pretty stupid yelling at her own stomach.

So whenever the two of you have a spare moment together, such as when you're waiting to cash a check at the bank, the man should lean over and yell, in the general direction of the woman's uterus, something like "THE CAPITAL OF NORTH DAKOTA IS PIERRE." Or maybe that's South Dakota. I can never keep the state capitals straight, because when I was in the uterus, back in 1946, Phil Donahue hadn't been invented yet.

The Baby Shower

Probably the single most grueling ordeal a woman must endure during pregnancy is the baby shower. What happens is you have to sit in the middle of a group of women and repeatedly open gifts, and every time you

THE BABY SHOWER

open one, you have to adopt a delighted expression, then hold the gift up—even if it is disposable diapers—and exclaim, "Oh! How cute!" In some cases this goes on for hours, and all you are permitted to eat is tiny sandwiches with the crusts cut off.

At one time, most women relied on drugs to get through their showers. But more and more, women are practicing "natural" shower techniques, which allow them, through careful preparation, to have perfectly safe showers without the use of artificial substances.

The key is teamwork between you and your husband. Well in advance of the expected shower date, the two of you should practice regularly at home. Sit on the sofa while your husband hands you various objects, and practice holding them up and exclaiming, "Oh! How cute!" You must practice this every night until no matter what he hands you—an ashtray, a snow tire, a reptile, etc.—you can still appear to be genuinely delighted.

Chapter 3

Getting Ready for Baby

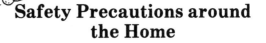

Safety Precautions around the Home

Babies are equipped at birth with a number of instinctive reflexes and behavior patterns that cause them to spend their first several years trying to kill themselves. If your home contains a sharp, toxic object, your baby will locate it; if your home contains no such object, your baby will try to obtain one via mail order. Therefore, you must comb through your house or apartment and eliminate all unsafe things, including:

dirt	forks	old copies of
germs	spittoons	*Penthouse*
attics	stairs	magazine
stoves	water	

You should also be sure to have the electrical system taken out. You cannot "childproof" it by plugging those little plastic caps into all the outlets. Children emerge from the womb knowing how to remove those caps by means of an instinctive outlet-cap-plucking reflex that doctors regard as one of the key indicators that the child is normal.

Baby's Room

Baby's room must be kept at a steady temperature of 72 degrees Fahrenheit and a relative humidity of 63 percent, and it must have wallpaper with clowns holding blue, red, and green balloons. Baby's room should be close enough to your room so that you can hear baby cry, unless you want to get some sleep, in which case baby's room should be in Peru.

Baby's Crib

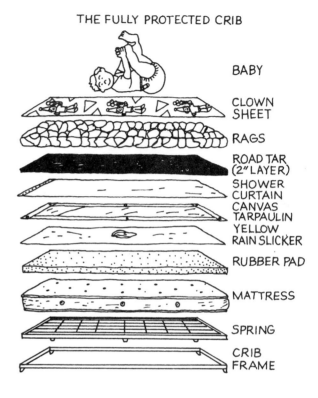

THE FULLY PROTECTED CRIB

BABY

CLOWN SHEET

RAGS

ROAD TAR (2" LAYER)

SHOWER CURTAIN

CANVAS TARPAULIN

YELLOW RAIN SLICKER

RUBBER PAD

MATTRESS

SPRING

CRIB FRAME

The important thing to remember here is that baby does not sleep in the crib. Baby sleeps in the car. Baby uses the crib as a place to cry and go to the bathroom, so the crib has to be fully protected. To make up the crib, first put down the mattress, then a rubber pad, then a yellow rain slicker, then a stout canvas tarpaulin, then a shower curtain, then a two-inch-thick layer of road tar, then a bale of highly absorbent rags, then a cute little sheet with pictures of clowns holding blue, red, and green balloons. You should have lots of spares of all these things.

Other Furniture for Baby's Room

Your best bet is an industrial dumpster.

Baby's Clothes

Have you ever stopped to ask yourself why so few high-level corporate executives are babies? The reason is that most babies do not dress for success.

Next time you're in a shopping mall, take a look at what these unsuccessful babies are wearing. Somewhere on virtually every

AN EXTENDED-WEAR DIAPER

A TYPICAL MALL-BABY

child's outfit will be embroidered either a barnyard animal or a cretin statement such as "Lil' Angel." Many of the babies will be wearing bib overalls, despite overwhelming scientific evidence that such garments reduce the wearer's apparent I.Q. by as many as 65 points. Some of the girl babies will be wearing tights and petticoats that stick straight out horizontally in such a way as to reveal an enormous unsightly diaper bulge, causing them to look like miniature ballerinas with bladder disorders. Really young babies will be encased in fluffy pastel zip-up sacks with no place for the poop to get out, so that after a few hours in the mall they are no more than little pastel sacks of poop with babies' heads sticking out.

You look at these babies, and you realize that they will never be considered for responsible positions until they learn to dress more sensibly. So when you're shopping for clothes for your baby, stick to the time-tested dress-for-success classics—your pin-stripes, your lightweight wool suits in blue or gray, stout brogans, etc. And don't neglect the accessories! A baby sucking on a cheap pink plastic rattle is likely to be passed over at promotion time in favor of a baby sucking on a leather rattle with brass fittings.

Baby's Toys

Your friends and relatives will buy your baby lots and lots of cute dolls and stuffed animals, all of which you should throw in the trash compactor immediately. Sure, they look cute to you, but to the baby they appear to be the size of station wagons. So all night long, while you're safe in your animal-free bedroom, your baby is lying there, surrounded by these gigantic creatures. Try to imagine sleeping with an eight-foot-high Raggedy Ann sitting just inches away, staring at you! Especially if you had no way of knowing whether Raggedy Anns were vicious! No wonder babies cry so much at night!

So you don't want cute creatures with eyes. You also don't want so-called educational toys that claim to teach "spatial relationships," because the only spatial relationship newborn babies care about is whether they can fit things into their mouths. This means you want toys that will fit safely and comfortably in a baby's mouth. The best way to select such toys is to try them out in your own mouth, bearing in mind that yours has eight times the volume of baby's. When you go to the toy store, ask to see eight of each potential toy; if you can stuff them all comfortably in your mouth, you should buy one. Remind the salesclerk to sterilize the other seven, so as not to pass infectious diseases on to the next shopper. The clerk will appreciate this thoughtful reminder.

In a later chapter, I'll talk about buying toys for you child when it has acquired the conceptual and manipulative skills necessary to break things.

THE "NO" TOYS   THE "YES" TOYS

Diapers: Cloth vs. Disposable

At one time, back during the Korean War, most people rejected disposable diapers because they preferred the natural soft feel of cloth. Then it finally began to dawn on people that the natural soft feel of cloth begins to lose some of its charm when it has been pooped and peed on repeatedly.

So now everybody uses disposable diapers. Oh, I realize there are diaper services that come to your house and drop off clean cloth diapers and pick up the dirty ones, but even those diapers are now disposable. The instant the driver is out of sight of your house, he hurls the dirty diapers into the street and drives off briskly.

The only problem with disposable diapers is that they are starting to overflow the world's refuse-disposal facilities; scientists now predict that if the present trend continues, by the year 1997 the entire planet will smell like the men's room in a bar frequented by motorcycle gangs. But this is not really as serious as it sounds, because scientists also believe that several years before 1997 the polar ice caps are going to melt. Also, we could always have a nuclear war. So I would definitely go with the disposable diapers.

CLOTH DIAPER

← PINS

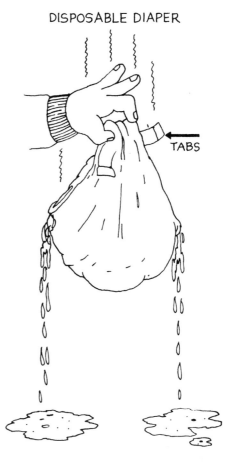

DISPOSABLE DIAPER

← TABS

Chapter 4

Preparing for Birth

An Important Message about Professional Childbirth-Preparation Terminology

Before you have your baby, you're going to be dealing with a number of professional childbirth experts, so you ought to know that they all have this very strict rule: when they talk about childbirth, they never use the word "pain." Granted, this is like talking about the Pacific Ocean without using the word "water," but the way they see it, if they were to tell you women, in clear language, what is really involved in getting this largish object out of your body, none of you would have babies, and the professional childbirth experts would have to find another source of income.

So they use the International Childbirth Professional Code Word for pain, which is "contraction." To the nonexpert, a "contraction" sounds like, at worst, maybe a mild muscle cramp, but it actually describes a sensation similar to that of having professional football players smash their fists into your uterine wall. In a "strong contraction," the players are also wearing skis.

It's quite natural for you to be apprehensive about the pain of childbirth. I was terrified of it myself, until I did a little research and learned there was no way I would ever have to go through it. So let's take a thorough, informed, scientific look at this much-misunderstood topic, and maybe we can clear up your concerns, although I doubt it.

Here are two actual diagrams, drawn with the aid of modern medical expertise, showing the insides of a woman just before and just after giving birth:

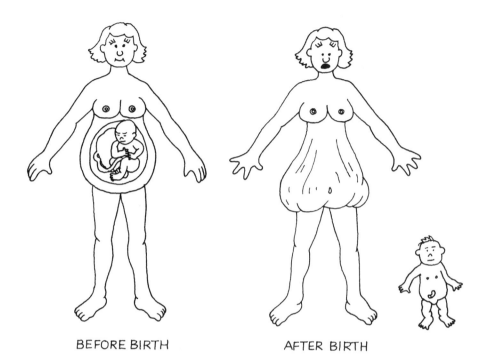

BEFORE BIRTH   AFTER BIRTH

What these diagrams reveal to those of us trained to understand them is that there is an entire baby inside the pregnant woman, and somehow during childbirth it comes out. This is the part that stumps us, because despite all of our modern medical expertise, we frankly cannot see how such a thing is possible. All we really know about it is that it seems to hurt like crazy.

If you'd like more technical details on the childbirth process, I suggest you view one of the many fine prairie dramas on television wherein some pathetic wispy-haired pioneer woman goes into labor during a blizzard in the most god-awful desolate prairie place, such as Kansas. Nothing brings on labor like a prairie blizzard. Women have been known to give birth in prairie blizzards even when they weren't actually pregnant.

Anyway, on these prairie dramas the pioneer woman lies around moaning and writhing, which should give you an idea of what childbirth is like, except that on television it takes about as long as an episode of "Little House on the Prairie," whereas in real life it can take as long as "Roots."

But don't worry, because later in this chapter we'll talk about a wonderful new modern natural technique for coping with contractions. I won't describe this amazing technique right away, because I don't want you to find out yet that it's really just deep breathing.

How Your Mother Had Babies, and Why We Now Feel It Was All Wrong

Here is the system that was used for having babies during the Eisenhower Administration: At the first sign of pregnancy, the husband would rush the wife to the hospital, where she would be given modern medical drugs that would keep her from

GROWN-UP DRUG-DAMAGED BABIES OF (LEFT TO RIGHT) THE 40s, 50s, AND 60s

feeling contractions or anything else, including a volcanic eruption in the delivery room. This way the woman felt very little pain. Often she didn't regain consciousness until her child was entering the fourth grade.

One big problem with this system was that drugs can have adverse effects on the baby, as is evidenced by the fact that every single person born during the 40s, 50s, or 60s is really screwed up. Another problem was that the father had very little to do with the birth. His job was to sit in the waiting room with the other fathers and smoke cigarettes and read old copies of *Field and Stream* and wonder what the hell was taking so long. When the baby was born, the nurses would clean it up as best as they could and show it to the father, then he'd go home to bumble around and have humorous kitchen episodes until his wife got back on her feet and could resume cooking. This system deprived the husband of the chance to witness the glorious moment when his child came into the world, not to mention all the other various solids and fluids that come into the world with the child.

So today we have a much better childbirth system. Federal law now requires the man to watch the woman have the baby, and the woman is not allowed to have any drugs unless she agrees, in writing, to feel guilty. In some ways, we're back to the old prairie method of baby-having, only we do it in modern hospitals, so the husband doesn't have to boil water. All the water-boiling is now done by trained health-care professionals for about $65 a gallon.

Choosing a Hospital

The most important thing to remember in choosing a hospital is that there must be no Dairy Queen between it and you. Medical science has been unable to develop a way to get a pregnant woman, even in the throes of labor, past a Dairy Queen without stopping for a chocolate milk shake. This could waste precious time on the way to the hospital. Even worse, the woman could start having the baby right there in the Dairy Queen, with nobody to help her except her husband and various teenage Dairy Queen employees all smeared with butterscotch and wearing those idiot hats.

Also, you should pick a hospital you feel comfortable in. Most people feel uneasy about hospitals, possibly because the instant you walk through the door medical personnel grab you and remove your blood and stick tubes up your nose. But in deciding where you're going to have your baby, you must overcome these fears. You must barge right into the hospital and ask questions. If you have no questions, use these:

1.   How much does this hospital weigh?
2.   What's that funny smell?

Don't leave until you get the answers!

Childbirth Classes: Learning to Breathe

Before you can have your baby, you have to attend childbirth classes wherein you openly discuss the sexual organs with people you barely know. You get used to it. You'll get so that when your instructor passes around a life-size plastic replica of the cervix, you'll all hold it up and make admiring comments, as if it were a prize floral arrangement. You'll get to know the uterus so well that you'd recognize one anywhere. Also, you'll see actual color movies of babies being born, so that you'll be prepared for the fact that they come out looking like Mister Potato Head.

But the main thing you'll do in childbirth classes is learn the amazing new modern natural technique for getting through contractions, namely deep breathing. Now I will admit that when our instructor first talked about getting through labor with nothing but deep breathing, my immediate impulse was to rush out and buy three or four quarts

THE CERVIX

of morphine, just in case. But after several weeks of practicing the breathing techniques, my wife and I became convinced that, by golly, they really worked! Obviously we were hyperventilating.

The key to the technique is to breathe in a different way for each stage of labor, as is illustrated by the accompanying simple chart.

The Magic Word

One last thing. In childbirth classes, you will be taught, with much ceremony, a Se-

Correct Way to Breathe during Labor		
NAME OF LABOR STAGE	SYMP-TOMS	CORRECT BREATHING TECHNIQUE
Early	Pain	Inhale for 11 sec.; exhale through teeth in six sharp, 2-second gasps, forming mouth as if to say "carnivorous"
Orienta-tion	Pain	Inhale for 55 sec.; exhale towards Mecca with mouth formed in shape of a lowercase "r"
Transmis-sion	Pain	Inhale for 3 sec.; exhale gradually for 107 sec. through partner's teeth; hum "Turkey in the Straw" (but NOT the chorus)
Baby Coming Out	Really aw-ful pain	Do not inhale; exhale for 25–30 min. with mouth formed as if to shriek

cret Magical Anti-Contraction Word that the woman is supposed to say when things get really awful, when the professional football players in her uterus are wearing skis *and* carrying sharpened poles. Technically, this word is supposed to be revealed only in childbirth classes, but I have decided to print it below for use in case of emergency.

WARNING: THE NEXT PARAGRAPH CONTAINS THE SECRET MAGICAL ANTI-CONTRACTION WORD. DO NOT READ THIS PARAGRAPH UNLESS YOU ARE SINCERELY IN THE PROCESS OF HAVING A BABY.

The word is "hout." Rhymes with "trout." It may not look like much, but it has been scientifically shown to be over twice as effective against contractions as the next leading word, "Ohmigod." You may hear another secret word in your childbirth classes, but "hout" did it for us. Our instructor had us practice it for hours in class—you have to get the tip of your tongue right on the edge of your front teeth—and it really helped my wife get through those first few contractions. After that, she switched over to "AAAAAAAARRRRRRGGGUUU-NNNNH," which is not an officially approved word, but seemed to work well for her.

Chapter 5

The Actual Blessed Event

Childbirth is like vampires: it never strikes before sundown. If you feel something that seems like contractions during the day, you're actually having what is called "false labor." Sometimes false labor can be very realistic, in which case you may have to go to the hospital, where you will be examined by a false doctor, who may even deliver an anatomically correct doll.

But real labor always begins at 3:15 A.M. eastern standard time, because that is when every obstetrician in the country is in deepest sleep. As soon as the contractions start, you should call your obstetrician, who will answer the phone and, without even waking up, say: "How far apart are the contractions?" You can give any answer you want

("About two feet," for example), and then the obstetrician will say, "You'd better come on in to the hospital." Then he'll roll over onto his side, still completely unconscious, and resume snoring.

At this time, you should gather up the things you'll need in the hospital (don't forget your passport!) and set off. Husbands, here is how you should drive: Sit on the edge of the driver's seat with your face one inch from the windshield and grip the steering wheel so firmly that little pieces of it keep breaking off in your hands. Every eight or nine seconds, jerk your head down violently to look at the gas gauge, then give your wife's knee a firm clench for one-tenth of a second and grimace at her and say,

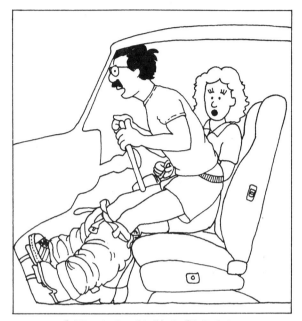

CORRECT DRIVING POSITION

"Everything's going to be fine." But despite this reassuring exterior, husbands, you must be alert and prepared for any problem that could prevent you from getting to the hospital in time.

What to Do If You Can't Get to the Hospital

At all costs, you must not panic. Stay calm. A good way to do this is to play word games, such as the one where you start with a letter, and then the other person adds a letter, and so on, the idea being that you are spelling an actual word, but you don't want to supply the last letter. For extra fun, you can say that the loser has to get out and run around the car backwards three times at a red light. Besides livening up the game, this will attract the attention of the police, who might help deliver your baby in a gruff but kindly manner, the way they do in anecdotes from *Reader's Digest*. Or they might beat you with clubs.

What Will Happen to You If You Get to the Hospital

At the maternity ward, you will be greeted by kindly nurses who will do a number of unspeakably degrading things to you while the hospital operator tries to wake up your obstetrician. Then you will be placed in a little room where your husband can sit with his little clipboard and stopwatch and time your contractions, just like you learned in childbirth class, until you swat his goddamn clipboard and stopwatch across the room and demand to be killed, which is the sign that you have gone from "contractions" to "strong contractions."

Three Problems That Could Prevent You from Getting to the Hospital in Time

1. Your car radio could explode for no apparent reason.

2. You could be stopped by police who are looking for escaped radicals, and who think your wife's stomach is a bomb and call in the Explosives Disposal Unit to cover her with sand.

3. You could get stuck behind a member of the Elderly People with Enormous Cars Club, driving smack dab in the middle of the road at two miles an hour in search of an all-night drugstore to buy new batteries for his hearing aid, so he can't hear you honk.

At this time, you will be taken to the delivery room, where you will be placed in the Standard Childbirth Position, illustrated below. Medical researchers have tried for decades to come up with a childbirth position even more humiliating than this one, but they have had no success. Two of the alternative childbirth positions are diagramed on the following page.

STANDARD CHILDBIRTH POSITION

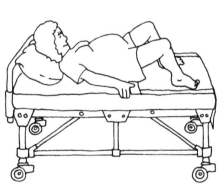

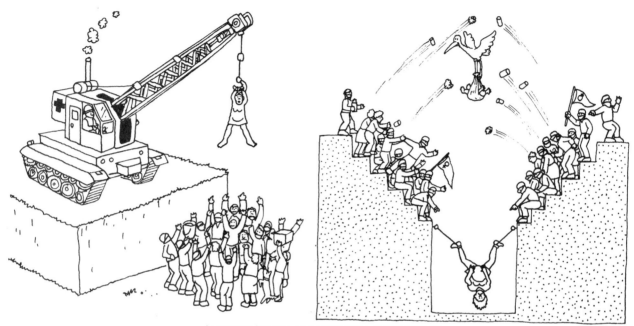

ALTERNATIVE CHILDBIRTH POSITIONS

While you're in this delicate position in the delivery room, you may be a bit embarrassed, especially since there are people standing around wearing masks and watching you. So let me explain who these people are. You have your obstetrician, of course, unless the hospital operator has been unable to rouse him, in which case he will actually be a life-size obstetrician puppet operated from behind by a nurse trained to mimic obstetricians' voices. You also have your husband, assuming he has been able to wash away the little crumbled bits of steering wheel embedded in his hands.

Then you have your pediatrician, and an anesthesiologist to stand by in case the doctors decide that the delivery is not costing enough. Also you have at least one nurse to assist each of these doctors; you have three medical students; you have one law student;

and you have Billy Ray Johnson, who is actually a retired beet farmer who just happens to like hanging around delivery rooms and watch people have babies.

So that's it, just 12 of you, unless Billy Ray has brought friends to share this wondrous moment.

The Big Moment

And what is it like? That, of course, is what you want to know: What is it *really* like?

I don't have the vaguest idea, of course. But I do remember what it sounded like when my wife had our son. I was at one end of my wife, shouting words of encouragement to her head, the doctor and nurse were shouting to the other end of her body. It sounded like a group of extremely sincere people trying to help an elephant dislodge a Volkswagen from its throat:

DOCTOR: You're doing just great, Beth! Just great! Really! Isn't she doing great?
NURSE: She sure is! She's doing just great!
ME: You're really doing great, honey! Really!
BETH: AAAAAAAAAAAAARRRRRRRR RRRRRRRRUUUUNNNNNNNNNNNNN NNNGGGGGGGGGGGGGGGGGGGGGGGG GHHHHHHHHHHHH.
DOCTOR: That was just great! Really!

And so on, for quite a while, until finally Robert came out, and immediately demanded to be put back in. My wife and I were very happy. I remember hugging her head.

What to Do Immediately after Birth

Close your eyes tightly. This is in case the doctor takes it into his head to show you the placenta, which is a highly unattractive object that comes out close on the heels of the baby. In the old days, when people were decent, the placenta was disposed of quickly and quietly and was never talked about in polite society. But now people bandy it about openly in public, as if it were a prize-winning bass.

Bonding

While the obstetrician is finishing up, the pediatrician will wrap your baby in a blanket and hand it to you so that you can marvel at the miracle of birth and everything. My only warning here is that you should not hold your baby too long, or you will become "bonded" to it and have to be tugged apart by burly hospital aides.

Chapter 6

The Hospital Stay

A Reassuring Word for First-Time Parents about Hospital Baby-Identification Procedures

A common fear among new parents is that, as a result of a mix-up in the nursery, some kind of terrible mistake will be made, such as that they'll wind up taking home Yasser Arafat's baby. This fear is groundless. When a baby is born, a hospital person immediately puts a little plastic tag around its wrist with the words "NOT YASSER ARAFAT'S BABY" printed on it in indelible ink. So whichever baby you wind up with, you can be sure it isn't his.

Visitors in the Hospital

Maternity ward visitors are an excellent source of amusement, because they always feel obligated to say flattering things about newborn babies, which of course look like enormous fruit fly larvae. One fun trick is to show your visitors somebody else's baby. "She definitely has your eyes!" your visitors will exclaim. For real entertainment, have the nurse bring you a live ferret, wrapped in a baby blanket. "She's very alert!" your visitors will remark, as the ferret lacerates their fingers with needle-sharp teeth.

How Long Should the Mother Stay in the Hospital after the Baby Comes Out?

As long as possible. For one thing, as long as you're in the hospital you can wear a bathrobe all day. This means you won't have to face up to the fact that even after expelling the baby and all the baby-related fluids and solids, you still have hips the size of vending machines from all the Mallomars you ate back when you thought you were going to be pregnant forever.

For another thing, the hospital employs trained professional personnel to change the baby's diapers, etc., so all you have to do is lounge around in your bathrobe looking serene and complaining about the food. If you go home, you'll have to take care of the baby *and* confront the fact that you did not once clean behind any of the toilets during the last four months of your pregnancy because you couldn't bend over.

The hospital personnel will try to make you leave after a couple of days, but all you have to do is waddle off to another room and plop down on the bed. There are so many comings and goings in a maternity ward that it will be several days before they catch on to you and try to make you leave again, at which time you can just waddle off to another room. You can probably keep this up until your baby starts to walk unassisted from the nursery to your room at feeding time.

Naming Your Baby

A good way to pass the time while you're in the hospital is to argue loudly with your husband about what to name the baby. You should get started on this as soon as possible, because both of you are likely to have strong views. For example, he may want to name the baby "John," after a favorite uncle, while you may hate "John" because it reminds you of a former boyfriend, not to mention that the baby is a girl.

There are some names new parents should avoid altogether. You shouldn't name a boy "Cyril" or "Percy," because the other boys will want to punch him repeatedly in the mouth, and I can't say as I blame them. And you shouldn't give a girl's name a cute spelling, such as "Cyndi," because no matter how many postgraduate degrees she gets she will never advance any further than clerk-typist.

In recent years, it has become fashionable to give children extremely British-sounding names, such as "Jessica." I think this is an excellent idea. Despite the fact that Great Britain has been unable to produce a car that can be driven all the way across a shopping mall parking lot without major engine failure, Americans think that any-

ATYPICAL CYRIL   ATYPICAL PERCY

thing British is really terrific. So I recommend you give your baby the most British name you can think up, such as "Queen Elizabeth" or "Big Ben" or "Crumpet Scone-Hayes."

Some Heavy Thoughts to Think during the Hospital Stay

The hospital stay is a good time for you, as new parents, to share some quiet moments together listening to the woman on the other side of the curtain discuss her bowel movements with her mother via telephone. This is also a time for you to marvel at your baby's incredibly small feet and hands and to reflect on the fact that this is a real human life, a life that you have created, just the two of you; a tiny, helpless life that you are completely responsible for. Makes you want to hop right on a plane for the Azores, doesn't it? I mean, what do the two of you know about being responsible for a human life? The two of you can't even consistently locate clean underwear, for God's sake!

Mother Nature understands this. That is why she has constructed babies so that even the most profoundly incompetent person, even a person who takes astrology seriously and writes angry, semiliterate letters to the television station when it changes the time at which it broadcasts "Family Feud," can raise babies successfully. All a newborn baby really needs is food, warmth, and love, pretty much like a hamster, only with fewer signs of intelligence.

So don't worry; you'll do fine. Some day, when your child has grown into a teenager and gotten drunk and crashed your new car into the lobby of the home for the aged during the annual Christmas party, you'll look back on the hamster era and laugh about how worried you were.

In the next chapter, we'll talk about how laughably easy it is to take care of a newborn baby, provided you don't do anything else.

Chapter 7

Maintenance of a New Baby

Finally will come the big day when the hospital authorities order the wife to leave, and the two of you take your new baby home. There is nothing quite like the moment when a young couple leaves the hospital, walking with that characteristic new-parent gait that indicates an obsessive fear of dropping the baby on its head. Finally! It's just the three of you, on your own!

This independence will last until you get maybe eight feet from the hospital door, where you'll be assaulted by grandmothers offering advice. The United States Constitution empowers grandmothers to stop any young person on the street with a baby and offer advice, and they take this responsibility very seriously. If they see your baby without a little woolen hat, they will advise you that your baby is too cold. If your baby has a hat, they will advise you that your baby is too warm. Always they will offer this advice in a tone of voice that makes it clear they do not expect your baby to survive the afternoon in the care of such incompetents as yourselves.

The best way to handle advice from random grandmothers is to tell them that you appreciate their concern, but that you feel it is your responsibility to make your own decisions about your child's welfare. If that doesn't work, try driving them off with sticks. Otherwise, they'll follow you home and hang around under your windows.

Now let's talk about maintaining your new baby.

The Basic Baby Mood Cycle

This is the Basic Baby Mood Cycle, which all babies settle into once they get over being born:

MOOD ONE: Just about to cry
MOOD TWO: Crying
MOOD THREE: Just finished crying

MOOD ONE   MOOD TWO   MOOD THREE

Your major job is to keep your baby in Mood Three as much as possible. Here is the traditional way to do this. When the baby starts to cry, the two of you should pass it back and forth repeatedly and recite these words in unison: "Do you suppose he's hungry? He can't be hungry. He just ate. Maybe he needs to be burped. No, that's not it. Maybe his diaper needs to be changed. No, it's dry. What could be wrong? Do you think maybe he's hungry?" And so on, until the baby can't stand it any more and decides to go to sleep.

When your baby is awake and not crying, it will follow specific air molecules around the room with its eyes. For years, scientists thought the reason newborn babies waved their eyes around in such seemingly random ways was that they couldn't really focus on anything, but we now know that, thanks to the fact that they have such small eyes, they can actually see molecules whooshing around, which is a much more interesting thing to watch than a bunch of parents and relatives waving stupid rattles in their faces.

Also, babies receive signals from outer space, bringing messages from other galaxies that only babies can detect. These messages cause the baby to smile (if the message is a joke) or look startled (if it is bad news, such as the explosion of a popular star).

When Should You Feed Your Baby?

During the day, you should feed your baby just before the phone rings. At night, you should feed your baby immediately after you have fallen asleep. After each feeding, you should pat your baby gently on the back until it pukes on your shoulder.

BABY THROWING UP IN CHURCH

Should You Breast-Feed or Bottle-Feed Your Baby?

I'm surprised you even have to ask. All of us modern childbirth experts feel very

BABY'S VIEW OF A BREAST AND A BOTTLE

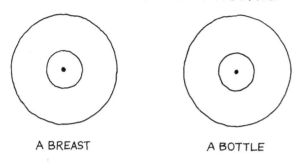

A BREAST   A BOTTLE

strongly that you should breast-feed your child. There are two major reasons:

1.   Your mother *didn't* breast-feed, and as I pointed out in the chapter on childbirth, we now know that everything your mother did was wrong.

2.   Breast-feeding is better for the baby. Much has been written on this subject, reams and reams of information in hundreds of excellent books and articles which I frankly have been unable to read because I would never get this book finished on time. But the basic idea, as I understand it, is that *bottle* milk is designed primarily for baby *cows*, whereas your baby is not a cow at all! It can't even stand up! Am I getting too technical here?

Anyway, all your really smart, with-it trendsetters are into breast-feeding today. Go into any swank New York City night spot and you'll see dozens of chic women such as Leona Helmsley breast-feeding, many of them with rented babies.

Learning to Breast-Feed

Like many new mothers, you may feel ashamed that you don't just automatically know how to breast-feed. You know there must be more to it than just shoving the breast into the baby's mouth, because otherwise people wouldn't keep writing enormous books about it. But just what *are* you sup-

posed to do? You look at pictures in *National Geographic* of women in some primitive South American jungle tribe, women who have never even seen Tupperware, casually breast-feeding their infants, and you think: "How come *they* know how to do it and I don't? What's *wrong* with me?"

136

Don't be so hard on yourself. Those primitive women have undergone hours and hours of intensive breast-feeding instruction at special training centers funded by the United Nations, and only the top graduates are chosen to appear in *National Geographic* photographs. Yes, they have to be taught, too, so don't be the least bit

GIVING BABY A BOTTLE

STEP 1: INSERT BOTTLE.

STEP 2: BABY SHOULD SUCK.

STEP 3: IF BABY DOESN'T SUCK,
CHECK BOTTLE. IF BOTTLE
IS OK...

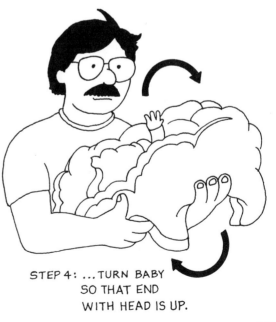

STEP 4: ...TURN BABY
SO THAT END
WITH HEAD IS UP.

ashamed to ask a nurse for help. My wife finally had to ask a nurse, who came in and stuck her (my wife's) breast into my son's mouth. Without the nurse's technical know-how, my wife might have stuck her breast into my son's ear or something, and serious nutritional complications could have developed.

Common Problems with Breast-Feeding

Well, for one thing, you're supposed to switch the baby from one side to the other, but usually the baby wants to stay where it is, and babies develop suction that has been measured at upwards of 6,000 pounds per square inch. You can't get them off with crowbars.

Another common problem is milk supply. Babies love to play little pranks wherein one day they drink about six gallons of milk, which causes a mother to produce like crazy, and the next day the baby drinks maybe an ounce and a half. Some mothers have been known to explode from the pressure.

What Is Colic?

Colic is when your baby cries all the time, and people keep telling you how their kid had the colic for 71 straight months. If your baby gets colic, you should take it to the pediatrician so he can say, "There's nothing to worry about," which is of course absolutely true from his perspective, since he lives in a colic-free home many miles from your baby.

"There's nothing to worry about" is a typical example of the kind of easy-for-you-to-say remarks that pediatricians like to make. Another one is, "Take his temperature rectally every hour," an instruction which, if actually followed, would scar both parent and child emotionally for life. If your baby has diaper rash, your pediatrician may say, "Just leave the diaper off for a while." This would be a wonderful idea if the baby would stop shooting wastes out of its various orifices, but of course the baby cannot do this, which is why it is wearing a diaper in the first place. Not that the pediatrician knows about any of this. His baby is tended by domestics from third world nations.

Changing Your Baby's Diapers

First of all, you must understand that as far as your baby is concerned, you never have to change its diapers. There is no creature on earth so content as a baby with a full diaper. Pooping is one of the few useful skills that very small babies have mastered, and they take tremendous pride in it, especially when they have an audience, such as grandparents or the assembled guests at the christening. They'll wrinkle their little faces up into determined frowns, and they'll really *work* at it, with appropriate loudish grunting noises that will at times drown out the clergyman. After all that effort, they want some time to enjoy their achievement, to wriggle and squirm until poop has oozed into every wrinkle and crevice of the cute little $45 designer baby outfit you bought especially for the christening. So when you change your baby's diaper, don't think you're doing your baby any great favor. As far as your baby is concerned, you're taking away the fruits of its labor. "Why don't you get your own poop?" is what newborn babies would say if they could talk, which thank God they can't.

Now let's talk about diaper-changing technique. The problem with most baby books is that when they show you how to change diapers, they use photographs showing a clean changing table in a well-lit room, and a baby that is devoid of any sign of bodily eliminations. Why would *anybody,* except maybe some kind of pervert, want to change such a baby? No, what you need to know is how to change a really filthy baby, and under difficult conditions, such as in bus station rest rooms where even the germs have diseases.

I'd say restaurants pose the biggest dia-

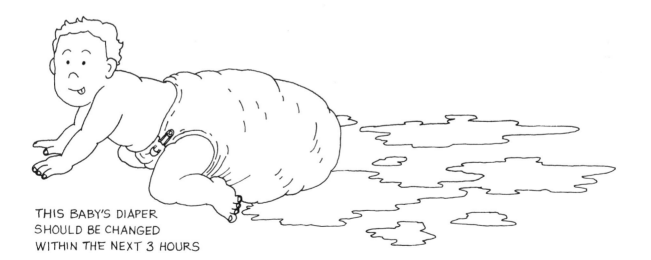

THIS BABY'S DIAPER
SHOULD BE CHANGED
WITHIN THE NEXT 3 HOURS

DINING OUT WITH BABY

per-changing challenge. When my son was three months old, my wife and I took him to a dimly lit, semielegant restaurant, and by the time we examined him closely he had managed to get poop up as far as his *hat*. I mean, we had a major failure of the containment vessel, and there was no sterile little changing table around, just lots of people hoping to dine in a romantic environment. So what you have to do in these situations is go on laughing and chatting as though nothing is wrong, but meanwhile work away like madmen under the table with moist towelettes, which you should buy in freight-car loads.

What I'm saying here is that you need to learn to change diapers furtively, in the dark, and you need to be able to saunter unobtrusively carrying huge wads of reeking towelettes past amorous couples to the rest room trash container, and you do not learn these things in books.

How to Get Your Body Back into Shape after Childbirth the Way All the Taut-Bodied Entertainment Personalities Such As Jane Fonda Do

Don't kid yourself. Those women have never had babies. Their children were all borne by professional stunt women.

Chapter 8

The First Six Months

Baby's Development during the First Six Months

The first six months is a time of incredibly rapid development for your baby. It will learn to smile, to lift its head, to sit, to play the cello, and to repair automatic transmissions.

Ha ha. Just kidding here, poking a little fun at new parents who watch like hawks for their babies to pass the Major Milestones of Infant Development, when the truth is that during the first six months babies mainly just lie around and poop. They haven't even developed brains at this point. If you were to open up a baby's head—and I am not for a moment suggesting that you should—you would find nothing but an enormous drool gland.

Nevertheless, this is definitely the time to buy your baby its first computer. It's never too soon to start learning about computers,

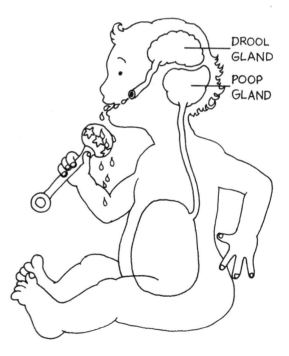

BASIC INFANT ANATOMY

DROOL GLAND

POOP GLAND

as you know if you have been watching those television commercials wherein children whose parents didn't buy them computers at an early age wind up as ragpickers with open sores all over their bodies.

Computers are the way of the future. You can buy them at K-Mart, for God's sake. You see families wandering through the computer department, clutching K-Mart purchases such as huge bags of caramel popcorn manufactured in Korea, and they're saying things like, "I think we should get this computer, because it has a built-in modem and the software support is better." These are not nuclear physicists talking this way; these are K-Mart shoppers, and if they know about computers, your kid damn well better know about them, too.

What kind of computer is best for a baby aged 0 to 6 months? There are many models, ranging widely in memory size, telecommunications facilities, and expansion capabilities, but the critical thing is that your baby's computer should be red, and it should have no sharp edges. Also, you should immediately cut off the plug, because otherwise your baby could receive a dangerous electrical shock from drooling on the keyboard.

Disciplining a New Baby

During the 1950s and 60s, parents were told to be permissive with their children, and the result was juvenile delinquency, drug abuse, Watergate, Pac-Man, California, etc. So we experts now feel you should start disciplining your baby immediately after birth. At random intervals throughout the day, you should stride up to your baby and say, in a strict voice, "There will be no slumber party for *you* tonight, young lady."

You may think this is a waste of time, but scientists have determined that babies as young as three days old can tell, just from the tone of an adult's voice, when they are being told they can't go to a slumber party. You should keep up this tough discipline until your child is in junior high school and thus has access to weapons.

Baby-Tending for Men

During the first six months, your baby will need more care than at any other time in its life except the following 30 months. We modern sensitive husbands realize that it's very unfair to place the entire child-care burden on our wives, so many of us are starting to assume maybe three percent of it. Even this is probably too much. I know I'll be accused of being sexist for saying this, but the typical man has had his nurturing instincts obliterated by watching professional football, and consequently he has no concept of how to tend a baby. He feels he's

A FATHER'S PRIMER

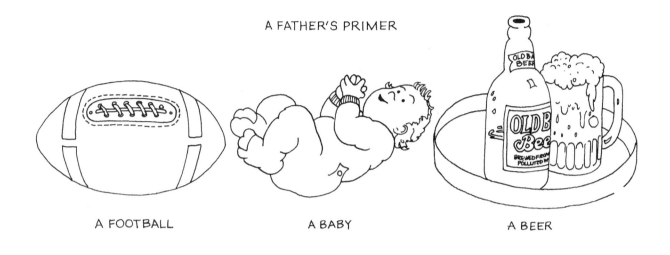

A FOOTBALL   A BABY   A BEER

done a terrific job if the baby isn't stolen by gypsies. You'd get better infant care from an affectionate dog.

But men keep reading articles in the newspaper Style section about how they're supposed to help. So what happens is the family goes to, say, a picnic, and on the way the man, feeling magnanimous, says, "I'll take care of the baby, honey. You just relax and enjoy yourself." So they get to the picnic, and the husband, feeling very proud of himself, tends to the baby by poking it affectionately in the stomach every 45 minutes on his way to the cooler for a new beer. Between pokes the wife comes over maybe 35 times to change the baby's diaper, feed it, cuddle it, arrange its blanket, put the pacifier back in its mouth, brush enormous stinging insects off it, etc.

On the way home, the man remarks on how easy the baby is to take care of, how it hardly cried at all, etc., and the woman plunges the red-hot car cigarette lighter deep into his right thigh. This is bad for a relationship.

So what I've done, men, is I've prepared a little automotive-style maintenance chart for you to follow when you're in charge of the baby.

Men's Baby-Maintenance Chart

INTERVAL	MAINTENANCE ACTIVITY
Every 5 minutes	Lean over baby and state the following in a high-pitched voice: "Yes! We're a *happy* boy or girl! Yes we *are*! Watcha watcha watcha!"
Every 10 minutes	Check all orifices for emerging solids and liquids; wipe and change containment garments as needed
Every 30 minutes	Attempt feeding and burping procedures
Every 60 minutes	Examine entire baby surface for signs of redness, flaking, major eye boogers, etc.
Every 2 hours	Call pediatrician about something

Advice to Women about Babies and Jobs

If you're like many young mothers who held jobs before childbirth, you face a cruel dilemma: Your family could really use another income, yet you feel strongly that you should stay home for at least the first few critical years.

The solution to this dilemma is to have your *baby* get a job. Under federal law, it is now illegal for employers to discriminate against any person solely because that person is a baby. And to their surprise, many employers are finding that babies often make excellent employees, the kind who are always at their desks and never make personal telephone calls. In fact, one major corporation now shows all of its financial proposals to a team of handpicked babies: If they cry at a proposal, it is rejected out of hand; if they attempt to eat it, it is sent on to the board of directors.

What kind of job should you seek for your baby? Your best bet is the kind of job that even the most pathetic incompetent can handle:

State legislator
Paperweight
Consultant
Anything in marketing
Vice president of anything
Clerk in a state motor vehicle bureau

Choosing a Pediatrician

You should choose your pediatrician carefully, for his job is to examine your baby, give it shots, weigh it, measure it—in short, to do everything except attend to the baby when it is actually sick. When the baby is sick, either you or your pediatrician will be on vacation. This is an immutable law of nature.

Babysitters

The best babysitters, of course, are the baby's grandparents. You feel completely comfortable entrusting your baby to them for long periods, which is why most grandparents flee to Florida at the earliest opportunity.

If no grandparents are available, you will have to rent a teenager. You don't want a modern teenager, the kind that hangs around the video-game arcade smoking Marlboros and contracting herpes. No, you want an old-fashioned, responsible teenager, the kind who attends Our Lady of Maximum Discomfort High School and belongs to the 4-H Club and wants to be a nun. Even then you don't want to take any chances. The first time she takes care of your baby, you should never actually leave the house. Drive your car until it's out of sight, then sneak back and crouch in the basement, listening for signs of trouble. In later visits, as you gain confidence in the sitter, you should feel free to eat sandwiches in the basement, and maybe even listen to the radio quietly. After all, this is your night out!

A GOOD BABYSITTER   A BAD BABYSITTER

Safety Tip

Be sure to leave the babysitter a first-aid kit with tourniquet; the phone numbers of the pediatrician, the ambulance, the fire department, the police, the Poison Control Center, all your neighbors, the Mayo Clinic, all your relatives, the State Department, etc; and a note telling her where you are ("We're in the basement") and what to do in the event of an emergency ("Pound on the floor").

Songs for New Babies

One fun thing to do with a small baby while it's lying around is to sing it the traditional baby songs, the ones your mother sang when you were a baby. The words sometimes seem strange to us now, because your mother learned them from her mother, who learned them from her mother, and so on back to medieval England, when most people had the intelligence of kelp. Here are three of my favorites:

LADYBUG
(Robert Frost)

Ladybug, Ladybug
Fly away home
Your children are all burned
They look like charred Raisinets

(Tickle baby under chin.)

HEG-A-LEG MOLLY
(Anonymous)

Heg-a-leg Molly
Daddy's got a bunting
Why do you sleep so soon?
Wet his bed
And he broke his head
And Myron has gone to Vermont.

(Hold baby up and laugh as if you have just said something immensely amusing.)

LAND OF 1,000 DANCES
(Cannibal and the Headhunters)

I said a na
Na na na na
Na na na na na na na na na na
Na na na na

(Check baby's diaper.)

Three Traditional Baby Games

OKLAHOMA BABY CHICKEN HAT

Grasp your baby firmly and place it on your head, stomach side down, then stride about the room, bouncing on the balls of your feet and clucking to the tune of "Surrey with the Fringe on Top."

HERE COMES THE BABY EATER

Place your baby on the carpet, face up, then crawl around on all fours and announce, "I'm so *hungry!* I could eat a *baby!*" Then crawl over and gobble up the baby, starting at the feet, and periodically raising your head and shouting, "Great baby! Delicious!" Babies love this game, but you don't want to play it when other grown-ups are around, because they will try to take custody away from you.

ATTACK OF THE SPACE BABIES

Lie on your back on the floor and hold your baby over you, face down. Move the baby around in the manner of a hovering spacecraft while making various high-pitched science fiction noises such as "BOOOOOOOWEEEEEEEOOOOO." Feign great fear as the baby attempts to land on the planet Earth. (NOTE: Wear protective clothing, as space babies often try to weaken the earth's resistance by spitting up on it.)

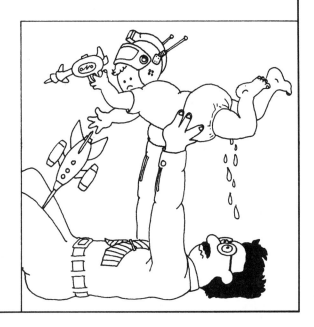

Babies and Pets

First of all, get rid of your cat. Cats are scum. You've read newspaper stories about elderly widows who die and leave their entire estates to their pet cats, right? Well, your cat reads those stories too, and has spent most of its skulking, devious little life dreaming about inheriting all your money. You know where it goes when it disappears for hours at a time? Investment seminars, that's where.

So if you bring a baby into the home, the cat will see the baby as a rival for your estate and will do anything to turn you against it. Many instances of so-called colic are really nothing more than a cat repeatedly sneaking into a baby's room in the dead of night and jabbing the baby in the stomach.

Dogs, of course, would never do anything like that. They're far too stupid to think of it. So you can keep your dog. In fact, many dogs come to love their masters' babies, often carrying them around gently by the scruffs of their necks, licking them incessantly and refusing to let anybody—even the parents!—near the baby. It's the cutest thing you ever saw, and it really cuts down on child-care costs. Of course, you have to weigh this against the fact that the child

CAT ATTENDING INVESTMENT SEMINAR

develops a tendency to shed and attack squirrels.

DRAWBACK OF CLOSE CHILD-DOG
RELATIONSHIP

Baby Albums

Baby albums are probably the single biggest cause of violent death in America today. The reason is that when people have their first baby, they record everything that happens:

January 5 — Today Rupert is exactly one and a half weeks old! He weighs 8 pounds, 3.587 ounces, up 2.342 ounces from yesterday! He had two poopy diapers today, but definitely not as runny as the ones he had January 3! Also not quite so greenish!

And so on. By the time these people have their *second* baby, they're sick of albums. Oh, they try to slap something together, but it's obvious that their hearts aren't really in it:

1966-74 — Byron was born and is now in the second grade.

So Byron grows up, seemingly normal on the outside, but knowing on the inside that he has this pathetic scrawny album while his brother's looks like the Manhattan telephone directory, and eventually he runs amok in a dentist's office with a Thompson submachine gun. So if you want to do a baby album, fine, go ahead, but have the common decency to notify the police first.

Chapter 9

Six Months to a Year

Development during the Second Six Months

During the second six months, your baby will begin to start crawling around looking for hazards. It will start to become aware of the mysteries of language, perhaps even learning to understand simple phrases such as "No!" and "Spit that out!"

Physically, you'll find your baby is getting hardier and more portable now, so that you can more easily take it to restaurants, although you still can't go inside. By now baby should have gotten over early medical problems such as the colic; if not, you should see your pediatrician and get something you can use to kill yourself.

So all in all, you can look forward in the next six months to a period of change and growth, with a 60 percent chance of afternoon or evening thundershowers.

Baby's First Solid Food

We're using the term "food" loosely here. What we're talking about are those nine

their bowel movements. We have enough trouble with the Congress.

How to Feed Solid Food to a Baby

The key thing is that you should *not* place the food in the baby's mouth. At this stage, babies use their mouths exclusively for chewing horrible things that they find on the floor (see below). The way they eat food

CIGAR BUTT

CHEWING TOBACCO WAD

CRUSHED PAPER TISSUE

CRUSHED COCKROACH

zillion little jars on the supermarket shelf with the smiling baby on the label and names like "Prunes with Mixed Leeks." Babies hate this stuff. Who wouldn't? It looks like frog waste.

Babies are people, too; they want to eat what *you* want to eat. They want cheeseburgers and beer. If we simply fed them normal diets, they'd eat like crazy. They'd weigh 150 pounds at the end of the first year. This is exactly why we don't feed them normal diets: The last thing we need is a lot of 150-pound people with no control over

is by absorbing it directly into their bloodstreams through their faces. So the most efficient way to feed a baby is to smear the food on its chin.

Unfortunately, many inexperienced parents insist on putting food into the baby's mouth. They put in spoonful after spoonful of, say, beets, sincerely believing they are doing something constructive, when in fact the beets are merely going around the Baby Food-Return Loop (see diagram), which all

humans are equipped with until the age of 18 months. After the parents finish "feeding" the baby, they remove the bib and clean up the area, at which point the baby starts to spew beets from its mouth under high pressure, like a miniature beet volcano, until its face is covered with beets, which it can then absorb.

What to Do When a Baby Puts a Horrible Thing in Its Mouth

The trick is to distract the baby with something even worse than what's in its mouth. Next time you're in a bus station rest room, scour the floor for something really disgusting that might appeal to a baby. Stick it in your freezer, so you can quickly defrost it in a microwave oven (allow about 40 seconds) and wave it enticingly in front of the baby until the baby spits out its horrible thing and lunges for yours.

Of course, as your baby catches on to your tricks, you'll need new and different things to entice it with, which means you'll have to spend a great deal of time on your hands and knees in bus station rest rooms. This is a perfectly normal part of being a responsible parent. Remember to say that when the police come.

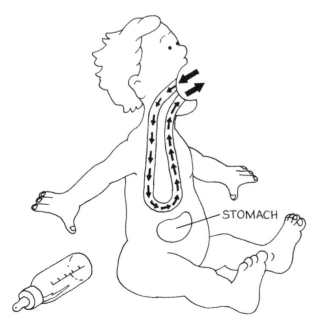

THE BABY FOOD-RETURN LOOP

TEACHING BABY TO SWIM

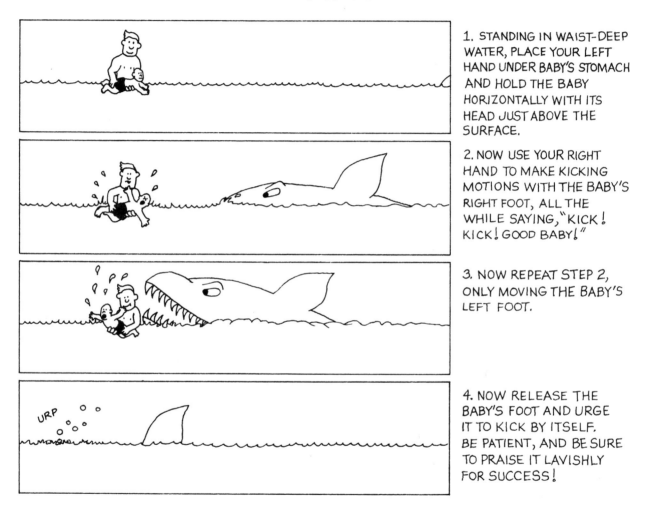

1. STANDING IN WAIST-DEEP WATER, PLACE YOUR LEFT HAND UNDER BABY'S STOMACH AND HOLD THE BABY HORIZONTALLY WITH ITS HEAD JUST ABOVE THE SURFACE.

2. NOW USE YOUR RIGHT HAND TO MAKE KICKING MOTIONS WITH THE BABY'S RIGHT FOOT, ALL THE WHILE SAYING, "KICK! KICK! GOOD BABY!"

3. NOW REPEAT STEP 2, ONLY MOVING THE BABY'S LEFT FOOT.

4. NOW RELEASE THE BABY'S FOOT AND URGE IT TO KICK BY ITSELF. BE PATIENT, AND BE SURE TO PRAISE IT LAVISHLY FOR SUCCESS!

Traveling with Baby

By now you're probably thinking how nice it would be to take a trip somewhere and stay in a place where there isn't a hardened yellowish glaze consisting of bananas mixed with baby spit smeared on every surface below a height of two feet. Great idea! My wife and I took many trips with our son, Robert, when he was less than a year old, and we found them all to be surprisingly carefree experiences right up until approximately four hours after we left home, which is when his temperature would reach 106 degrees Fahrenheit. Often we didn't even have to take his temperature, because we could see that his pacifier was melting.

Almost all babies contain a virus that activates itself automatically when the baby is 200 miles or more from its pediatrician. The first time this happened to Robert, we wound up in a pediatric clinic where the doctor got his degree from the University of Kuala Lumpur Medical School and Textile College. He said, "Baby very hot! Bad hot! Could have seezhah!" And we said, "Oh no! My God! Not seezhah!" Then we said, "What the hell is 'seezhah'?" We were afraid it was some kind of horrible Asian disease. Then the doctor rolled his eyes back in his head and went, "Aaaarrgh," and we said, "Oh! *Seizure!*"

The lesson to be learned from this is that when you travel with a baby, you must be prepared for emergencies. Let's say you're planning a trip to the seashore. Besides baby's usual food, formula, bottles, sterilizer, medicine, clothing, diapers, reams of moist towelettes, ointments, lotions, powders, pacifier, toys, portable crib, blankets, rectal thermometer, car seat, stroller, backpack, playpen, and walker, don't forget to take:

- One of those things that look like miniature turkey basters that you use to clear out babies' noses, for when your baby develops a major travel cold and sounds like a little cauldron of mucus gurgling away in the motel room six feet away from you all night long.

- A potent infant-formula anti-cholera drug, for when you're lying on the beach and look up to discover that baby has become intimately involved with an enormous buried dog dropping.

- Something to read while you're sitting in the emergency ward waiting room.

- Plenty of film, so you can record these and the many other hilarious adventures you're bound to have traveling with a baby. You might also take a camera.

Taking a Baby on an Airplane

First, you should notify the airline in advance that you will be traveling with an infant, so they can use their computers to assign you a seat where your baby will be in a position to knock a Bloody Mary into the lap of a corporate executive on his way to make an important speech.

Also, you should be aware that your baby will insist on standing up in your lap all the way through the flight, no matter how long it is. If you plan to fly with a baby to Japan, all I can say is you'd better have thighs of steel.

Some people try to get their babies to sit down on flights, by giving them sedatives. On our doctor's suggestion, we tried this on a cross-country flight, and all it did was make Robert cranky. The only thing that cheered him up was to grab the hair of the man sitting in front of us, who tried to be nice about it, but if you have a nine-month-old child with a melted Hershey bar all over his pudgy little fingers grabbing your hair all the way from sea to shining sea, you'd start to get a little cranky yourself. So I think it might be a good idea if, on flights featuring babies, the airline distributed sedatives to all the adults, except maybe the pilot.

Teething

Teething usually begins on March 11 at 3:25 P.M., although some babies are off by as much as 20 minutes. The major symptom of teething is that your baby becomes irritable and cries a lot. Of course, this is also the major symptom of everything else, so you

Quick-Reference Baby Medical-Emergency Chart

SYMPTOM	CAUSE	TREATMENT
Baby is chewing contentedly	Baby has found something horrible on floor	Follow enticement procedure described on page 61
Baby is crying	It could be teething, colic, snake bite, some kind of awful rare disease or something	Don't worry: most likely it's nothing
Baby has strange dark lines all over face and body	Baby has gotten hold of laundry marking pen	Wait for baby to grow new skin
Baby's voice sounds muffled	Baby's two-year-old sibling, jealous of all the attention the New Arrival is getting, has covered the New Arrival with dirt	Vacuum baby quickly; explain to sibling that you love him or her just as much as baby, but you will kill him or her if he or she ever does that again

might try the old teething test, which is to stick your finger in baby's mouth and see whether baby bites all the way through to your bone, indicating the presence of teeth.

Most teething babies want to chew on something, so it's a good idea to keep a plastic teething ring in the freezer, taking care not to confuse it with the frozen horrible things from bus station rest rooms (see above).

The first teeth to appear will be the central divisors, followed by the bovines, the colons, the insights, and the Four Tops, for a total of 30 or 40 in all. Your pediatrician will advise you to brush and floss your baby's teeth daily, but he's just kidding.

Chapter 10

The Second Year

Major Developments during the Second Year

Your baby will learn to walk and talk, but that's nothing. The major development is that your baby will learn how to scream for no good reason in shopping malls.

What to Do when a One-Year-Old Starts Screaming in a Shopping Mall, and the Reason Is That You Won't Let It Eat the Pizza Crust That Somebody, Who Was Probably Diseased, Left in the Public Ashtray amid the Sand and the Saliva-Soaked Cigar Butts, but the Other Shoppers Are Staring at You as if to Suggest That You Must Be Some Kind of Heartless Child-Abusing Nazi Scum

First of all, forget about reason. You can't reason with a one-year-old. In fact, reasoning with children of any age has been greatly overrated. There is no documented case of any child being successfully reasoned with before the second year of graduate school.

Also you can't hit a one-year-old. It will just cry harder, and women the age of your mother will walk right up and whap you with their handbags. So what do you do when your child decides to scream in pub-

lic? Here are several practical, time-tested techniques:

■ Explain your side to the other shoppers. As they go by, pull them aside, show them the pizza crust, and talk it over with them, adult to adult ("Look! The little cretin wants to *eat* this! Ha ha! Isn't that CRAZY?").

■ Threaten to take your child to see Santa Claus if it doesn't shut up. All children are born with an instinctive terror of Santa Claus.

■ Let your child have the damn pizza crust. I mean, there's always a chance the previous owner wasn't diseased. It could have been a clergyman or something.

Walking

Most babies learn to walk at about 12 months, although nobody has ever figured out why they bother, because for the next 12 months all they do is stagger off in random directions until they trip over dust molecules and fall on their butts. You cannot catch them before they fall. They fall so quickly that the naked adult eye cannot even see them. This is why diapers are made so thick.

During this phase, your job, as parent, is to trail along behind your child everywhere, holdings your arms out in the Standard Toddler-Following Posture made popular by Boris Karloff in the excellent parent-education film *The Mummy,* only with a degree of hunch approaching that of Neanderthal Man (see diagram) so you'll be able to pick your child up quickly after it falls, because the longer it stays on the ground the more likely it is to find something to put in its mouth.

THE MUMMY
(ANGLE OF HUNCH: 15°)

MODERN MAN
(ANGLE OF HUNCH: 30°)

TODDLER

NEANDERTHAL MAN
(ANGLE OF HUNCH: 45°)

Talking

There are two distinct phases in the baby's language development. The second phase is when the baby actually starts talking, which is at about 18 months. The first phase is when the parents imagine that the baby is talking, which is somewhere around 12 months, or even earlier if it's their first baby.

What happens is that one day the baby is holding a little plastic car, trying to get it all the way into his mouth, and he makes some typical random baby sound such as "gawanoo," and the parents, their brains softened from inhaling Johnson's Baby Oil fumes, say to each other: "Did you hear that? Teddy said 'car'!!!!!" If you've ever been around young parents going through this kind of self-delusion, you know how deranged they can get:

YOU: So! How's little Jason?
PARENT: Talking up a storm! Listen!
JASON: Poomwah arrrr grah.
PARENT: Isn't that incredible!
YOU: Ah. Yes. Hmmm.
PARENT: I mean, 13 months old, and already he's concerned about restrictions on imported steel!
YOU: Ah.
JASON: Brrrrrooooooooooooooooooooper.
PARENT: No, Jason, I believe that was during the Kennedy administration.

Eventually, your child will start to learn some real words, which means you'll finally find out what he's thinking. Not much, as it turns out. The first words our son, Robert, said were "dog" and "hot," and after that he didn't seem the least bit interested in learning any more. For the longest time, our conversations went like this:

ME: Look, Robert. See the birds?
ROBERT: Dog.
ME: No, Robert. Those are birds.
ROBERT: Dog dog dog dog dog dog dog dog dog.
ME: Those are *birds,* Robert. Can you say "bird"?
ROBERT (emphatically):   Dog dog dog dog dog dog dog dog dog dog dog dog dog dog dog dog dog dog.
ME (giving up):   Okay. Those are dogs.
ROBERT: Hot.

Sometimes we'd think we were making real progress on the language front. I remember once my wife called me into the living room, all excited. "Watch this," she said. "Robert, where's your head?" And by God, Robert pointed to his head. I was stunned. I couldn't believe what a genius we had on our hands. Then my wife, bursting with pride, said, "Now watch *this.* Robert, where's your foot?" Robert flashed us a brilliant smile of comprehension, pointed to his head, and said, "dog."

Books for One-Year-Olds

The trouble with books for small children is that they all have titles like, *Ted the Raccoon Vists a Condiments Factory* and are so boring that you doze off after two or three pages and run the risk that your child will slide off your lap and sustain a head injury. So what you want to do is get a book that has more appeal for adults, such as, *Passionate Teenage Periodontal Assistants,* then cut out the pages and paste them over the words in your child's book. This way you can maintain your interest while the child looks at the pictures:

YOU (pretending to read out loud): "My, my," said Ted the Raccoon. "These pickles taste good!" Just look at all those pickles, Johnny!

(While Johnny looks at the pickles, you read: "Brad looked up from *U.S. News and World Report* as a blond, full-breasted periodontal assistant swayed into the waiting room on shapely, nylon-sheathed legs. 'My name is Desiree,' she breathed through luscious, pouting lips, 'and if you'll follow me, I'll show you how to operate the Water Pik oral hygiene appliance.' ")

Teaching Small Children to Read

Children are capable of learning to read much earlier than we give them credit for. Why, Mozart was only two years old when he wrote *Moby Dick!*

When our son was about 18 months old, my wife, who has purchased every baby-improvement book ever published, got one called *How to Teach Your Baby to Read.* The chapter headings started out with "Can Babies Learn to Read?" and worked up to "Babies Definitely Can Learn to Read" and finally got around to "If You Don't Teach Your Baby to Read Right Now, You Are Vermin,"

Me, I was dubious. I thought it was better to teach our child not to pull boogers out of his nose and hand them to us as if they were party favors. But my wife gave it the old college try. She did what the book said, which was to write words like DOG in big letters on pieces of cardboard, then show them to Robert and say the words out loud as if she were having a peck of fun. She did this conscientiously for a couple of weeks, three times a day, and then she realized that Robert was paying no attention whatsoever, and her I.Q. was starting to drop, so she stopped.

My theory is that there is a finite amount of intelligence in a family, and you're supposed to gradually transfer it to your children over a period of many years. This is why your parents started to get so stupid just at the time in your life when you were getting really smart.

How to Put a One-Year-Old to Bed

Children at this age move around a lot while they sleep. If we didn't keep them in cribs, they'd be hundreds of miles away by dawn. So the trick is to put the blankets as far as possible from the child, on the theory that eventually the child will crawl under them.

Bedtime Songs

I advise against "Rock-a-Bye Baby," because it's really sick, what with the baby getting blown out of the tree and crashing down with the cradle. Some of those cradles weigh over 50 pounds. A much better song is "Go to Sleep":

Go to sleep
Go to sleep
Go right straight to sleep
And stay asleep until at least 6:30 A.M.

"ROCK-A-BYE BABY"

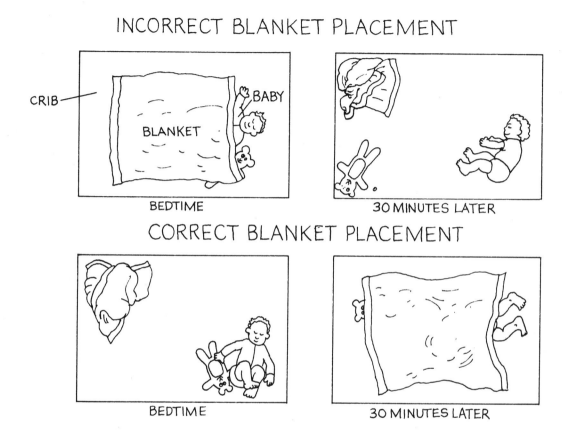

Potty Training

Child psychologists all agree that bodily functions are a source of great anxiety for children, so we can safely assume this isn't true. It certainly wasn't true for our son. He was never happier than when he had a full diaper. We once took him to a department store photographer for baby pictures, and just before we went into the studio, when it was too late to change his diaper, he eliminated an immense quantity of waste, far more than could be explained by any of the known laws of physics. The photographer kept remarking on what a happy baby we had, which was easy for him to say, because he was standing 15 feet away. The pictures all came out swell. In every one, Robert is grinning the insanely happy grin of a baby emitting an aroma that would stun a buffalo. So much for the child's anxiety.

I'll tell you who gets anxious: the parents, that's who. Young parents spend much of their time thinking and talking about their children's bodily functions. You can take an educated, sophisticated couple who, before their child was born, talked about great literature and the true meaning of life, and for the first two years after they become parents, their conversations will center on the consistency of their child's stool, to the point where nobody invites them over for dinner.

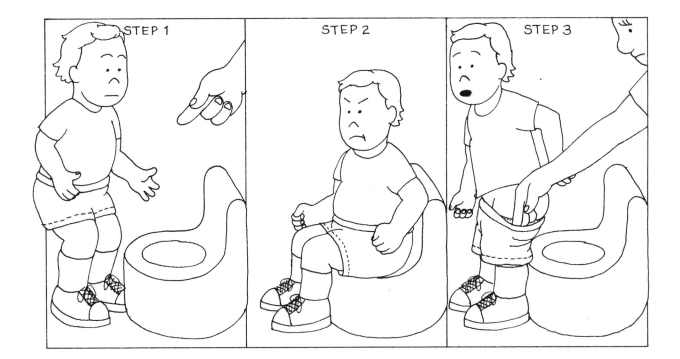

Around the child's second birthday, the parents get tired of waiting for the child to become anxious about his bodily functions, and they decide to give him some anxiety in the form of potty training. This is probably a good thing. A child can go only so far in life without potty training. It is not mere coincidence that six of the last seven presidents were potty trained, not to mention nearly half of the nation's state legislators.

The Traditional Potty Training Technique

The traditional potty training technique is to buy a book written by somebody who was out getting graduate school degrees when his own children were actually being potty trained. My wife bought a book that claimed we could potty train our child in one day, using a special potty that (I swear this

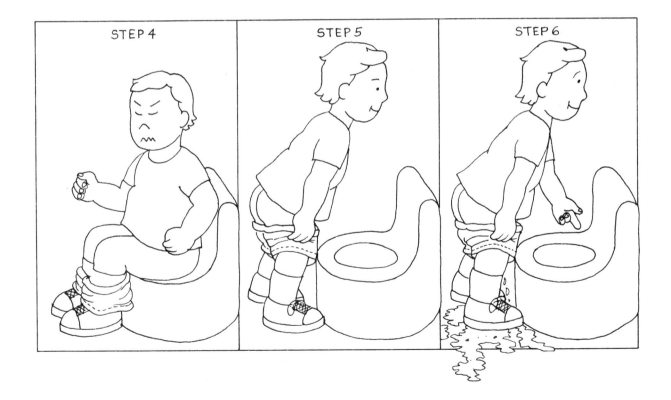

is true) played "Twinkle, Twinkle Little Star" when the child went in it. She also got a little book for our son that explained potty training in terms that a small child could understand, such as "poo-poo."

Now there may well be some parents, somewhere, who managed to potty train their child in one day, but I am willing to bet they used a cattle prod. My wife read that book all the way through, and she did exactly what it said, which was that you should feed your child a lot of salty snacks so that it would drink a lot of liquids and consequently would have to pee about every 20 minutes, which would give it lots of opportunities to practice going in the musical potty, so that it would have the whole procedure nailed down solid by the end of the day. That was the theory.

When I left home that morning, my wife was reading the poo-poo book to Robert. She had a cheerful, determined look on her face. When I got home that evening, more than ten hours later, there were cracker crumbs everywhere, and piles of soiled child's underpants, seemingly hundreds of them, as if the entire junior class of St. Swithan's School for Incontinent Children had been there on a field trip. My wife was still in her nightgown. I don't think she had even brushed her teeth. It is extremely fortunate for the man who wrote the potty training book that he did not walk in the door with me, because the police would have found his lifeless body lying in the bushes with an enormous bulge in his throat playing "Twinkle, Twinkle Little Star."

We did, in the end, get Robert potty trained. We did it the same way everybody does, the same way you will, by a lot of nagging and false alarms and about 30,000 accidents and endless wildly extravagant praise for bowel movements ("Honey! Come and see what Robert did!" "Oh Robert, that's *wonderful!*" etc.).

The big drawback to potty training is that, for a while, children assume that all adults are as fascinated with it as their parents seem to be. Robert would walk up to strangers in restaurants and announce, "I went pee-pee." And the strangers would say, "Ah." And Robert would say, "I didn't do poop." And the strangers would say, "No?" And Robert would say, "I'm gonna do poop later." And so on.

Nutrition

By the middle of the second year, your baby's Food-Return Loop has disappeared, so its mouth is connected directly to its stomach. At this point, you want to adjust its diet to see that each day it gets food from all three Basic Baby Food Nutrition Groups (see chart). You also should encourage your baby to feed itself, so that you won't have to be in the room.

The Basic Baby Food Nutrition Groups

FOODS THAT BABIES HURL AT THE CEILING

- Anything from jars with babies on the labels
- Anything the baby ate the day before, so you went out and bought $30 worth of it

FOODS THAT BABIES HURL AT THE DOG

- Anything in a weighty container
- Taffy
- Zwieback (NOTE: Zwieback has sharp edges, so the dog should wear protective clothing)

FOODS THAT BABIES EAT

- Anything from vending machines
- Caulking
- Anything with dead ants on it
- Sand

Chapter 11

The Third Year

This period is often referred to as the "terrible twos," not so much because children this age start behaving any worse than before, but because they reach the size where if they swing at you, they'll hit you square in the crotch.

The important thing to remember here is that your child is only trying to establish its independence. This is a necessary part of its development: It must learn to make its own decisions, to interact with the world directly rather than through the protective mediation of its parents. Your child must also learn that when it hits a bigger person in the crotch, it should pretend to be very, very sorry.

How to Discipline a Two-Year-Old

Discipline during this phase consists of choosing the appropriate Escalating Futile Parental Disciplinary Threat. A handy reference chart is printed here for your use.

Remember that when your two-year-old "misbehaves," it's usually becaue of his natural curiosity. It is not cruelty that causes him to thrust a Bic pen deep into the dog's nostril; it is a genuine desire to find out how you will react.

The time-tested way to react is to work your way up the ladder of Traditional Escalating Futile Parental Disciplinary Threats.

BABY WITH NORMAL CHILDHOOD FEAR
OF GIANT LOBSTERS

The Traditional Escalating Futile Parental Disciplinary Threats

1. "You're going to poke somebody's eye out."
2. "You're going to make me very angry."
3. "You're going straight to your room."
4. "I'm going to tell your father."
5. "I'm going to tell Santa Claus."
6. "I'm not going to give you any dessert."
7. "I'm not going to buy you any more Hot Wheels."
8. "I'm very angry now."
9. "I'm going to give you a good smack."
10. "I mean it."
11. "I really mean it."
12. "I'm not kidding."
13. (SMACK).

NOTE: If there's a real discipline emergency, such as your child has somehow gotten hold of an acetylene torch, you may have to start right in at Threat Number 8.

Fears

All of us are born with a set of instinctive fears—of falling, of the dark, of lobsters, of falling on a lobster in the dark, of speaking before a Rotary Club, and of the words "Some Assembly Required." These fears help protect your child from real danger, and you should encourage them. ("Run!" you should shout. "Lobsters are coming!")

But many two-year-olds also develop seemingly irrational fears. They get these from Mister Rogers. He tries to reassure his young viewers about standard childhood fears, but the children would never have thought of them if Mister Rogers hadn't brought them up. My son and I once watched Mister Rogers sing this song in

Fears Your Mother Teaches You during Childhood

You needed these fears to become a responsible adult, and now it's time to start passing them on to your child.

- The fear that if you cross your eyes, they'll get stuck that way.

- The fear that if you go in the water less than an hour after eating, you will get a cramp and sink to the bottom, helpless, and possibly catch cold.

- The fear that public toilet seats have germs capable of leaping more than 20 feet.

- The fear that if you wear old underwear, a plane will crash on you and rip your clothes off and your underwear will be broadcast nationally on the evening news. ("The victim shown here wearing the underwear with all the holes and stains has been identified as . . .")

- The fear that if you get in trouble at school, it will go on your Permanent Record and follow you for the rest of your life. ("Your qualifications are excellent, Mr. Barry, but I see here in your Permanent Record that in the eighth grade you and Joseph DiGiacinto flushed a lit cherry bomb down the boys' room toilet at Harold C. Crittenden Junior High School. Frankly, Mr. Barry, we're looking for people with more respect for plumbing than that.")

MR. ROGERS   NOT MR. ROGERS

grits in seconds. Aided by this kind of understanding and support from us, Robert eventually stopped imagining his horse, which was good because it was ruining the carpet.

So unless you want your child to develop a set of irrational fears, I advise you not to let him watch Mister Rogers. A far better alternative is the Saturday morning cartoon shows, which instill the healthy and rational fear that evil beings with sophisticated weapons are trying to destroy the planet.

which he said over and over, in the most cheerful voice imaginable, that "You can never go down the drain." By the time he finished, we were both very concerned about going down the drain. And this came at a time when I had just gotten over the fear of being stabbed to death in the shower, which I got from *Psycho.*

Recently, my son became convinced that a horse was coming into his bedroom at night to get him. The way to cope with this kind of fear is to allow the child to confront it openly. We took Robert to visit some real horses, so he could see for himself that they are nothing more than huge creatures with weird eyeballs and long teeth and hard feet that could stomp him to the consistency of

Toys for Two-Year-Olds

Pay no attention to the little statements on the boxes that say things like "For Ages 1 to 3." If you heed these statements, all you'll buy for the first few years are little plastic shapes that the child is supposed to put in corresponding little holes, which is so exceedingly boring that after five minutes the child will develop an ear infection just for a change of pace. The best toys for a child aged 0 to 3 is a toy that says "For Ages 10 to 14." The best toy for a child aged 10 to 14 is cash, or its own apartment.

You should also buy Fisher-Price toys. Not for your child. For your own protection. Every Fisher-Price toy has been approved by a panel consisting of dozens of child psychologists and pediatricians and Ralph Nader and Mister Rogers, and in most states failure to own at least a half dozen of these toys is considered legal proof of child abuse.

Another reason why you should buy Fisher-Price toys is that they are built better than any other products you can buy, even in Japan. They're made out of some plastic-like substance that Fisher-Price imports from another planet, and nothing can harm it. If Fisher-Price had any marketing sense, it would make its cars much bigger and put real engines in them and change the seats so that real people could sit in them. Right now, the seats are designed for little toy ball-headed Fisher-Price people, which have no arms or legs (the Fisher-Price factory employees whack off the arms and legs with little machetes just before shipment). Consumers would snork these cars up like hotcakes. We'd forget all about Toyota.

How to Hold a Birthday Party for Two-Year-Olds

Not in your house. Outdoors, I don't care if you live in Juneau, Alaska, and it's January. You want to hold it outdoors, and you want the fire department to stand by to hose the area down immediately after you put the ice cream in front of them. And you want all the adults inside the house where they can drink in relative safety.

A Word about Smurfs, Snoopy, Strawberry Shortcake, and All the Other Nauseating Little Characters That You Swear You Will Never Allow in Your Home

Forget it. These toys are creatures of the multibillion-dollar Cuteness Industry, which is extremely powerful and has

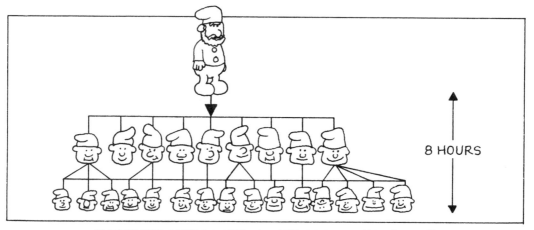

8 HOURS

OVERNIGHT REPRODUCTION RATE OF OBNOXIOUS TOYS

influence everywhere. The *Voyager II* space probe found traces of a Snoopy toothbrush on Mars. If you fail to buy Smurfs, agents of the Smurf Corporation will mail them to you, or smuggle them into your house baked inside loaves of bread, until you reach the national average of 24 Smurfs per child under eight.

So you have to live with them. The only defense you have is to encourage your child to play hostile games with them, such as "Smurf War Tribunal" and "Mr. Smurf Visits the Toaster Oven."

Questions

Starting at around age two, your child will start asking you a great many questions. This can be annoying, but you must remem-ber that if children couldn't ask questions, they would have no way to irritate you when they're strapped in the car seat.

The most popular question for small children is "Why?" They can use it anywhere, and it's usually impossible to answer:

CHILD: What's that?
YOU: That's a goat.
CHILD: Why?

Our son would lie awake at night thinking of questions that nobody could answer:

ROBERT: Which is bigger, five or six?
ME (confidently):   Six.
ROBERT: What if it's a great big five made out of stone?
ME: Um.
ROBERT: And a little six made out of wood.

Once I hauled out my guitar to sing traditional folk songs to Robert. It was going to be togetherness. It was going to be meaningful. It was going to be just like on "The Waltons." Here is a verbatim transcript:

ME (singing):   "Puff, the Magic Dragon, lived by the sea . . ."
ROBERT: What's a dragon?
ME: It's a great big animal that has fire coming out of its nose. (Singing) "Little Jackie Paper, loved that rascal . . ."
ROBERT: Did Jackie Paper have fire coming out of his nose?
ME: No, he was a little boy, like you. Do you have fire coming out of your nose?
ROBERT (thoughtfully):   No. Boogies.
ME: Um. Right. (Singing) "Little Jackie Paper, loved that . . ."
ROBERT: Did Jackie Paper have boogies coming out of his nose?

The point here is that your child will never ask you where babies come from, or why the sky is blue, or any other question that has a real answer. Your child is going to want to know whether Jackie Paper had boogies coming out of his nose, and whether you answer "yes" or "no," your child will want to know why.

Preschool Programs

Near the end of the second year, most parents start thinking about putting their child in a preschool program, which is a place that has all these little tables and chairs where your child makes these pathetic drawings that you put on your refrigerator. Also they eat snacks and take naps. That's the core of the curriculum.

You must choose your child's preschool program carefully, because it determines how well the child does in kindergarten, which affects how well the child does in grade school, which is an important factor in how well the child does in junior high school, which forms the basis for how well the child does in high school, which of course determines which college the child gets into.

On the other hand, all the child will do in college is listen to loud music and get ready for dates, so you don't have to be all *that* careful about choosing the preschool program. Just kick the little chairs a few times to make sure they're sturdy, and say a few words to the staff to let them know you're a Concerned Parent ("Anything happens to my kid, I come in here and break some thumbs. Got it?").

Also, make sure the preschool doesn't have any guinea pigs. I don't know why, but somewhere along the line, preschool educators picked up the insane notion that guinea pigs are educational, when in fact all they do is poop these little pellets that look exactly like the pellets you give them to eat. You don't want your child exposed to that.

The Little Boy and the Toad (A Child-Participation Bedtime Story)

It's good to encourage your child to participate in making up stories. Here's a bedtime story I used to tell Robert, with his help:

ME: Once upon a time, there was a little boy named John.

ROBERT: No. Lee.

ME: Okay. There was a little boy named Lee, and one day he was walking along, and he . . .

ROBERT: No. He was driving.

ME: Okay, he was driving along, and he saw . . .

ROBERT: In a Jeep.

ME: He was driving along in a Jeep, and he saw a little toad.

ROBERT: No. He saw a dump truck.

ME: And they all lived happily ever after. Now go to sleep.

ROBERT: Why?

Epilogue:
Should You Have Another?

Well! So here we are! We've taken your baby from a little gourdlike object with virtually no marketable skills to a real little human being, capable of putting the cat in the dryer and turning it on all by himself or herself!

Sure, it's been a lot of work for you. Sure, you would have liked to have had a few more quiet evenings alone, just the two of you sipping wine and talking instead of sitting in the hospital X-ray department, waiting to find out whether your child had, in fact, swallowed the bullets that it snatched out of the belt of the policeman who was writing a traffic ticket because you smashed into the furniture store when your child threw your glasses out the car window. But take a minute to look at the positive side of parenthood.

(Pause)

Give it time. You'll come up with something. And when you do, think about how much fun it would be to do the whole thing over again. Not with the same child, of course; there is no way you could get it back into the uterus. I'm talking about a completely new baby, only this time around you'll have a chance to avoid the mistakes you made last time, such as labor. I understand from reading the publications sold at supermarket checkout counters that you can now have a baby in a test tube! I don't know the details, but it sounds much less painful than the usual route, although you'd have to balance that against the fact that the baby would be extremely small and cylindrical. It would look like those little Fisher-Price people.

But whether you have another child or not, the important thing is that you've experienced the fulfillment that comes with being a parent. You may feel your efforts will never be rewarded, but believe me, you have sown the seeds of love and trust, and I guarantee you that there will come a time, years from now, when your child—now an adult with children of his or her own—will come to you, and, in a voice quaking with emotion, ask for a loan for a down payment on a house much nicer than yours.

Index

A

Ann, Raggedy, 113

B

Benz, Mercedes, 101
Boogers
eye, 145
Little Jackie Paper and, 177
nose, 177
Burr, Raymond, 100

C

Claus, Santa, 160, 171
Condom Lady, 97

D

Dick, Moby, 163
Donahue, Phil, 106
"Dragon, Puff the Magic," 177

E

Easygoing Deaf People's Night, 95
Eisenhower Administration, 118
Elderly People with Enormous Cars Club, 124

F

"Family Feud," 131
Ferret, 129
Field and Stream, 119
Fonda, Jane, 141
Four Tops, 158
Frog waste, 152

G

Grandmothers, U.S. Constitution and, 133
Gypsies, 144

H

Head, Mister Potato, 120
Headhunters, Cannibal and the, 147
Helmsley, Leona, 135
"Hout," 121

I

Ice caps, polar, 115

J

Johnson, Billy Ray, 127

K

K-Mart, 143
Kansas, 117
Karloff, Boris, 161
Korean War, 114

L
"Little House on the Prairie,"
  118

M
Mallomars, 104, 130
Mary, Bloody, 156
Mastodons, 93
Mecca, 121
"Molly, Heg-a-Leg," 147
Motor Vehicles Bureau, 145
Mozart, 163

O
Oklahoma Baby Chicken Hat,
  148

Our Lady of Maximum Discomfort High School, 146

P
Pacific Ocean, 116
Penthouse, 110
Peru, 111
Pierre, N. Dak., 107

Q
Queen, Dairy, 97, 119

R
Racoon, Ted the, 163
Raisinets, charred, 147
Rogers, Mister, 171, 173
"Roots," 118

S
Scone-Hayes, Crumpet, 131
Space, outer, 134

T
Teeth, wisdom, 99
"Turkey in the Straw," 121

V
Vampires, 122
Vermont, 147

W
Watergate, 143
Webster Groves, Mo., 104
Welles, Orson, 104
Wheels, Hot, 171
Wives, old, 99–100

STAY FIT
& HEALTHY

UNTIL YOU'RE DEAD

Contents

Foreword .... page **187**

Introduction.. page **188**

Chapter 1   **How Your Body Works**.......................... page **195**

Chapter 2   **Getting Ready to Get Started** .... page **200**

Chapter 3   **Women's Total Complete Aerobic Fitness Workout**   page **210**

Chapter 4   **Running** .... page **215**

Chapter 5   **Popular Sports** .... page **222**

Chapter 6   **Bodybuilding**.................................... page **231**

Chapter 7   **Nutrition** .... page **239**

Chapter 8   **Dieting and Weight Control** .... page **244**

Chapter 9   **Women's Beauty and Grooming** .... page **250**

Chapter 10   **Men's Beauty and Grooming** .... page **256**

Chapter 11   **When You Get Sick**............................. page **262**

Chapter 12   **Fitness Q and A** .... page **268**

Index .... page **275**

Inspirational Opening Anecdote Explaining the Author's Lifelong Personal Commitment to Health and Fitness

Thirty-one years ago, when I was a mere boy of seven, my mother fell very, very sick. She called me to her side and, in a voice weakened by pain, said, "Bob, whatever happens to me, I want you to remember that . . ."

"David," I corrected. "My name is David."

"I know that, you little snot," she said. "I'm your mother."

I have always remembered those words, despite the fact that my mother recovered completely and is fine today.

Hi, Mom.

Introduction

Four Reasons Why You Must Get Fit Immediately

1. YOU OWE IT TO YOUR COUNTRY. You can bet that the enemies of your country are fit. People in Communist nations are on a strict fitness program

of waiting in line a lot and darting their eyes about nervously. We, too, must be fit, in case these Communists invade us. We must be ready to fight them in the streets and the alleys. The problem is that many of you have eaten so many Enormous Economy Size bags of corn chips and so much bean

dip that you probably couldn't fit into the alleys without the aid of powerful hydraulic devices. So you'd have to fight them in the streets, where you'd be easy prey for their blimp-seeking missiles.

2. YOU OWE IT TO YOUR CAREER. In the old days, your successful business executive was generally a spectacular tub of lard who had to be transported from business deal to business deal via private railroad car. But today's top executives are lean, sleek, and fit. They eat nutritionally balanced meals, run ten miles every day, play tennis and racquetball, and work out regularly on Nautilus machines. Consequently, they have no time whatsoever for their work. Many of them don't even know where their offices are. This is why the entire U.S. economy is now manufactured in Japan.

3. YOU OWE IT TO YOUR SELF-ESTEEM. There is no feeling in the world quite as wonderful as the feeling of being physically fit, except the feeling of eating pepperoni pizza. No! Wait! Disregard that last remark! What I'm trying to say is, when you become fit, everything about you changes. You have to buy new pants, for example. And you develop a whole new attitude about yourself. Instead of constantly thinking, "I am pasty and flabby and disgusting and nobody likes me," you think, "People like me now, but only as long as I can keep from becoming pasty and flabby and disgusting again. I wish I had a pepperoni pizza."

4. YOU OWE IT TO YOUR FUTURE. There's nothing like regular, vigorous exercise to prepare you for the pain you'll inevitably have to endure when you get older. Let's say you're in your mid-20s to mid-30s. Most of the time you feel pretty good, right? The only time you feel lousy is when you ingest huge quantities of alcohol and wake up the next day in an unfamiliar city naked with unexplained chest wounds. But as you grow older, you're going to start feeling more aches and pains caused by the inevitable afflictions of age, such as the Social Security Administration, condescending denture adhesive commercials, and your children.

People who exercise regularly are prepared for this pain. Take joggers: you see them plodding along, clearly hating every minute of it, and you think, "What's the point?" But years from now, when you're struggling to adjust to the pains of the aging process, the joggers, who have been in constant agony for 20 years, will be able to make

the transition smoothly, unless they're already dead (see Chapter 12, under "Fitness and the Afterlife").

How Insects Stay Fit

We can learn a great deal about fitness from observing insects. You have probably noticed, for example, that most ants are in excellent shape. You almost never see a fat ant. What makes this especially interesting is that ants are always lugging around disgusting junk food, such as discarded Cracker Jacks many times the ants' own size.

So how do ants stay so fit? The answer is surprisingly simple: they have no mouths.

And this is a good thing, really, because it means they can't scream when you spray them with Raid, although they do their best to writhe around in a piteous manner.

So anyway, what we have, in the ant, is a creature that engages in strenuous physical exercise all day long and never eats any-thing. This is Nature's Way to fitness, and we should emulate it if we wish to have the kind of taut, firm bodies that make ants the envy of the insect kingdom. Of course, we must always weigh this against the fact that they have a life span of maybe six weeks and are subject to attack by vicious beetles.

TRUE TESTIMONY FROM AMERICA'S LEADING PHYSICAL FITNESS BUFFS...

ARNOLD SCHWARZENEGGER BEFORE READING THIS BOOK: "IT READ REAL GOOD"

JANE FONDA BEFORE READING THIS BOOK: "DAVE WHO?"

MR. T BEFORE READING THIS BOOK: "IT'S BAD, REAL BAD"

TRIGGER BEFORE CHEWING ON THIS BOOK: "NAY"

WOODY ALLEN BEFORE READING THIS BOOK: "PLAY IT AGAIN, DAVE"

DOLLY PARTON BEFORE READING THIS BOOK: "LEARNED ME REAL GOOD"

So the Bottom Line Is . . .

. . . now is the time to start that fitness program! Fitness is more than just another new "craze," like flavored popcorn or parenthood. Fitness is a philosophy of life, a revolutionary new concept in personhood, and, ultimately, a way for people like me to become wealthy via the sales of fitness-related items such as this book.

But people like me can do only so much. We can take your money. After that, it's up to you. If you don't follow the diet and exercise program outlined in this book, it won't do you a bit of good. Even if you do follow it, it may not do you any good. Nobody really knows what will happen. You'll be the first person who ever actually tried this particular program. I meant to try it myself, before the book got published, but I had to buy snow tires. So maybe it would be a good idea to have a friend try it first, as a sort of test, and watch to see whether he actually does become fit, or starts lapsing into lengthy comas or something.

Well, that's enough of a pep talk. Let's square our shoulders and take that first step toward Becoming a Fitter You. Those of you who are unable to simultaneously square your shoulders and take a step may do them one at a time.

How Fit Are You?

The first step in your new fitness program is to take the three simple tests below so we can find out how fit you are right now. Be sure to write down the results as you go along, so the police will be able to figure out what happened.

1. BODY FAT TEST

You'll need:

A swimming pool

A dozen concrete blocks

Some stout rope

A knife

A primitive denizen of some remote fungal island in the South Pacific

Directions: Fat tends to make you float, so the idea here is to determine how many concrete blocks have to be lashed to your body to make you stay on the bottom of the pool for at least a minute without bobbing to the surface. Have your denizen perch by the side of the pool with the knife clenched in his teeth so he can dive down to cut you loose after the minute elapses.

(Caution: Some of your more primitive denizens have no understanding whatsoever of time, so their concept of a minute may in fact be closer to what we in Western Civilization think of us a fortnight. Also, whatever you do, don't give your denizen one of those Swiss army knives with all the various confusing attachments. You don't want him swimming down there and sawing at your rope with the spoon.)

How to score: Count the number of blocks required to keep you submerged. More than eight is very bad.

2. HEART TEST
You'll need:
A friend
A job at an office building with elevators
A scorpion

Directions: Give the scorpion to your friend, and instruct him or her to wait a couple of weeks, until you've completely forgotten about it, then sneak up behind you at work and hurl it into the elevator with you just as the doors close. What we're looking to determine here is whether your heart is strong enough to handle the rigors of an exercise program.

How to score: Give yourself a 5 if your heart continues to beat unassisted. If

you score any lower than that, you probably shouldn't do this particular test.

3. AEROBICS TEST
You'll need:
A stopwatch
Gerald Ford

Directions: The word "aerobics" comes from two Greek words: *aero,* meaning "ability to," and *bics,* meaning "withstand tremendous boredom." This is the difference between a world-class marathon runner and a normal person: a world-class marathon runner has undergone sufficient aerobic conditioning that he can run for nearly three hours without falling asleep, whereas a normal person will quit after a few minutes and look for something interesting to do.

What you want to do in this test is start your stopwatch, then see how long you can listen to Gerald Ford discuss the federal deficit before you doze off. If Gerald Ford is unavailable, you can use televised golf.

How to score: 15 seconds is excellent. More than 30 seconds indicates some kind of brain damage.

CALCULATING YOUR FINAL "FITNESS QUOTIENT"

Divide your age by the number of blocks it took to hold you on the bottom of the pool, then add the number of seconds it took for Gerald Ford to sedate you multiplied by your scorpion score, unless you are claiming two or more exemptions. This will give you your "fitness quotient"; store it wherever you keep the instructions for operating your various digital watches.

Important Medical Note

Before you begin any fitness program, you should, of course, have your doctor give you a thorough physical examination in which he shoves cold steel implements into your various bodily orifices and sticks needles directly into your skin and makes you put on a flimsy garment apparently made from a cocktail napkin and parade through the waiting room carrying a transparent container filled with your own urine past several people you hope to someday ask for jobs. Or, if you'd prefer not to undergo this procedure, you may simply send your doctor some money.

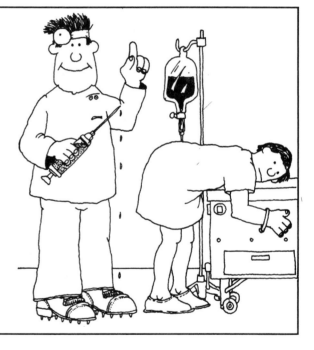

Chapter 1

How Your Body Works

Your body is like a superbly engineered luxury automobile: if you use it wisely and maintain it properly, it will eventually break down, most likely in a bad neighborhood. To understand why this is, let's take a look inside this fascinating "machine" we call the human body.

Your body is actually made up of billions and billions of tiny cells, called "cells," which are so small that you cannot see them. Neither can I. The only people who can see them are white-coated geeks called "biologists." These are the people who wrote your high-school biology textbooks, in which they claimed to have found all these organs inside the Frog, the Worm, and the Perch. Remember? And remember how, in Biology Lab, you were supposed to take an actual dead frog apart and locate the heart, the liver, etc., as depicted in the elaborate color diagrams in the textbook?

Of course, when you cut it open, all you ever found was frog glop, because that is what frogs contain, as has been proven in countless experiments performed by small boys with sticks. So you did what biology students have always done: you pretended you were finding all these organs in there, and you copied the diagram out of the book, knowing full well that in real life a frog would have no use whatsoever for a liver.

Anyway, biologists tell us that the human body consists of billions of these tiny cells, which combine to form organs such as the heart, the kidney, the eyeball, the funny bone, the clavichord, the pustule, and the hernia, which in turn combine to form the body, which in turn combines with other bodies to form the squadron. Now let's take

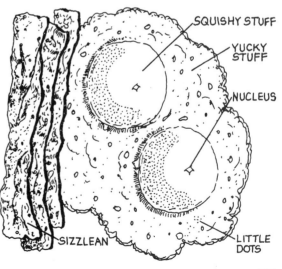

a closer look at the various fitness-related organs and see if we can't think of things to say about them.

The Skin

Your skin performs several vital functions. For example, it keeps people from seeing the inside of your body, which is repulsive, and it prevents your organs from falling out onto the ground, where careless pedestrians might step on them. Also, without skin, your body would have no place to form large facial zits on the morning before your wedding.

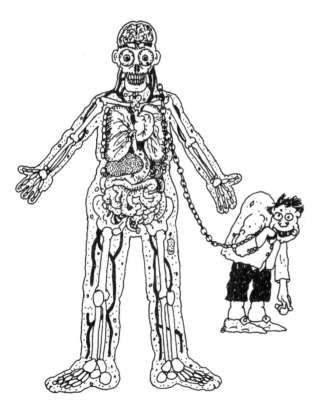

But for fitness-oriented persons like yourself, the important thing about skin is that it acts as your Body's Cooling System. Whenever you exercise or get on an elevator, sweat oozes out of millions of tiny skin holes so it can evaporate and cool the area. Unfortunately, virtually all of these holes are located in your armpits, which is stupid. I mean, you hardly ever hear people complaining about having hot armpits. So what we seem to have here is one of those cases where Mother Nature really screwed up, like when she developed the concept of nasal hair.

The Muscle System

Your muscles are what enable you to perform all of your basic movements, such as bowling, sniping, pandering, carping, and contacting your attorney. Basically, there are two kinds of muscle tissue: the kind that people in advertisements for fitness centers have, which forms units that look like sleek and powerful pythons writhing just beneath the surface of the skin, and the kind you

FITNESS AD MUSCLES   YOUR MUSCLES

have, which looks more like deceased baby rabbits.

The beauty of muscle tissue, however, is that it responds to exercise. In a later chapter, we'll talk about how, using modern exercise equipment such as the Nautilus machine in a scientific workout program, you can stretch those pudgy little muscle tissues of yours to the point where you won't even be able to scream for help without the aid of powerful painkilling drugs.

The Skeletal System

How many bones do you think your skeletal system has? Would you say 50? 150? 250? 300? More than 300?

If you guessed 50, you're a real jerk. I would say it's around 250, but I don't really see why it's all that important. The only important part of your skeleton, for fitness purposes, is your knees.

Knees are God's way of telling mankind that He doesn't want us to do anything really strenuous. When we do, our knees punish us by becoming injured, as you know if you've ever watched professional football on television:

ANNOUNCER: The handoff goes to Burger; he's tackled at the six. . . . Uh oh! He's hurt!
COLOR COMMENTATOR: Looks like a knee injury, Bob, from the way that bone there is sticking out of his knee.
ANNOUNCER: Burger's teammates are bending over him. . . . Uh oh! Now *they're* down on the field!
COLOR COMMENTATOR: Looks like they've all injured their knees, too, Bob.
ANNOUNCER: Here comes the team physician, who is. . . . Uh oh! Now *he's* down on the. . . .

So one of the things we're going to stress in our fitness program is knee safety. We're going to get you so aware of this important topic that you won't even discuss racquetball over the telephone without first putting on knee braces the size of industrial turbines.

The Digestive System

Your digestive system is your body's Fun House, whereby food goes on a long, dark, scary ride, taking all kinds of unexpected twists and turns, being attacked by vicious secretions along the way, and not knowing until the last minute whether it will be turned into a useful body part or ejected into the Dark Hole by Mister Sphincter. You must be careful about what you eat, unless you want your body making heart valves out of things like bean dip.

The Central Nervous System

The central nervous system is your body's Messenger, always letting your brain know what's going on elsewhere in your body. "Your nose itches!" it tells your brain. Or, "Your foot is falling asleep!!" Or, "You're hungry!!!" All day long, your brain hears messages like these, thousands of them, hour after hour, until finally it deliberately rests your hand on a red-hot stove just for the pleasure of hearing your nervous system scream in pain.

Your Respiratory System

Your respiratory system takes in oxygen and gives off carbon monoxide, a deadly gas, by a process called "photosynthesis." This takes place in your lungs, yam-shaped organs in your chest containing millions of tiny little air sacs, called "Bernice." In a normal person, these sacs are healthy and pink, whereas in smokers they have the wretched, soot-stained, anguished look of the people fleeing Atlanta in *Gone with the Wind*. This has led many noted medical researchers to conclude that smoking is unhealthy, but we must weigh this against the fact that most of the people in cigarette advertisements are generally horse-riding, helicopter-flying hunks of major-league manhood, whereas your noted medical researchers tend to be pasty little wimps of the variety that you routinely held upside down over the toilet in junior high school.

The Circulatory System

This is, of course, your heart, a fist-sized muscle in your chest with a two-inch-thick layer of greasy fat clinging to it consisting of every Milky Way you ever ate. Your heart's job is to pump your blood, which appears to be nothing more than a red liquid but which, according to biologists (this should come as no surprise), is actually teeming with millions of organisms, some of them with tentacles so they can teem more efficiently.

The only organisms that actually belong in your blood are the red cells and the white cells. The red cells are your body's Room Service, carrying tiny particles of food and oxygen to the other organs, which snork them up without so much as a "thank you." The only reward the red cells get is iron in the form of prunes, which the other cells don't want anyway. If you don't eat enough prunes, your red cells get tired—a condition doctors call "tired blood"—and you have to lie down and watch "All My Children."

The white cells are your body's House Detectives. Most of the time they lounge around the bloodstream, telling jokes and forming the occasional cyst. But they swing into action the instant your body is invaded by one of the many enemy organisms that can get into your bloodstream, these being bacteria, viruses, rotifers, conifers, parameciums, cholesterol, tiny little lockjaw germs that dwell on the ends of all sharp objects, antacids, riboflavin, and the plague. As soon as the white cells spot one of these, they drop whatever they're doing and pursue it on a wild and often hilarious chase through your various organs, which sometimes results in damage to innocent tissue. Eventually they catch the invader and tie its tentacles behind its back with antibodies, which are the body's Handcuffs, and deport it via the bowel.

Of course this is just a brief rundown on your various organs and systems; in the short space I have here, it's very difficult for me to explain all of your body's complexities and subtleties in any detail, or even get any facts right. For more information, I suggest you attend Harvard Medical School, which I believe is in Wisconsin.

Meanwhile, let's turn the page and really get started on our fitness program! Or at least limber up.

Chapter 2

Getting Ready to Get Started

One of the most exciting aspects of getting into fitness is that you get to wear modern fitness-oriented clothing, clothing that makes a statement to the world around you. "Look," it states, "I have purchased some fitness-oriented clothing."

Up until about 15 years ago, the only fitness clothing available for men was the plain grey sweat suit, which we fitness experts now recognize as totally inadequate in terms of retail markup. Fitness wear for females consisted of those high-school gym outfits colored Digestive Enzyme Green; there was no fitness clothing available at all for adult women, because the only forms of exercise deemed appropriate for them were labor and driving station wagons.

As the fitness craze developed, however, all kinds of "active sportswear" became available from famous designers who think

STANDARD 1965 (OR SO) MALE GYM SUITS

STANDARD 1965 (OR SO) FEMALE GYM SUITS

nothing of putting their names on your clothing, but who would have the servants set the dogs on you if you ever tried to put your name on *their* clothing. Today it's not uncommon for people to wear their active sportswear to the shopping mall, to work, to the opera, to state funerals, etc. Recently, an attorney argued a major case before the U.S. Supreme Court while wearing a puce jogging outfit! The justices didn't seem to mind at all, although this could also have been partly because they had fallen asleep.

The point is, you want to choose your fitness-program clothing carefully because chances are you'll be wearing it to do much more than just exercise. In fact, you'll probably be wearing it to do everything *but* exercise, since there is growing medical evidence that exercise can make you tired and sweaty, as we'll see in later chapters.

The Basic Fitness Fashion Look for Women

This is, of course, the leotard and tights, which is the preferred outfit because it shows every bodily flaw a woman has, no matter how minute, so that a woman who, disguised in her street clothes, looks like Victoria Principal will, when she puts on her leotard, transform herself into Bertha the

Choosing the Correct Leotard Size

The correct leotard size for you depends, of course, on your body type. Use this handy chart as a guide:

BODY TYPE   LEOTARD SIZE

Amazing Land Whale. This encourages her to exercise vigorously and watch what she eats. She cannot, of course, drink anything, as there is no way to go to the bathroom in a leotard and tights.

Many a woman who suffers an exercise-related injury during an aerobic workout is forced to lie in great pain for hours on her exercise mat, trapped, while frustrated rescue personnel wait for the helicopter to bring the various specialized torches, saws, and other equipment they need to free her from her tights and leotard so they can render medical treatment.

Extremely Important Advice Concerning Danskin Brand Thermal Calf Protection Devices

Several years ago, a crack team of medical fashion experts determined that cold air tends to form pockets around the calves of fashionable, fitness-oriented women (see illustration). This breakthrough discovery explained the sudden upsurge in calf-related hospitalizations that occurred at the onset of the fitness craze and soon reached epidemic proportions. As one nationally reknowned physician, whose name is available upon request, put it, "Never in my 600 years of practicing medicine had I seen so

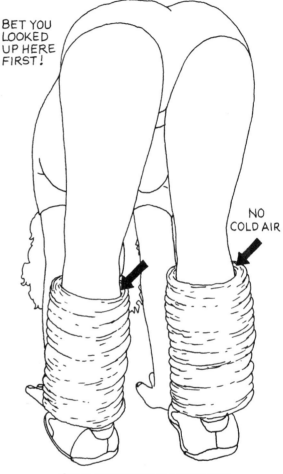

BET YOU LOOKED UP HERE FIRST!

NO COLD AIR

CALF PROTECTION DEVICES

many deaths directly attributable to calf coldness. If only we had known then the importance of wearing Danskin brand thermal calf protection devices!"

So the bottom line is: Do not view these devices as just another semiretarded fashion trend. View them as essential medical protection, every bit as important as lip gloss.

Fitness Fashion for Men

What you want, men, is a fashion look that gives you freedom of movement but at the same time displays, in large letters, the names of at least three major manufacturers of sporting equipment. Also you want to wear a headband and wristbands to absorb the tremendous outpouring of sweat that we males emit when we are engaged in strenuous masculine physical activity. (If you are one of those unfortunate males who does not emit tremendous outpourings of sweat, you should purchase, from the Nike Corporation, a container of "Pro-spiration" spray-on sweat droplets, which you apply discreetly in the locker room before you begin your workout.)

Ideally, of course, you will also sport some evidence of a semicrippling football injury. The best kind is a medical knee contraption of such enormous size and complexity that your racquetball opponent will feel like absolute pond scum if he hits the ball anywhere other than directly to you. Or you might want to look into a new product from the Adidas Corporation called "The All-

Scars," which are large, realistic, and extremely repulsive synthetic removable knee scars patterned after those belonging to famous battered sports legends such as Joe Namath.

Fitness with Computers

Can you use a personal home computer in your fitness program? You bet! Computers are incredibly versatile machines that can do everything from screw up your airplane reservation to cause an income tax blunder that gets you sentenced to a life term in a slimy walled federal prison so utterly desolate that the inmates pay rodents for sex! So they're a "natural" for the fitness movement!

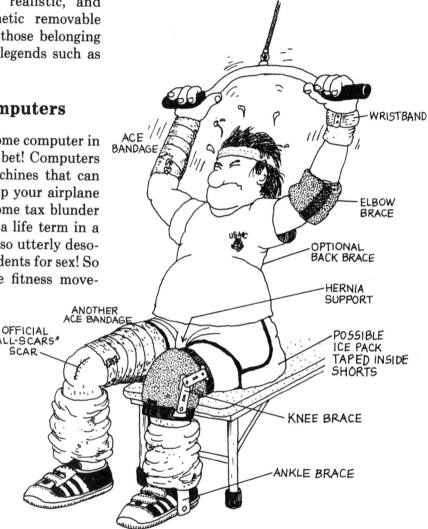

WRISTBAND

ACE BANDAGE

ELBOW BRACE

OPTIONAL BACK BRACE

HERNIA SUPPORT

POSSIBLE ICE PACK TAPED INSIDE SHORTS

KNEE BRACE

ANKLE BRACE

ANOTHER ACE BANDAGE

OFFICIAL "ALL-SCARS" SCAR

TYPICAL FAKE INJURY EQUIPMENT

One obvious way to use a computer, of course, is to record your daily fitness statistics such as weight, height, age, etc., on it, using a felt-tipped marker (see illustration). But the best way to really unleash the power of a computer is to lift it up and set it down repeatedly, thus building muscle mass and definition. As you become stronger, you can gradually add weight, in the form of "disk drives," until eventually you move up to a heavier computer—and perhaps someday even reach the point where you can hoist what computer bodybuilding enthusiasts call a "mainframe" computer!

For the average person who does not have a background in data processing, I generally

DON'T OVERLOOK THE COMPUTER'S PACKING BOX
AS A SURFACE TO ENTER YOUR STATISTICS

recommend starting out with a 35-pound computer. Unfortunately, computer weights are measured not in pounds, but in "K's" (as in 512K), which stands for "kilograms." There is a way to convert kilograms to pounds, but it is almost always fatal, so I recommend, as a wise consumer tip, that you go through your entire planned computer-lifting routine right at the store with several reputable computers, checking each for heft, balance, and tendency to break into 600,000 tiny pieces when you lift it over your head and drop it, before you actually purchase anything.

Of course, some of you, and here I am talking about the technically oriented ones, the ones with a thin layer of mechanical-pencil dust on your clothing—in a word, the geeks—may even want to plug your computer directly into the wall, thus allowing electricity to flow through it. In this case, you'll also need to purchase a "program," or "software," which comes on a "floppy disk," an object the size of a 45 RPM record such as "Shake, Rattle and Roll," which we used to dance to at "record hops" back when Dwight "Ike" Eisenhower was president.

Fortunately for you and the entire fitness movement in general, I have developed a special piece of fitness-oriented software called the "Dave Barry Total Diskette Workout Program." The way it works is, you

THE GEEK

put it in the computer, which asks you to type in your name. Then you type in your name, and the computer forgets it immediately because the truth is that the computer really doesn't give a damn what your name is. It was just trying to be polite.

Next, the computer holds an Interactive Fitness Dialogue with you, wherein it elicits certain facts from you regarding your specific fitness situation, then it evaluates the facts and reports its findings, as follows:

COMPUTER: ENTER THE LAST TIME YOU ENGAGED IN A WORKOUT.
YOU: (Enter the last time you engaged in a workout, such as "just before Thanksgiving" or "World War II.")

COMPUTER   (thinks for a minute, and proceeds): SOUNDS TO ME LIKE YOU'VE DONE ALL THE WORKING OUT YOU NEED TO DO FOR THE FORSEEABLE FUTURE. ALL WORKING OUT MAKES JACK A DULL BOY! HA HA! PLEASE ENTER A LIST OF THE FOODS YOU WOULD LIKE TO EAT TODAY.
YOU: (Enter a list consisting of no more than 100 foods which you would like to eat on that particular day.)
COMPUTER: I DON'T SEE ANY PROBLEM WITH THE FOODS YOU HAVE LISTED. HAVE A NICE DAY.

That's all there is to it! In less than five minutes, you have accomplished, using a computer, a data-processing feat that would take 60,000 trained mathematicians 1.3 billion years to accomplish, and even longer if you let them go to the bathroom! And you will be pleased to learn that this program will also do your income taxes ("YES! YOU CAN DEDUCT THAT! I'M SURE OF IT!").

Choosing the Right Place to Get Fit

Basically you have two options: your living room, or a fitness club. The advantage of getting fit in your living room is that it's free

THE FITNESS CLUB

and you can scratch yourself openly. The disadvantage is that your living room is where you keep your little dish of M&Ms for guests, which means you'll actually gain roughly a pound of ugly fat for each week of your home fitness program.

So you should probably join a fitness club such as you see advertised in the newspapers by photographs of attractive models wearing leotards fashioned from a maximum of eight leotard molecules. Before you join such a club, you should take a tour conducted by one of the fit and muscular staff persons. This person will show you the various rooms and pieces of equipment, then hold your head under the whirlpool until you agree to buy a membership.

Here's a useful checklist of the features a good fitness club should have:

A powerful odor of disinfectant

Various species of hairs in the sinks

Signs all over the place reminding you that the management is not responsible

A loudspeaker system playing soothing musical numbers as performed by the Dentist's Office Singers

A door that says "WEIGHT ROOM" that you never venture through because large sweating men go in there and emit noises like oxen with severe intestinal disorders

Two women in the sauna who are always there, no matter what hour of the day or night, talking loudly about growths in their pelvic regions

Saunas

The word "sauna" is Finnish for "very hot little room with strangers in it breathing funny," and people who've tried it agree that it's a very invigorating experience, provided you get out in time. If the door sticks or anything, you have about as much chance of survival as the unfortunate corals who happened to be residing on that reef where we detonated the original hydrogen bomb, because the usual temperature inside a sauna is 180 degrees, which you may recognize as the recommended final temperature for cooked turkeys, very few of which live to tell about it.

This high temperature is, of course, very good for you because your body contains traces of toxic minerals such as lead, which get in there when you get drunk and eat paint, and the heat helps you sweat them out. Really, I'm not making this up. Here's a direct quote from *Shape* magazine, an authoritative journal:

"Sweating is now a significant route for eliminating trace elements from the body."

So that's the good news. The bad news, of course, is that these trace elements have to go somewhere, presumably onto the sauna seat, which means if you use a spa sauna, you're lounging around on a lot of other people's trace elements.

So what I recommend is that you build your own sauna at home, which is a lot easier than you might think. All you need is a few simple hand tools. (No! I'm *not* going to tell you which ones! I'm *sick* of making all the decisions!)

Using your hand tools, construct a handcrafted little wooden room that has a bench inside it and a sign on the door that says "WARNING! REMOVE ALL CLOTHING AND JEWELRY AND DENTAL FILLINGS AND PACEMAKERS!" Now all you need is a way to raise the internal temperature to 180 degrees. You could always set fire to the sauna, of course, but then you'd have to handcraft a new one every time you wanted to use it, which would leave you with

A FEW FRIENDS, A FEW BEERS, A HOT SAUNA, AND THOU...

very little time in which to eliminate your elements. So I suggest that you take the more practical route, which is to plug in 40 toasters set to "medium brown." They'll give you all the heat you need, plus you'll get a healthy aerobic workout clambering around in there trying to keep all the little levers pushed down. Keep the number of the Burn Unit handy.

Okay! Now you've bought your fitness outfits, you've found a place to do your workout, and you've built your own sauna. The only remaining question is . . .

When to Actually Start Your Fitness Program

Not today, certainly. You've done enough today! I would rule tomorrow out, also, seeing as how it comes so soon after today. You rush into these things, and the next thing you known you've strained a ligament or something. So I would say the best time to begin would be first thing after Easter, although not the one coming up.

Chapter 3

Women's Total Complete
Aerobic Fitness Workout

Warming Up

To understand the importance of warming up, let's take a look inside a typical human muscle:

As we can see, it's very dark inside a typical human muscle. This means that most of the time the individual muscle cells are fast asleep. The purpose of your warm-up routine is to allow these cells to wake up gradually—to stretch, to scratch, to go to the bathroom, etc. If you just start jerking them around, they're going to be very cranky, and they may develop a condition that professional medical doctors call a "Charley horse," which is usually fatal.

WARM-UP NUMBER ONE: CLEARING YOUR MIND OF WORRISOME THOUGHTS

You can't loosen up effectively if you're worried about nuclear war, or the likelihood that somebody might steal your wallet while you're doing your exercise routine. So your initial warm-up step should be to lie down on your back with your knees bent and your feet planted 17 inches apart, then, with your left hand overlapping your right, clasp your wallet to your chest, raise your head to an angle of about 36 degrees Fahrenheit, and watch "Happy Days" or a similar television situation comedy rerun where they never talk about the likelihood of nuclear war, as shown in Figure 1. Hold this position until

FIGURE 1

about a minute and a half before your neck develops a "crick," which is usually fatal.

WARM-UP NUMBER TWO: LETTING YOUR MUSCLES KNOW YOU'RE ABOUT TO START MOVING

Lie facedown on your wallet with your legs together and your arms away from your body at an angle of about 7 degrees, then have a friend or hired servant place his or her face about an inch from your various major muscle groupings, as shown in Figure 2, and say, in a pleasant, musical voice, "Everybody up! Time to start warming up for a Fitness Workout!" Then have your friend listen closely to your muscle groupings for the sound of good-natured cellular grumbling. If necessary, he or she should prod them very gently with the eraser of a number 2 pencil, such as you used on your college boards.

FIGURE 2

WARM-UP NUMBER THREE: PUTTING A TAPE OF LOUD ROCK 'N' ROLL–TYPE WORK-OUT MUSIC ON A GHETTO BLASTER–TYPE STEREOPHONIC LISTENING DEVICE

One thing you have probably wondered about for many years is why musicians who sing rock 'n' roll tend to be extremely thin, if not actually dead, whereas those who sing, say, opera, tend to be humongous wads of cellulite. The reason for this phenomenon, scientists now believe, is that fat cells are actually destroyed by stupid lyrics. In one recent experiment, scientists at the University of Iowa reduced a live 450-pound hog to an object the size of a harmonica in less than six hours by repeatedly playing the chorus to "Shake Your Groove Thing" at it. Other songs with proven fat-reduction lyrics that you'll want to have on your workout tape are:

"My Baby Does the Hanky Panky"

"Yummy Yummy Yummy I've Got Love in My Tummy"

The verse of "We Wish You a Merry Christmas" that refers to "figgy pudding"

Everything Barry Manilow ever wrote

"Ballad of the Green Berets"

"Da Doo Ron Ron"

"My Way"

To put your tape on your ghetto blaster, lie on your back with your legs about 7¾ inches apart and your wallet clamped in your left armpit, raise your right arm gradually until you can insert the workout tape into the ghetto blaster device, press the "play" button, as shown in Figure 3, then gradually return your arm to the floor and just lie there for a while, spent.

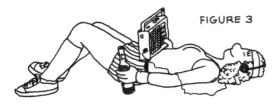

FIGURE 3

The Actual Workout

All warmed up? Great! Let's start getting fit! Do each of the exercises below twice on the first day, 4 times the second day, 8 times the third day, and so on, each day doubling the previous day's number until, after just two weeks, you're doing each exercise over 1,000 times! And hemorrhaging internally! So let's get started!

EXERCISE NUMBER ONE: LEG HEFT

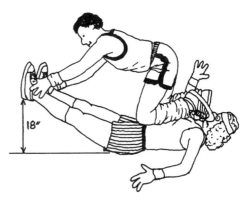

Lie on your back, legs slightly spread, arms resting on the floor, palms down. Have an accomplice grasp you by your ankles and lift your legs about 18 inches then attempt to guess their combined weight.

EXERCISE NUMBER TWO: THIGH GRASP

Lie on your stomach with your face resting on a *New York Times* "Fall Fashion Supplement" opened to a photograph of a model who consumes fewer calories in an entire year than you do at a single wedding

reception. Slowly reach your hands down and grasp yourself by the left thigh, then the right, and then close your eyes and moan quietly in despair for a count of about eight seconds.

EXERCISE NUMBER THREE: SINCERE ANNOUNCEMENT OF INTENTION TO CHANGE DIETARY HABITS

You and a partner stand facing each other about three feet apart, legs comfortably spread, knees slightly bent, eating from individual one-pound bags of Wise brand potato chips. You say, "First thing tomorrow I swear to God I am definitely going to go on a diet, I really mean it." Your partner responds, "Yes, me too. I definitely will go on a diet also. I believe there is a vat of Lipton brand California-style onion dip in the refrigerator." Then you exchange places and repeat the exercise.

EXERCISE NUMBER FOUR: BREAST DEVELOPMENT

Originally, I was going to use this space to describe an amazing new Scientific Discovery exercise that enables any woman to develop, within minutes, two large, firm breasts such as are regularly featured on television star Loni Anderson. But then I said to myself, "Hey, isn't it time that we, as a liberated society, got over this juvenile and demeaning fixation with breasts?" So I have decided to omit this particular amazing, risk-free, 100 percent effective exercise, although of course if you wish to obtain a copy for the purpose of scientific research, I'd be happy to send it to you just for the asking, plus $29.95 for postage and handling. If you act right now, I'll also send several grainy before-and-after photographs of women who used to look like Olive Oyl but now, thanks to this Amazing Breast Exercise Discovery, cannot walk erect unless preceded by native bearers.

Cooling Down

As we discussed in Chapter 1, when you exercise, your muscle cells take in molecules of oxygen and give off molecules of sweat, which work their way to your armpits. For your cooling-down phase, lie on your back with your arms laced behind your head and your elbows on the floor, thus exposing a maximum of armpit area and allowing the sweat molecules to escape into the atmosphere as harmless BO vapors. This would be an excellent time to start worrying about nuclear war again.

DAVE BARRY'S AMAZING BREAST EXERCISE

BEFORE　　　　AFTER

Chapter 4

Running

An Important Safety Note about Running

In this chapter, I can give you only a cursory overview of running, which is without question the most difficult and complex form of exercise, as is evidenced by the fact that it is the subject of numerous lengthy books costing upward of $14.95. Unfortunately, many members of the general public still labor under the dangerous misconception that running is simply a matter of getting out and running. So before you attempt to do any actual running, I strongly urge you to read a minimum of several books on the subject and to take lessons from a trained running instructor. I also cannot overemphasize the importance of spending large sums of money.

What Kind of Person Should Take Up Running, and What Will Happen to This Person's Knees

Running is the ideal form of exercise for people who sincerely wish to become mid-dle-class urban professionals. Whereas the lower classes don't run except when their kerosene heaters explode, today's upwardly mobile urban professionals feel that running keeps them in the peak form they must be in if they are to handle the responsibilities of their chosen urban professions, which include reading things, signing things, talking on the telephone, and in cases of extreme upward mobility, going to lunch.

That's why at the end of the working day, when the lower classes have passed out face-down in the Cheez Whiz, you can drive down the streets of any middle-class neighborhood in America and see dozens of professionals out running with determined facial grimaces, burning off calories, improving the efficiency of their cardiovascular systems, increasing their muscle flexibility, and ultimately staggering off into the bushes to die. Even as you read these words, thousands of designer-sportswear-clad bodies are rotting in the bushes of suburban America, and the only reason you don't hear more about it is that the next of kin generally don't report the disappearances, because they are quite frankly pleased that they no longer have to listen to the runner blather on and on about his or her cardiovascular development.

Of course, not all runners die in the bushes. Many fail to make it that far, because of knee injuries. To understand why, let's look at this anatomical diagram of the interior of the human knee.

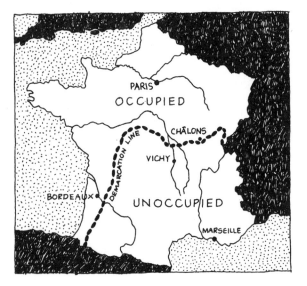

What we can learn from this diagram is that, although from the outside your knee feels like a croquet ball inserted in the middle of your leg, it is in fact a complex organ consisting of bone, muscle, thong, and mucilage, bounded on the west by Spain. The knee provides adequate support for everyday activities, such as renewing magazine subscriptions or gesturing at cretins in traffic, but it is not designed to withstand the strain placed on it by running, where each time the runner's foot hits the pavement, the knee is subjected to 650,000 kilocycles of torque, and even more if the runner has been dropped from a helicopter. This is why it is so very important to choose the right running shoe.

Choosing the Right Running Shoe

Time was, of course, when there were no running shoes, only "sneakers," which were bulky objects that cost $12 and said "U.S. Keds" on the side and had essentially the same size, weight, and styling characteristics as snow tires. But today's topflight running shoe is a triumph of sophisticated, computer-designed, laser-augmented, fully integrated, infrared, user-friendly technology and space-age materials, packed with dozens of medically proven health and safety features, and all combined into a small and lightweight unit that, surprisingly, costs no more than a black-market infant. Let's take a peek inside a typical running shoe and see how this technological miracle is accomplished.

ABEBE BIKILA MODEL STATIC-BALANCE "ROCKET THUNDERSQUAT" 3000-XT RUNNING SHOE
(INTERIOR VIEW) (SIZE 9-D) (ALSO COMES IN BEIGE)

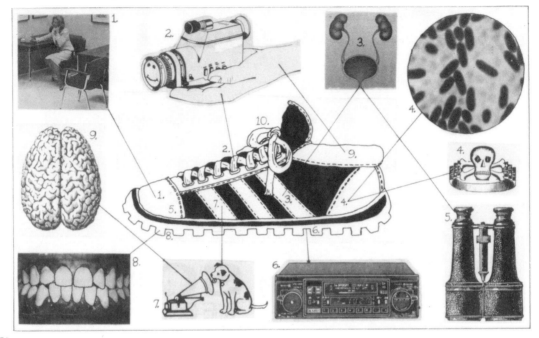

KEY8

1. MAIN STABILIZERS
2. STRESS AVERTERS
3. MAIN DESTABILIZERS
4. AFT MONTAGE SPLINE
5. TORQUE SUBVERTERS
6. ENCROACHMENT VALVES
7. PIGLET'S HOUSE
8. MODEM
9. WENCH INVERTERS
10. STAFF LOUNGE
11. NOT SHOWN
12. NOT SHOWN, EITHER

Choosing the Left Running Shoe

Most running experts and bankers recommend that you wait until you've completely paid for the right running shoe, including insurance, before you plunge in and buy the left. When you do, I urge you to shop around for a shoe that is as similar as possible to the other one, except insofar as which foot it goes on. This is assuming that you intend to wear both shoes simultaneously.

PROPER RUNNING SHOE ALIGNMENT

INTERNATIONAL HAND SIGNALS FOR RUNNERS PASSING EACH OTHER ON THE STREET

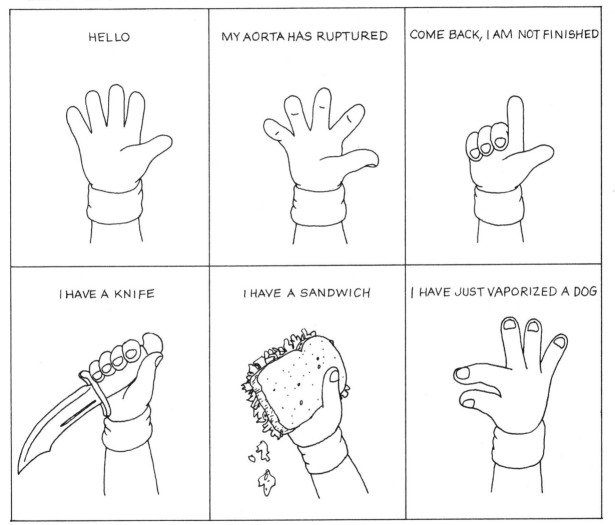

What to Wear on the Rest of Your Body

You should, of course, wear a specially designed $200 Running Garment made from a synthetic material that has a name like the leader of a hostile reptilian alien invasion force in a space movie, such as "Gore-Tex." The beauty of these materials is that they actually "breathe." Really. At night, if you listen very carefully to your closet, you'll hear your garment in there, breathing and occasionally chuckling softly at some synthetic joke it heard from your dress slacks.

Where to Run

One good place to run is in the Olympic marathon, because (a) you have to do it only once every four years, and (b) you have an armed motorcycle escort, so if people try to thrust liquids and fruits at you, which is a

IN-HOME JOGGING TREADMILL

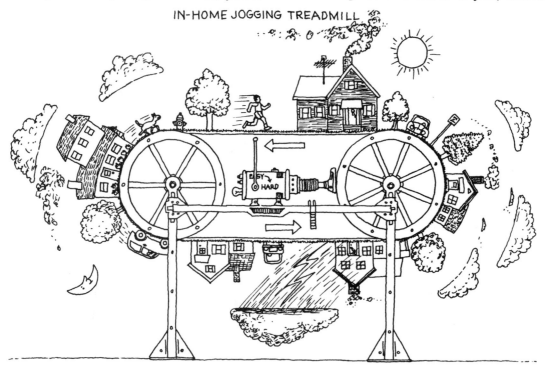

common problem in marathons, you can order your escort to fire a few warning rounds into their chests. The big drawback with running in the marathon, however, is that you have to consort with a bunch of sunken-eyed running wimps, some of whom are not even United States citizens.

This is why many people prefer to run, unescorted, on the streets of their own neighborhoods. The big problem here is dogs, which will view you as an intruder and may attack you, especially if they can smell fear on your body. This is why the wise runner carries a small spray can of a chemical originally designed for use by mail carriers. If a dog attacks, you simply spray this chemical into your nose, and within seconds you don't feel any fear of any damn dog. Be careful that you don't stare directly into the sun.

Chapter 5

Popular Sports

Mankind's need to compete in sports goes back to that fateful prehistoric day, hundreds of thousands of years ago, when a primitive man first picked up a club and a primitive ball fashioned from animal hide, tossed the ball aloft, then whomped the club into the sloping forehead of a primitive umpire. Since then, there has never been a civilization that did not engage in sports. Archeologists digging in what was once ancient Sumeria recently found the remains of a primitive stone jockstrap (see illustration). This goes a long way toward explaining why you see so few Sumerians around.

In ancient Greece, the Olympic games were considered so important that when it was time to hold them, the Greeks would lay down their arms and invite their enemies to do the same. Then the Greeks would snatch up their arms again, whack their enemies into pieces the size of candy corn, and celebrate by having the Olympic games.

Back then, of course, the only events were running naked, jumping naked, throwing things naked, and ice dancing. Today, we have hundreds of sports to choose from. In this chapter we're going to look at some of the more popular modern sports, so you can

ARCHAEOLOGIST FINDS
ANCIENT SUMERIAN STONE JOCKSTRAP

choose the ones you wish to incorporate into your overall fitness program. As I have stressed repeatedly throughout this book, before you embark upon any new form of physical activity, you should notify your doctor's answering service.

Ski Jumping

Ski jumping as a form of exercise has grown immensely in popularity in recent years, especially among people who, because of knee problems, cannot jog. This exciting sport got its start as a symptom of mental illness in northern climes such as Norway and Sweden, where it is cold and dark and there is very little to do except pay taxes. Life is depressing in these countries. Watch any movie by the famous Swedish director Ingmar Bergman, and you'll notice that all that ever happens in the entire two hours is

PORTABLE SKI JUMP SIMULATION DEVICE

depressed people sit around talking Swedish, which sounds like Fats Domino records being played backward, only a little too slow. This is what life in Sweden is actually like, except that it often lasts longer than two hours. After a while, the strain gets to people, and they suddenly leap up, barge out, don skis, and launch themselves off giant chutes.

Americans did very little ski jumping until the television program "Wide World of Sports" began showing a promotional film snippet in which a ski jumper hurtles off the edge of the chute, completely out of control, with various important organs flying out of his body (for a discussion of the various important organs and their functions, see Chapter 1). Fitness buffs saw this and realized that any activity with such great potential for being fatal must be very good for

you, so the sport began to catch on. Today, most major hotels offer ski jumping facilities for the convenience of business travelers. Also, thanks to a new, innovative portable device (see illustration), you can even engage in "simulated" ski jumping indoors! So there's really no excuse not to get into this popular sport, except a will to live.

Peewee Football

Although most people think of Peewee Football as a "kid's game," more and more fitness-oriented urban professionals with a love of physical contact and a sincere desire to lie about their ages have discovered that there's no better way to get rid of frustrations than to lean down, take a handoff (by force, if necessary) from a 48-pound quar-

terback, and plow through an entire team of 8-year-old boys on the way to a 97-yard touchdown run. Not only is it fun, but nutritionists (never mind which ones) tell us that the average 40-year-old male burns off ten extra calories for each child clinging to his ankles!

One word of caution here: If any other urban professionals have discovered your particular Peewee Football league, you want to make sure they play on your team. This is also a good practice to follow with any unusually large eight-year-old boys.

Racquetball

This is a popular sport wherein you and another person go into a white room, close the door, and attempt to injure each other in

TRADITIONAL
RACQUET

COMPETITIVE
RACQUETS

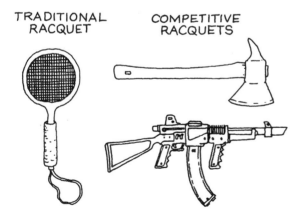

the eye. Originally, this was done by whacking a ball against a wall in such a way that it would bounce back and strike the other person, but your highly competitive modern player tends to ignore the ball and lunge straight for his opponent. This is why you first should determine the playing style of your potential opponent and then decide whether you need a "traditional" or a "competitive" racquet.

Professional Ice Hockey

Professional ice hockey is an ideal way for the entire family to keep fit. There's something for everyone: the kids will love participating in a loose, freewheeling sport where everybody makes the play-offs and the only activity that is specifically prohibited is selling narcotics to your opponents on the ice; Dad will appreciate the fact that he's improving his cardiovascular efficiency while at the same time fleeing large vicious toothless stick-wielding men whose frontal lobes have been battered into prune-sized masses of scar tissue; and Mom will be pleased to learn that many of the players come from Canada, so she'll have a chance to "brush up" on such French phrases as *Arretez vous! Je suis une femme! C'est ma balle d'oeil!* ("Stop! I am a woman! That is my eyeball!")

Golf

Although golf was originally restricted to wealthy, overweight Protestants, today it's open to anybody who owns hideous clothing. The basic idea is to stand on top of a hummock, squinting into the distance, wager, then saunter over to another hummock, and so on until it's time to drink. That may not sound like much exercise to you, but in fact every one of these activities except drinking consumes calories, as shown by this scientific chart.

Thus we see that in the course of a typical "round" of golf, lasting just four hours, you could burn off enough calories that you could then go out and eat the better part of a slice of Wonder bread with only a minor weight gain.

GOLF ACTIVITY	CALORIES CONSUMED
Ascending hummock	2.04959
Squinting	0.00035
Wagering	0.00102
Descending hummock	1.84958
Sauntering to next hummock	4.02013
Saying things like "You certainly did bogey that par-six eagle nine-iron wedge, Ted! Ha ha!"	0.00076
Tipping wiry youth who carries equipment	0.00007

Swimming

Swimming is one of the best forms of exercise, provided you remember to follow these simple safety rules:

1. NEVER SWIM IN A LAKE OR RIVER. These contain snapping turtles, which have no natural enemies and therefore grow to the size of motel units, plus they tend to be irritable because they mate for life. Lakes also contain giant lake-dwelling carp, which will watch you from the gloomy depths with their buggy eyes, wondering with their tiny carp brains whether you would fit into their mouths.

2. NEVER SWIM IN THE OCEAN. The ocean contains creatures that make the giant lake-dwelling carp look like Bambi.

3. NEVER SWIM IN A SWIMMING POOL. People pee in swimming pools. Oh, I know *you* don't pee in swimming pools, and I certainly don't, but *somebody* does, which promotes the growth of bacteria, which is why swimming pool owners are always dumping in toxic chemicals, to the point where there is virtually no actual water in the pool, just toxic chemicals and dead bacteria and old pee. This is why, as you may have noticed, the actual owner never gets into the pool. He's always off pretending he has to do something important involving the filter.

Pig Lifting

This is probably the quintessential fitness activity for today's upscale young urban professional, who more often than not will forsake the old-fashioned "three-martini lunch" in favor of going to his posh downtown club, sometimes with an important client, for a hard 45 minutes of pig lifting, followed by a soothing hose-down. More than one major business deal has been

forged this way, and the cry "Anyone want to hoist some pork?" is likely to echo down the corridors of power for many years to come.

Fitness for the Business Traveler

Anyone who travels a lot on business will tell you that it isn't easy: eating at a different restaurant every night, having the maid leave little chocolate mints on your pillow, ordering a late-night hors d'oeuvre platter from Room Service while you watch in-room movies such as *Nubile Olympic Gymnasts Visit the Petting Zoo,* and all the other little hassles and inconveniences that go with life "on the road." But for the businessperson who's into physical fitness, there's yet another problem: finding a way to work out. Here are some suggestions.

Without question, the best way to work out in your hotel room is to turn on the television at the crack of dawn and watch one of the morning workout shows featuring the Obscenely Cheerful Leotard Women. Believe me, there's no more invigorating way to start the day than to lie in a darkened hotel room and listen to these women leap around and shout encouragement at you until you work up the energy to hurl your hors d'oeuvre tray at the TV screen and

order Room Service to send up several orders of pancakes immediately.

Center-City Jogging

Although a few forward-looking hotels now offer a service whereby a staff person from a third-world nation will do your running for you while you are in meetings, in most cases you must still attend to this tiresome chore yourself. This isn't so bad if your hotel is located in, say, Nebraska, where the only danger you face on the street is that you might trip over a pig. But it can be a real problem if you're in a large urban area such as New York City, where the vast majority of the people on the street are drug addicts, pickpockets, muggers, rapists, murderers, or partners in advertising agencies.

This doesn't mean you can't run: it means you must take steps to protect yourself. A gun will do you no good. It would just be stolen. No, what you need is a safety device I designed especially to solve this problem—the Urban Runner's Simulated Gaping Chest Wound, which operates on the proven scientific principle that no urban resident will go anywhere *near* a person who is clearly in desperate need of help.

With your Simulated Gaping Chest Wound strapped on, you can jog anywhere you want in New York City, and you'll

attract no more attention than the apparently deceased persons sprawled on the sidewalks, or the random street lunatics holding lengthy debates with individual oxygen atoms. For extra privacy, you can purchase the optional 3,500 Simulated Maggots Eating Your Body accessory.

These devices, incidentally, are part of an entire Dave Barry line of Traveling Executive Fitness Products, which also includes the Heavy Briefcase. This appears from the outside to be a normal leather briefcase, but hidden inside is a 350-pound weight! (There's also a roomy compartment capable of holding your cigarette, or part of your pen.) Executives who regularly carry the

Heavy Briefcase report a dramatic improvement in arm length.

The In-Flight Workout Device is a portable device that, when folded up, fits inside a handy steamer trunk that can be carried on board a commercial aircraft, provided you purchase two adjacent first-class seats for it, yet unfolds after takeoff to form a complete "airborne gymnasium." It features a sophis-ticated electronic digital computer "brain" that not only monitors your pulse rate, but also has a new and improved electronic circuitry design which we sincerely believe and hope will correct the unfortunate problem whereby it was somehow seizing control of the automatic pilot and steering planes into various mountains, which is, of course, a violation of federal regulations.

Chapter 6

Bodybuilding

Most of us males, at one time or another, have felt like Joe, the scrawny little wimp in the old Charles Atlas advertisement who was humiliated in front of his girlfriend on the beach when the muscular bully kicked sand in his face. As you'll recall, Joe sent away for the Charles Atlas bodybuilding course, then came back to the beach with large, bulging, rippling muscles. When the bully returned, he was extremely impressed and suggested that Joe should also apply oil to his body so that it would have a satiny gleam, and perhaps shave his armpits. Before long, they were very close friends and often helped each other select posing outfits.

BEFORE

AFTER

You may feel that this is the kind of story that "only happens in comic books," but in fact it can happen to you, too—provided you have the discipline, drive, endurance, and just plain old-fashioned guts required to procure the necessary steroids.

Ha ha! Just a little fitness humor there. You don't need to ingest pharmaceutical substances to develop a major body; you simply have to follow the simple-to-follow instructions in this chapter. But first, let's answer some commonly asked questions about bodybuilding.

Q. I'm a man. How large should I let my muscles get?

A. This depends on the size of your head. See, your body has only a certain number (21,796,349,582) of cells. Each of these cells can be either part of your body or part of your head. This means if you make your body bigger, your head has to get smaller, as shown here in these actual unretouched photographs. So you should cease your muscle development as soon as you start noticing the warning signs of severe head reduction, such as:

ACTUAL UNRETOUCHED PHOTOGRAPH SHOWING HOW HEAD CELLS TURN INTO BODY CELLS

Buying lawn ornaments

Having trouble following the plot on "Dukes of Hazzard"

Answering to the name "Vinnie"

If you already meet any of these criteria, you probably shouldn't do any bodybuilding at all. Of course, if you already meet any of these criteria, you're probably still trying to figure out how to get this book open.

Q. Can a woman such as myself engage in bodybuilding?

A. Of course! Although experts have discovered that a woman can never achieve the large muscle mass and definition of a Mister Universe, she can still, with patience, dedication, and hard work, make herself look like this.

Or she can simply have large, realistic depictions of centipedes tattooed on her face.

Q. Once I become huge and muscular, will I still be able to operate a telephone?

A. Push-button, or rotary dial?

Q. Push-button.

A. Probably.

Now that we've answered your commonly asked questions, let's take stock of your current body. Take off all your clothes and stand in front of a mirror, and let's make an objective, professional, scientific assessment. Go ahead! Don't be shy! We can't help you if we can't see what we're working with!

(PAUSE)

So! That's your body, eh?Hahahahahahaha hahahahahahahahahahahahahahahahahaha

hahahahaha! Excuse me. I'm not (choke, gasp) laughing at you, really. I just, ummmmm, I just thought of something funny somebody said to me in 1967. Anyway, looking at your body, I would hahaha hahahahahahahahahahahahahahahaha hahahahahaha! Excuse me. I would say that you hahahahahahahahahahaha! Whew! Put your clothes back on, okay?

Using this scientific assessment of your current bodily needs as a guide, let's look at the various kinds of bodybuilding equipment.

Weights: A Stupid Idea

Forget about weights. For one thing, they're very heavy, and for another thing, they wreck your body. Look at what they do to your big-time weight lifters, who have turned into 400-pound hairy sweaty shapeless grunting masses of tissue. And the men are even worse. No, you want to take the new, high-tech, scientific route to a better body, with Nautilus equipment.

How Nautilus Equipment Works

Originally designed as a way to keep professional football players from having sex before a game, Nautilus equipment has become an extremely popular bodybuilding aid that not only is costly but also takes up a lot of room. This is because it's actually a series of machines, each specifically designed to develop one of the major muscle groupings (the abductors, the transponders, the trapezoids, the isobars, the quatrains, the bivalves, the Social Democrats, and the gerunds). The idea is that you work a grouping until it can no longer respond to signals from your brain, then you move on to the next machine, and so on until you've worked all your muscle groupings, at which time you signal the attendant, by blinking in a prearranged code, that you wish to be bathed.

I can't go into great detail here about how the various Nautilus machines work, because it would soon become obvious that I don't know. On the next page, however, is a diagram illustrating the operation of a typical Nautilus unit, this one designed to develop facial muscles.

The Trouble with Nautilus Equipment

The trouble with Nautilus equipment is that to use it, you have to join either a spa or a professional football team, which means you're going to spend a lot of time enveloped

in other people's bodily aromas. So what would be ideal, if only such a thing were possible, would be if somebody would develop a totally new amazing scientific affordable bodybuilding device that you could use in your own home.

Announcing a Totally New Amazing Scientific Affordable Bodybuilding Device That You Can Use in Your Own Home

I am very pleased to be able to announce at this time a major breakthrough in the field of home body devices: the Dave Barry Total Person Workout Device. I'd tell you how good it is, but I'd be violating numerous federal statutes, plus I think you'll be even more convinced by these actual testimonials from imaginary satisfied customers:

"Your Total Person Workout Device has completely changed my life! For example, I can no longer discern colors!"

A.B., Detroit, Michigan

"I was being constantly hassled by vicious youths in my urban neighborhood. I sent away for your device, and within a week they had stolen it!"

C.D., Toledo, Ohio

"What have you done with my wife!"

L.M.N.O.P., Eau Claire, Wisconsin

What's the cause of all this excitement? It's a device that actually costs less than a new home yet yields results like those shown here.

BEFORE

AFTER

Let's turn the page and see this amazing new product!

Both models come in an attractive designer cardboard box telling you which end is supposed to be up and whether or not you should drop it (no). The price is just $799 for the Basic Model and $1,099 for the Really Nice Model, the main difference being that we check the Really Nice Model for vermin. Of course, if you are in any way the least bit dissatisfied with your Device, you simply have to write an angry letter to the employees at your state Bureau of Helping the Consumer, who probably won't be there because they get just about every other day off for cretin holidays like Arbor Day.

FOUR BODYBUILDING EXERCISES USING THE DAVE BARRY TOTAL PERSON WORKOUT DEVICE

SQUAT   LEAN   TOSS   PUSH-UP

Chapter 7

Nutrition

Why You Should Watch What You Eat

In your great-great-grandfather's day, nobody had to worry about proper nutrition, because people lived on farms and ate wholesome, natural foods. Whenever they needed meat, they just went out and whacked off a sector of the family cow. When they needed bread, they just cut down some wheat, then they threshed it, then they took the grain and starting grinding it up, then they said, "Nah, the hell with it; let's just eat sector of cow tonight."

Today, unfortunately, most cows are grown by giant multinational corporations, who feed them harmful preservatives day and night for the express purpose of killing innocent consumers. Many cows are so full of toxic chemicals that they explode right in the pasture, leaving behind only billowing clouds of greenish fumes, which cause acid rain. You have the same kind of problems with white bread and refined sugar, both of which, if eaten, cause death within hours. This is why it's so important in today's world that you watch what you eat, at least until you get it inside your mouth. After that, it gets pretty disgusting.

How Your Digestive System Works

Your digestive system's job is to turn food into useful body parts. To save itself a lot of aggravation, your digestive system has a

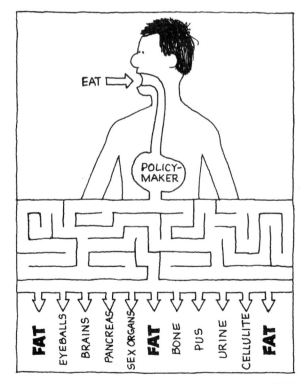

policy whereby it turns a given food into the body part most similar to it. Thus hard-boiled eggs become eyeballs, cauliflower becomes brains, mixed vegetables become the pancreas, Polish sausages become male sexual organs, candy canes become bone, little yellow-covered marshmallow Easter chickens become pus, beer becomes urine, and so on. If you eat a kind of food that does not resemble any known body part, such as a pink Good 'n' Plenty, your body turns it into fat.

Eating a "Balanced Diet"

To make sure your digestive system gets the "raw materials" it needs, at every meal you should eat at least 1 food from each of the 15 Basic Food Families: Fruits, Vegetables, Meats, Fishes, Loaves, Hors d'Oeuvres, Canned Goods, Jellies, Snacks, Shakes, Additives, Eels, Those Little Wax Bottles Filled with Colorful Sugar Water, Pez, and Spam.

What You Can Learn from Reading the Labels on Foods

Virtually nothing. I mean, if the product contains some dangerous chemical, you don't think the label writer, who has a mortgage and kids with braces just the same as you do, is going to risk his job by saying so, do you? Of course not. This is why all labels are written in label jargon, such as "This product contains not less than 0.02 percent of rehydroxylated glutonium or abstract of debentured soybean genitalia, whichever comes first." The more of this kind of jargon you see, the more likely it is that the label writer has something to hide.

So what I recommend is, instead of trying to understand the words on the label, you simply figure out the average number of syllables per word. If the average is two or below, the product is probably safe to eat in small quantities. If the average is three or four, you're probably dealing with a product that causes grave concern in laboratory rats. If the average is five or more, you should set the container down very carefully and flee the vicinity on foot.

About Vitamins

Vitamins are little pills named A, B, C, D, E, and K that the government recommends you have certain amounts of. These recommendations are based on the requirements of the Minimum Daily Adult, a truly pathetic individual that the government keeps in this special facility in Washington, D.C., where he is fed things with names like "riboflavin."

Physicians generally pooh-pooh the value of vitamins, but this is because you can get vitamins into your body without the aid of physicians. If the only way it could be done was for a team of eight surgeons to implant a special $263,000 trapdoor in your head, physicians would say vitamins were the best thing since luxury German automobiles.

The truth is that vitamins are very good for you, and each morning you should take a vitamin A pill, followed by a vitamin D, followed by an E, until you have spelled the healthful mnemonic phrase "A DEAD CAD BAKED A BAD CAKE, ACE." This will probably be plenty of vitamins for you, but be alert for the Four Major Warning Signs of Vitamin Deficiency, which are:

Nosebleeds

A sudden fondness for
Wayne Newton

Unusually thick coats on woolly
caterpillars

Death

If you notice any of these signs, you should add the phrase "A BEAKED DAD BEDDED A BEAD-BEDECKED BABE."

Vitamins in Food

Foods contain vitamins. Your mother told you this. She also told you that the vitamins are always in the most repulsive part of the food. If you were eating a potato, for example, she'd say, "Be sure to eat the skin, that's where the vitamins are." They learn this in Mother School. So with any given food, you should always eat the skin or, if it doesn't have a skin, the rind, the core, or the pit. If it doesn't have any of *these,* you should eat the wrapper.

Minerals in Food

Foods also contain minerals such as zinc, iron, magnesium, steel, and aluminum. At least, that's what I'm supposed to tell you. I personally think the whole idea that there is metal in food, especially blatantly soft food such as Twinkies, is absurd. The only idea more absurd is the deranged notion that eating metal is somehow good for you. If God had wanted us to eat metal, He would have given us much better teeth. Thank you.

What about Fiber?

Fiber is definitely the number one hot trend in the world of natural health, threatening to break all the old records set by "pH balance." Remember, back in the 70s, when every product you bought—food, shampoo, tires—was advertised as being pH balanced, even though nobody ever knew what the hell it meant? Well, it's like that with fiber today, and so naturally I recommend you eat all the fiber-rich foods you can shove down your throat. These would be mainly your cotton candy and your Slim Jims.

A Thoughtful Philosophical Discussion of Vegetarianism

This is a touchy subject for me to discuss without having the vaguest idea of what I'm talking about, but here goes. Many people feel it is wrong to eat animals, on the grounds that animals have souls. I would

have to say, although I certainly have nothing but the deepest respect for this position, that this is pretty stupid. I mean, I don't want to offend any religious group, especially if it is armed, but I frankly don't see how anyone can say that *all* animals have souls. Obviously, some animals do: Lassie clearly did, and probably so did Trigger. If anybody ever tries to eat Lassie, I'll be the first one to attempt a citizen's arrest.

But nobody's going to look me square in the eye and claim that, for example, toads have souls. I am not saying that it's okay to eat toads, of course, unless the alternative is starvation, or what they serve you under the

VEGETARIANS ARE EASY TO SPOT AT ROADSIDE REST STOPS

WHERE DOES HAMBURGER COME FROM ?

A. COWS, BULLS, STEERS?　　　B. PIGS, DOGS, CATS?　　　C. SHARKS, WHALES, RATS?

heading of "snack" on commercial airliners. I'm just saying we have to draw the line somewhere.

I, personally, follow what I call a "modified vegetarianism" system, under which it is okay to eat meat provided that it has been disguised so you can't tell what kind of creature it came from. A perfect example is hamburger. There is no way to tell, just by looking at a hamburger, where it originated. We believe it is from cows, because we are told this by burly cleaver-wielding men in Chicago with bloodstained garments, but we would not have come to this conclusion independently. So under my system, hamburger is fine.

Lobster, on the other hand, is out. There is no way you could *not* know you were eating a lobster. When you walk into a restaurant, often the first thing you see is a large tank containing lobsters wearing handcuffs and trying to scuttle behind each other so you won't pick them. If you order a lobster, you don't get to use the kind of euphemisms you use with cows, such as "beef" or "steak": you say, "I'll have a lobster," and when they bring it to you, you just get this naked *lobster,* and you're supposed to *eat* it. I think this is wrong, and I imagine it goes without saying that I also feel very strongly about blatant organs, such as tongue.

Chapter 8

Dieting and Weight Control

Do You Weigh the Proper Amount?

To answer that question, locate yourself on the medical chart provided here. Chances are the chart shows that you're above your proper weight. The reason is that you eat too many foods that are high in "calories," which are little units that measure how good a particular food tastes. Fudge, for example, has a great many calories, whereas celery, which is not really a food at all but a member of the plywood family, provided by Mother Nature so that mankind would have

	FEMALE			MALE		
AGE	SMALL	AVERAGE	BIG	SMALL	AVERAGE	BIG
18–25	E	F	A	B	C	D
26–31	F	A	B	C	D	E
32–39	A	B	C	D	E	F
40–50	B	C	D	E	F	A
Over 50	C	D	E	F	A	B
Dead	D	E	F	A	B	C

A—You could definitely stand to lose weight.
B—No question about it, you have a weight problem.
C—Based on your weight, you should get on a diet.
D—It would certainly not hurt you to lose some weight.
E—You are carrying too much weight for your body type.
F—You must make more of an effort to control your weight.

a way to get onion dip into his mouth at parties, has none.

The Simple, Basic, Obvious Truth about Losing Weight

Obviously, the only sane way to lose weight, and to keep it off, is to . . . *Hey!* Who *are* you guys?!! Wait a minute!! You can't just barge in here and . . .

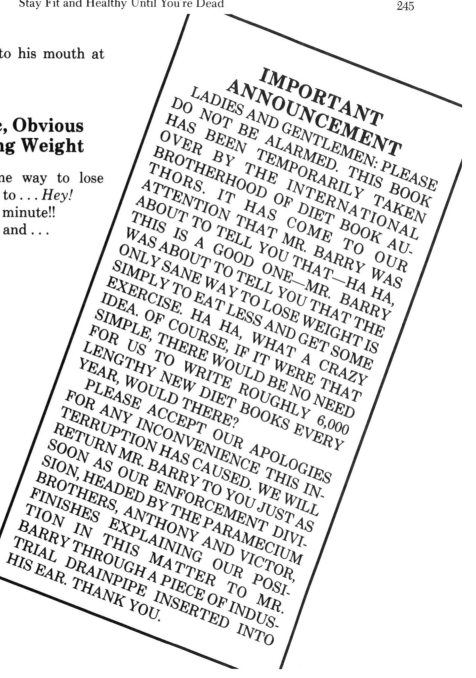

IMPORTANT ANNOUNCEMENT LADIES AND GENTLEMEN: PLEASE DO NOT BE ALARMED. THIS BOOK HAS BEEN TEMPORARILY TAKEN OVER BY THE INTERNATIONAL BROTHERHOOD OF DIET BOOK AUTHORS. IT HAS COME TO OUR ATTENTION THAT MR. BARRY WAS ABOUT TO TELL YOU THAT—HA HA, THIS IS A GOOD ONE—MR. BARRY WAS ABOUT TO TELL YOU THAT THE ONLY SANE WAY TO LOSE WEIGHT IS SIMPLY TO EAT LESS AND GET SOME EXERCISE. HA HA, WHAT A CRAZY IDEA. OF COURSE, IF IT WERE THAT SIMPLE, THERE WOULD BE NO NEED FOR US TO WRITE ROUGHLY 6,000 LENGTHY NEW DIET BOOKS EVERY YEAR, WOULD THERE? PLEASE ACCEPT OUR APOLOGIES FOR ANY INCONVENIENCE THIS INTERRUPTION HAS CAUSED. WE WILL RETURN MR. BARRY TO YOU JUST AS SOON AS OUR ENFORCEMENT DIVISION, HEADED BY THE PARAMECIUM BROTHERS, ANTHONY AND VICTOR, FINISHES EXPLAINING OUR POSITION IN THIS MATTER TO MR. BARRY THROUGH A PIECE OF INDUSTRIAL DRAINPIPE INSERTED INTO HIS EAR. THANK YOU.

So as I was saying, the only sane way to lose weight is to get yourself on, and then stick to, a regular, planned, conscientious program of purchasing newly published diet books. Here are some that I especially recommend:

The Handsome Sincere Random Doctor Medical Diet

Poop Yourself Thin

The Elvis Presley Memorial Diet

The Total Tapeworm Diet

How to Lose Weight in the Coming Depression

Shed Unwanted Ounces the Orson Welles Way

The Dead Preppy Cat Microcomputer Diet Book

The All-Goat-Products Diet

The Frequent Casual Motel Sex Diet

The Amazing Mother Theresa Weight Loss Plan

All of these books are very excellent, and there are thousands more that are just as good, many of them offering such proven and time-tested features as consecutively numbered pages.

Perhaps the best diet book is *Dessert Makes You Fat,* by Ernst Viewfinder, who

DR. VIEWFINDER EXPLAINING HIS THEORY TO MOTEL FOOD ADMINISTRATOR STUDENTS

has several credits toward his Associate's Degree in Motel Food Administration from Southwest Buford County Community College ("Where the Leaders of Tomorrow Are Frowning at Blackboards Today, Visa and MasterCard Accepted"). His theory is that people get fat because they eat too many desserts, so he has developed a diet designed to encourage you to skip the dessert. Here is a typical day's menu:

BREAKFAST
Froot Loops
Eclairs with side orders of bacon
DESSERT: One slice whole wheat toast

LUNCH

Snickers

Fries

Any number of cheeseburgers

DESSERT: Cottage cheese

DINNER

Dixie cup filled with sugar

Melted Turkish taffy soup

Big lumps of chocolate with fudge sauce

DESSERT: That really pathetic lettuce that looks like lichen, festooned with clearly visible insect eggs (no dressing)

I personally tried this diet for several weeks, and I found that not only was I able to skip many desserts, but I didn't need to sleep at all, although near the end they tried to make me.

Common Questions Often Asked about Losing Weight

Q. Do I actually have to read my diet books?

A. No. There is no medical evidence that reading leads to weight loss. Simply keep the books in a prominent location in your home, and occasionally press them against your thighs and buttocks.

Q. Is there any kind of operation I can have that will help me lose weight?

A. There are quite a few such operations, but probably the most effective one, with the fewest negative side effects, is to have an airline pet transporter bonded to your skull with fast-drying epoxy cement (see illustration). This encourages you to eat only those foods which will pass through the mesh door, such as fettuccine and licorice.

Q. What about absurd mechanical weight loss devices, such as those motorized belts that were always shown jiggling the massive hips of pasty middle-aged female character actresses in comedy movies and television shows up through the 1950s?

A. These devices are extremely effective. The fat just melts away. Two of those character actresses, in fact, went on to become Bo Derek and Victoria Principal. This is why you never see those machines in health clubs any more: the clubs took them out because their members were leaving at an alarming rate to accept lucrative film contracts. This is a shame, really, because it leaves the weight-conscious person without any kind of guaranteed, surefire, safe, proven weight loss device. If only somebody would make such a device available to the general public!

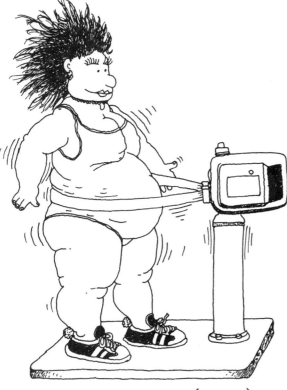

VICTORIA PRINCIPAL (BEFORE)

Announcing the Dave Barry Guaranteed, Surefire, Safe, Proven, Medically Unusual Weight Loss Device for Human Beings Belonging to the General Public

The concept for this truly revolutionary device, which came to me one evening while I was throwing up on my shoes, is amazingly simple: If you go around with an object that weighs approximately 350 pounds strapped to your body, you can't help but lose weight! Assuming you don't have a serious accident! So I designed this device with You, the Consumer, in mind, such that you can wear it virtually undetected to work, around the home, on the tennis court . . . even to executions, if these are permitted in your state!

THE DAVE BARRY
WEIGHT-LOSS DEVICE
FITS INTO YOUR
ACTIVE LIFE-STYLE

What the Experts Say about the Dave Barry Weight Loss Device

"Yes! Okay! It is very good! People should buy it! Now please, let us go!"

> —A team of leading physicians speaking in unison from inside a concrete structure

"The water used in Tokyo, Yokohama, Kawasaki, and other parts of the metropolitan area is supplied by aqueduct systems!"

> —*The Encyclopaedia Britannica* Volume 18 (Taylor-Utah)

Chapter 9

Women's Beauty and Grooming

Thus far in this book, we've concentrated on improving your body. But let's face it: having a great body does you no good whatsoever if you have the kind of face where people are always saying you have a Nice Personality, meaning you can cause crops to fail just by looking at them.

So in this chapter, we're going to take a look at some of the things you can do to your face and hair to give yourself that feeling of inner confidence that says, in the words of the song Maria sang in *West Side Story* just before her lover stabbed her brother to death, "I Feel Pretty." You'll see that you don't have to have been born with great genes to look beautiful; there are lots of simple little "beauty secrets" that can turn even a real woofer into an extremely presentable person, although in your case I would not necessarily rule out plastic surgery.

The First Step toward a More Beautiful You

The most important step, of course, is to recognize that whatever you're currently doing is totally wrong. What you need is a New Look, as you know if you read any of the major women's beauty magazines. Month after month, year after year, they publish the same article, which is "Several Dozen New Ways to Put Makeup on Your Face and Style Your Hair in a Lifelong Futile Effort to Look Like the Model on the Cover."

The reason the beauty experts keep coming up with new looks is that the old ones are all repulsive. You look back at your high school yearbook or, heaven help you, your mother's yearbook, and you see the Looks that were popular years ago, and you wonder how the human race managed to reproduce. You wonder why men and women didn't take one look at each other and sprint in opposite directions until they dropped from exhaustion. Someday your children will say the same thing about the way you look today, which is why we here in the beauty industry are always pushing back the frontiers of knowledge, coming up with New Looks, with no real hope of personal financial benefit beyond the sale of beauty products that cost more per ounce than all but the finest narcotics.

Sometimes, out of the goodness of our hearts, we beauty experts make guest appearances on those morning television shows devoted to a wide range of topics that the folks who run television feel are of interest to women, namely these:

Sex problems

Fashion and beauty tips

Problems that involve sex

Tips on beauty and fashion

Various sexually involved problems

Discussions of how you can become more sexually fashionable and beautiful by means of certain tips

Pasta

What the beauty experts generally do on these shows is select a woman from the audience and point out how she has committed several dozen common major beauty blunders due to the fact that she is not a knowledgeable beauty expert. Their technique is to pick somebody who looks perfectly normal—perhaps even attractive—to the unprofessional eye, then harp away at her until the audience begins to marvel that she managed to get past the studio guards without being mistaken for an escaped boar and shot.

Then they take this pathetic woman, and they give her a completely New Look, offering all kinds of professional beauty tips as they go along:

"Now the most unfortunate facial characteristic of Rhonda here," they say, "is that she has a nose you could hang a garment bag on, so we are going to begin by applying about five-eighths of an inch of base coat to the rest of her head in an effort to make it appear larger. We'll top that off with two coats of sealant, then we'll remove all of Rhonda's current eyebrows and start applying the first few coats of skin dye while we try to think up something we can do about her mouth."

And so on, until Rhonda's face is encased in congealed cosmetic substances to the

A NORMAL BEAUTY MAKE-OVER

BEFORE: BASICALLY REALLY UGLY ROUNDED FACE   AFTER: ADDED BROWNS, SHADOWS, AND SQUARED-OFF FEATURES

point where her own dog wouldn't recognize her. As the studio audience applauds her New Look enthusiastically, Robert Redford walks onstage and asks her to marry him, and they walk off together, living proof of the advantages of knowledgeably applied beauty products, at least until Rhonda's sealant weakens and her base coat starts falling off in slabs the size of French toast.

What You, Personally, Need to Do about Your Appearance

Unfortunately, we are dealing with the print medium here, so I am unable to consult individually with you in regard to your specific beauty needs, except to say that from this particular angle it appears you ought to give a bit more thought to booger removal. However, I can offer these helpful beauty guidelines for you to bear in mind as you try to achieve your New Look:

GUIDELINE 1

YOUR FACE IS MUCH TOO FAT.

It looks like a weather balloon, for God's sake. Try some puce blush on your cheekbones, if you can locate them, and accentuate those little lines coming out of the

BASIC FACIAL TYPES

MUCH TOO FAT   MUCH TOO THIN

sides of your mouth by filling them in lightly with an Accountant's Fine Point Bic pen.

GUIDELINE 2

I CAN'T BELIEVE WHAT HAS BEEN DONE TO YOUR HAIR.

I am assuming that you didn't pay for that cut. I am assuming that a deranged, near-blind, palsied person wielding pruning shears burst into your room in the dead of night and cut your hair after beating you unconscious. The only thing I can suggest until it grows back out is that you join some sort of religious order that has a mandatory head covering. And when it does grow back, you want to decide which of the three common head shapes, shown below, you have and choose a hairstyle that compliments it.

GUIDELINE 3
I WOULD SAY YOUR EYES ARE YOUR BEST FEATURE.

This is assuming I have to pick something. You want to draw attention to your eyes through subtle use of your lipstick, as this

SHAPE #1   SHAPE #2   SHAPE #3

WRONG   WRONG   WRONG

RIGHT   RIGHT   RIGHT

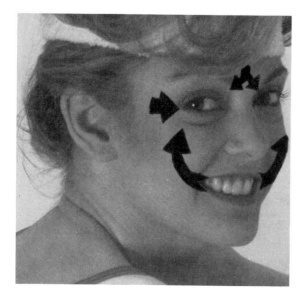

top New York fashion model has done. Note that when I say your eyes are your best feature, I am speaking of them as independent organs. Taken as a set, they are maybe three-quarters of an inch too close together.

Personal Hygiene

After going to all that trouble with your face and hair, the last thing you want to do is go around smelling like a billy goat with a flatulence problem. This is why good personal hygiene habits are so important. Let's review them briefly.

TEETH

You should brush them immediately before having conversations, using a tube of toothpaste with these words printed on the side: "The American Dental Association has found this to be an effective tube of toothpaste when squeezed from the bottom in conjunction with a program of regular payments to a member of the American Dental Association."

GUMS AND ARMPITS

Floss them regularly. If you use the same floss, do your gums first.

HAIR

Shampoo regularly with a shampoo bearing the name of a reputable beauty snot, such as Vidal Sassoon. Also, be alert for dandruff, an incurable disease where little pieces of your head keep falling off until eventually all you have left is two eyeballs on stalks protruding from your neck and you look like a gigantic lobster walking around wearing clothes. Scratching only makes it worse.

FEET

There's an old saying about feet that goes: "I had no shoes, and I pitied myself. Then I met a man who had no feet; so I took his shoes." Better than anything I could think of, this saying illustrates the importance of proper foot care. Each day, you should spend a minimum of an hour examining your feet closely under a 200-watt light bulb and picking at your toenails with various foot care implements available at Woolworth's. This is something the whole family can do together. Stress to your children that they should not mention it to the authorities.

FEMININE HYGIENE

At one time, this important subject would have been considered "too delicate" for a book like this, but all that has changed, thanks to the efforts of the fine people who sell vaginal deodorants via television commercials featuring two Good Friends having a Frank Discussion:

DEBBIE (hesitantly): Sue, may I ask you something?
SUE: Sure, Debbie. What is it?
DEBBIE: Sue, are you aware that for the past seven years, including at formal affairs such as funerals, you've been emitting an aroma that would fell a buffalo at 90 feet?
SUE (frowning slightly): Why no, Debbie, I didn't know! Perhaps that is why I have remained a housewife, rather than winning the Nobel Prize for Physics!
DEBBIE: Why not try this?
SUE (examining the label thoughtfully): Hmmm. New Improved Crotch Bouquet. By golly, I'll try it!
DEBBIE: Not here, for God's sake!

Chapter 10

Men's Beauty and Grooming

As recently as 20 years ago, a man was considered well-groomed if he remembered to remove the little pieces of toilet paper he stuck on his face where he cut himself shaving. But today we live in a liberated era, an era in which men are not afraid to make themselves more attractive by means of beauty aids formerly limited to women—hair coloring, makeup, totally alien plastic substances inserted into the body so as to form bulges, designer dresses, etc.

This is basically a healthy social development. For, as the saying goes, "A man who cares about his personal appearance is a man who is always checking his reflection in store windows." So in this section, men, we're going to suggest some grooming "tips" to help you look more like the lean and cruelly handsome male models in the "Fall Fashion Supplement," and less like the people in your immediate gene pool.

Hair

I will assume that you already shampoo your hair at frequent intervals, that you are not one of those repulsive males who, apparently feeling that there is some sort of grave threat to the world's grease supply, let their hair go for weeks at a time without washing it, such that if one of their pillows ever caught fire, it would burn for days. But men, even if you do use shampoo regularly, it's probably the wrong kind, by which I mean it

GREASER   NEW WAVE MAN

probably consists mainly of shampoo, with perhaps a dash of pH.

This is not good enough. Women discovered years ago that if you want true hair beauty, your shampoo must contain foodstuffs. Some women prefer fruits and vegetables, such as apricot and avocado; others prefer poultry products, such as egg; others prefer liquor, such as beer. Some even prefer—this is the absolute truth coming up here—human placentas, which makes for a *very* expensive shampoo because, believe me, the shampoo factory has to pay the workers a *lot* of money to stuff those suckers into the bottles.

(For a more complete discussion of placentas, see my *Babies and Other Hazards of Sex,* which many experts consider to be, of all the many books available about birth and child rearing, the one that took the least time to write.)

And why is it so important to have foodstuffs in shampoo? I can answer that science question in three syllables: follicles. Follicles are little organs that live in your skull, thousands of them, and produce your hair. To produce hair, they need protein, and to get protein, they need to eat, just as you do. Women are constantly shoving egg and beer down their tiny throats, which is why, as you have no doubt noticed, women generally have gobs of hair. Men, on the other hand,

HAIR FOLLICLES

practically starve them to death—you can eat only so much pH, and then you just don't want to *see* another bite—which is why so many men go bald.

A Sincere Discussion of Baldness

Too often in our insensitive society, baldness is treated as a joke, so let me begin this sincere discussion by stating that, although I am fortunate enough to be blessed with a very full and attractive head of hair, I am very much aware of the anguish and inner torment experienced on a daily basis by you chrome domes out there. I mean, it's not *your* fault you're bald, is it? Well, okay, it *is* your fault because you let your tiny helpless innocent follicles, which had never so much as said a mean word to anybody in their whole lives, suffer a horrible death by starvation while you were out laughing and eating pizza with friends, but there's no point in dwelling on that now. The question is: What can you do about your unfortunate condition?

One approach, of course, is to get a wig. The advantage of wearing a wig is that you don't look quite as stupid as you would if you went around with a giant red clown nose on. The main disadvantage is that a wig costs a lot more than a large, hand-lettered sign around your neck that says "WIG," which is equally effective.

Another approach is to get a hair transplant. This is a procedure whereby a person who has completed all three weeks of Hair Transplant School, which he enrolled in because he flunked Whack-a-Mole-Game-Machine Maintenance School, takes hair from somewhere else on your body and puts it on top of your head. The advantage of this approach is that you do, in fact, end up with

CAN YOU GUESS WHICH MAN IS WEARING AN ACTUAL WIG? (ANSWER BELOW)

A. TYPICAL ARTIST

B. TYPICAL MINISTER

C. TYPICAL HENCHMAN

D. TYPICAL REPUBLICAN

ANSWER: E

hair growing on your head. The disadvantage, of course, is that it has to come from somewhere else on your body, which means either (a) you have hair growing up there that originated in your armpit or some other locale so disgusting I don't even want to talk about it, or (b) they have to take the hair off the side of your head, which is not necessarily a great stride forward for you in the looks department (see illustration).

HAIR TRANSPLANTS ARE BECOMING COMMON

Finally, there are ads for all kinds of alleged "miracle" hair-growing pills, creams, lotions, and potions in the backs of sleaze-ball publications such as *Penthouse* and *American Beet Farmer,* which make all kinds of outrageous claims such as they can "stop the spread of baldness" and "restore lost hair" and even "grow hair on a billiard ball." These claims, of course, are totally false, except the one about the billiard ball, which government researchers recently discovered is true, the drawback being that many of the balls also developed tumors.

So unfortunately, balding men, there is little to offer you in the way of hope at this time. If only somebody would develop a proven scientific guaranteed effective totally safe miracle hair-growth substance!

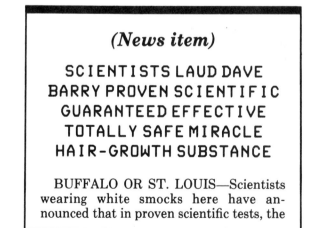

(News item)

SCIENTISTS LAUD DAVE BARRY PROVEN SCIENTIFIC GUARANTEED EFFECTIVE TOTALLY SAFE MIRACLE HAIR-GROWTH SUBSTANCE

BUFFALO OR ST. LOUIS—Scientists wearing white smocks here have announced that in proven scientific tests, the

Dave Barry Miracle Hair-Growth Substance did, in fact, bring new life to dead hair follicles belonging to volunteer bald persons who were scientifically monitored as they slept on street grates.

"As this enlarged photograph shows," explained Chief of Research Dr. Ernst Viewfinder, "most of the follicles of the untreated volunteers are small and dead—not unlike, I might add by way of a humorous aside, some of the untreated volunteers themselves, ha ha. But in these photographs of the treated volunteers, we can see that the Dave Barry Miracle Hair-Growth Substance has brought their scalps back to life, with sleek and happy follicles the size of adult mice, in some cases completely crowding out the brain! This could well be what happened to Vidal Sassoon."

Skin

What do women find attractive when they look at a man's skin? Bumps. Yes, bumps. Why do you think women fall all over Robert Redford while virtually ignoring you and me? Go watch Redford in a movie sometime, and you'll see that he has a number of facial bumps, which look during the extreme close-ups to be big enough to play polo on, and which, as far as I can tell, are the only major physical characteristic in which Robert Redford and I differ.

So what I am recommending, men, is that as part of your daily grooming ritual, you apply small globulets of Silly Putty to your face, as shown in the illustration, so as to render yourself irresistible to the opposing sex. I regret to point out, however, that Silly Putty comes in only the Caucasian skin hue,

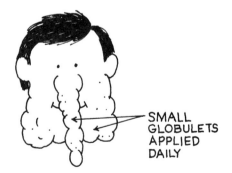

SMALL
GLOBULETS
APPLIED
DAILY

which is blatant discrimination against those members of minority groups who also wish to install facial bumps, and I think those of us who are still liberals ought to sit right down and write hostile letters about this to our Congresspersons.

Makeup

Makeup is definitely the coming thing in male grooming. Oh, I know what you're saying. You're saying, "No *way*. No *way* am I going to put on makeup!" But of course that's exactly what you said about bikini underwear, and hair spray, and blow-dryers, which, if you had used them in a locker room 15 years ago, would have resulted in a situation where if you entered the shower, the other men would have fled from you in very much the way the residents of Tokyo fled from Godzilla, but which are common grooming articles today.

Yes, men, you might as well face it: it won't be long before we're *all* wearing makeup. And the last thing you want to do is get left behind on this trend and end up looking ludicrously out of date, like the unfortunate individuals you occasionally see who still wear white patent leather shoes and matching belts and always look like assistant deputy sewage commissioners from small towns where the highest form of cultural activity is reading the drive-thru menu at Burger King. So what I recommend you do is gradually start introducing makeup into your grooming routine—a little blusher, a little eye liner, a touch of lipstick—and see if you don't start making a big impression at your office, maybe even start attracting the attention of people as high up as vice president, people who once seemed unaware you even existed, but who suddenly start looking at you for 20 and 30 seconds at a time on the elevator and trying to discreetly read your security badge.

Chapter 11

When You Get Sick

Even the healthiest person, if he follows the fitness program described in this book, will eventually need medical care. Fortunately, we Americans live in a nation where the medical-care system is second to none in the world, unless you count maybe 25 or 30 little scuzzball countries like Scotland that we could vaporize in seconds if we felt like it.

What we're going to talk about in this chapter is how you can become more aware of the various problems that your body can develop, so that you'll be better able to worry about them. We'll also talk about how, if you actually do become sick, you can explain your problems to the medical-care establishment in such a way that it does not immediately yank out a useful organ.

How You Can Tell When There Is Something Wrong with You

Trained medical personnel detect illness or other bodily problems by looking for "symptoms," the major ones being these:

Aches

Pains

A total absence of aches or pains

Bullet holes

A feeling of not keeping up with inflation

A leg bone sticking out through the skin

Never having the correct change

A stoppage of heart or brain activity

Irritability

Get in the habit of checking yourself every 20 minutes or so for these symptoms. When you notice one, you should immediately follow this emergency procedure:

1. Take two pills containing a Scientifically Proven Painkilling Formula that has been advertised on television by a reliable avuncular spokesperson such as Robert Young.

2. Phone your office to tell them that you won't be in for several days and could somebody please remember to discard any interoffice memoranda aimed at you. If you have no office, you should phone your

mother and have her confirm that there is definitely Something Going Around.

This course of treatment will cure you most of the time. If it doesn't, you probably have a serious illness, which means you should call your physician's answering service and make an appointment to go into his office the following month and sit in the waiting room for an hour and 45 minutes reading *National Geographic*. If *that* doesn't work, you should go to a hospital emergency ward and inflict a gunshot wound on yourself, thus increasing the odds that you will see an actual doctor to nearly 40 percent.

Dealing with Doctors

To get the most out of a doctor, you have to understand how he perceives the world, which is best summed up by the last sentence of the Hippocratic Oath:

"AND ABOVE ALL, REMEMBER THAT THE PATIENT HAS NABISCO BRAND SHREDDED WHEAT FOR BRAINS."

YOU MUST BE PREPARED TO TAKE EXTREME ACTION IN AN EMERGENCY WARD SITUATION

Yes, doctors tend to feel just a tad superior to the general public, but this is understandable. Doctors are generally smart people, the kind who were attending meetings of the National Honor Society while you were leaning out the study hall

SOME GUYS FROM HIGH SCHOOL WERE EASY TO PEG...

DAVID BARRY
Business Education

May 16 – "David" – Band, 9; Chorus, 9; Gentlemen Songsters, 9; Model Club, 10; Future Journalists of America, 10; Likes mashed potatoes, hot dogs, typewriters, and pet fish. Parents: Mr. and Mrs. Sylvester Barry.

PRESTON BAINBRIDGE, III
Academic

July 4 – "Little Doc" – Football, 9, 10, 11, 12; Basketball, 9, 10, 11, 12; Golf, 9, 10, 11, 12; National Honor Society, 9, 10, 11, 12; Future Doctors of America, 9, 10, 11, 12; National Medical Merit Scholarship Recipient; Band, 9, 10, 11, 12; Gentlemen Songsters, 9, 10, 11, 12; Homecoming King; Varsity Club President, 10, 11, 12; Student Council, 9, 10, 11, 12; Student Council President; Play, 9, 10, 11, 12; All-American Golfer, 9, 10, 11, 12; National Drug Institute Academic Award, 12; Likes blondes, weejuns, Corvettes, white clothes, and chasing ambulances in his red Triumph. Parents: Dr. and Mrs. P. Bainbridge, II.

window seeing if you could spit on passing nuns. In college and medical school, doctors spend years associating with other smart people and learning complicated things like the location of the pituitary gland. When they get out, the last thing they feel like doing is consorting with a bunch of cretin patients, who not only have no idea where the pituitary gland is, but also are often sick besides.

So the important rule to remember when you're dealing with a doctor is this: *never* tell him what you think the problem is, even if you're absolutely certain. If you tell him what you think, he'll become irritated and go out of his way to prove you're wrong:

YOU: Doctor, I think I have suffered a knife wound to the stomach.
DOCTOR (sneering):   Oh you do, do you? And what makes you think that?
YOU: Well, several hostile urban youths accosted me on the street and stuck a knife in my stomach. See? Here's the knife handle, sticking out of my stomach.
DOCTOR (examining your foot):   That could be caused by any number of conditions, such as an amalgamation of the pyloric valve or an interdiction of the right epistolary oracle. I'm going to send you to the hospital for some tests next week.

The phrase "send you to the hospital for some tests" is medical code for "drain all the blood out of your body." Blood removal is the primary form of health care in the United States, and it has been ever since April 4, 1906, when the founder of the Mayo Clinic, Dr. Ted Clinic, happened to be cutting open diseased woodland creatures, as was his wont, and made an amazing discovery: all of the creatures contained blood. He concluded that blood must be a leading cause of disease, which is why today when you go into the hospital, various personnel are always lunging at you with needles. They are very conscientious about this because they don't want to get a nasty note from the doctor ("3 PM—Patient still contains traces of blood! Let's not let this happen again").

If blood removal doesn't work, they start taking out your organs. Usually they start

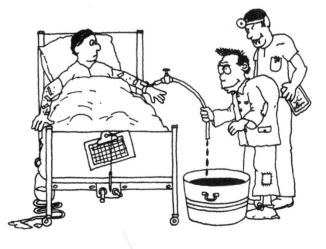

with organs you have two of, such as kidneys, then move up to the really vital ones, so it's very important that you convince the doctor you're getting better while you still have a chance to survive:

DOCTOR: So! How are we feeling today?
YOU (hastily):   Fine! Great! Never felt better!
DOCTOR (frowning at your chart):   Really? Are you sure? Because I see by your chart here that you still have several organs left, and we could . . .
YOU (staggering out of bed, trailing intravenous tubes):   No! No! Look! I feel terrific! (You attempt a deep knee bend, then collapse in agony.)
DOCTOR: Okay, but I'll be back to check on you in an hour.

Paying for Your Hospital Treatment

Always examine your hospital bill closely. It should look like this:

Aspirin tablet $11.05

Little Dixie cup for water to wash aspirin tablet down with 6.80

Water... 31.80

Removal of childproof cap from aspirin bottle (Dr. Viewfinder) 460.00

Removal of little tuft of cotton from aspirin bottle (Dr. Beaner) 385.00

CAT scan from when Dr. Spinnaker thought he might have heard a little whistling noise in the patient's chest that was probably nothing but You Always Want to Be Sure about These Things 87,354.50

Consultation among Dr. Spinnaker, Dr. Viewfinder, Dr. Beaner, Dr. Whelk, Dr. Pilsner, and Dr. Frackmeyer while they were peeing (per doctor)... 275.00

Also Dr. Whelk mentioned it to Dr. Hogworth at the polo match... 340.00

Gratuity....................................... 85.00

If, after examining the bill carefully, you feel satisfied that all the dollar amounts are lined up neatly on the right-hand side, you should submit it to your insurance company, which will, without even looking at it, send it back to you with a testy note telling you that you filled out the forms all wrong. This will give you time to sell your house and children to raise the cash you'll need for when you finally get everything filled out right and the insurance company notifies you that the only thing you're actually covered for is 60 percent of the Dixie cup.

Home Emergency First-Aid Chart to Be Kept Posted on the Bulletin Board underneath the Coupons That, If You Save Up Ten of Them, Get You a Free Medium Pizza

HOME EMERGENCY	TREATMENT
Decapitation.	Elevate head; shriek for assistance.
Victim has swallowed fabric softener.	Induce vomiting by showing the victim a videotape of that speech Richard Nixon gave about his mother after he resigned.
Victim has swallowed a can of chicken gumbo soup.	So? What's so bad about that?
You don't understand. Victim has swallowed the actual *can*.	Oh. Is this by any chance the same victim that swallowed the fabric softener?
Yes, it is.	Boy, that victim has a real problem.
I'll say.	Say, you're kind of cute. What are you doing for dinner?

Chapter 12

Fitness Q and A

Fitness and the Expectant Mother

Q. I am currently pregnant to a considerable degree. Instead of trying to keep fit, may I just lounge around watching "Days of Our Lives" and reading _Glamour_ Magazine?

A. No! These are the 80s, for God's sake, and _nobody_ is excused from being fit! _Especially_ you expectant women! If you just let your body go during pregnancy, after the baby comes, you're going to look as though a team of plastic surgeons have implanted a 35-pound mass of Wonder bread dough under the skin around your hips and thighs. But if you continue to care for your body, if you exercise regularly and maintain your muscle tone, the mass will have a much firmer consistency, like congealed rubber cement.

Of course, a pregnant woman can't do the same exercises as a normal person. Most gynecologists, for example, frown on the pole vault after about the seventh month. But there are still some exercises that work very well for the mother-to-be, such as:

1. TRY TO TOUCH THE WALL. Stand in a relaxed fashion with your arms over your head and your abdominal area forming a large tissue mass directly between you and the wall. Now gradually lean for-

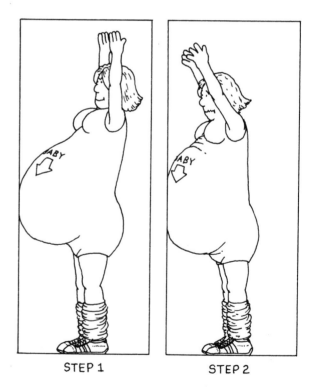

STEP 1   STEP 2

ward until your arms touch the wall, if such a thing is possible, and then return to the full standing position.

2. TRY TO GET OUT OF A CAR. Have several burly friends somehow place you behind the wheel of a 1979 Chevrolet Chevette, or some equally absurd little car, then have them time you as you attempt to get out of it in such a way that your undergarments are not clearly visible from other planets. Eight minutes is the world's record.

3. KNEE CLENCH. Go to a nice restaurant with friends and attempt to get all the way to the appetizers without going to the bathroom more than twice.

Q. What about fitness for the fetus?

A. You should indeed embark upon a rigorous program of fetal fitness, for otherwise the fetus will be born pasty and flabby and lacking in muscle definition, and in later life it may have trouble getting accepted by the better aerobic dancing institutes. Of course, getting the fetus to exercise is not easy, any more than teaching the fetus to read is easy, but if you truly are a Concerned Parent, you will find a way.

I particularly recommend a new product developed by the fine people who make Nautilus equipment. It's called the "Feta-

lus" (see illustration), and it's specially designed for the fetus to use in the womb. It's a very effective device and well worth the cost, although to be perfectly frank the insertion process is not everybody's cup of tea.

Some Helpful Answers for People Who Smoke

Q. I'm a smoker, and . . .

A. You're a what?

Q. I'm a smoker, and I'd really like to . . .

A. You are slime, you know that? You are raw industrial sewage.

Q. Yes, I know. I really want to quit. I just hate . . .

A. Why don't you just suck on the exhaust pipe of a poorly tuned automobile, huh? Why don't you just go around spraying Agent Orange on your fellow restaurant patrons?

Q. Of course you are absolutely right. It's just that it's so hard to stop, and I'm getting desperate, and I was hoping that maybe you'd have some tips on how . . .

A. I'll tell you one thing. If you *ever* try to ignite one of those repulsive toxic objects in a restaurant where I am dining, I shall order a reputable brand of designer carbonated water and forcibly pour it into your nasal passages. Do I make myself clear?

Q. Yes, and I can certainly understand why you feel that way.

A. Well, you'd damned well better.

Q. Thank you.

A. Get out of my sight before I vomit.

Fitness and the Afterlife

Q. I am very, very proud of my body. I have calluses on the top of my head formed by bumping into things because I walk around looking down at my various major muscle groupings. My question is: What will happen to my body when I die? Who will take care of it? Will it become soft and shapeless?

A. You will be pleased to learn that the long-neglected field of postmortem fitness has received a real "shot in the arm" lately with the emergence of the EternaBody chain of fitness centers, each equipped with the patented Cryo-Physique Room, which is very much like a sauna, except that instead of exposing living people to heat, it lowers the temperature of dead people to approximately 325 degrees below zero, at which temperature they acquire a firmness of muscle tone that we normally associate only with world-class bodybuilders and certain minerals.

Fitness and Sex

Q. About a year ago, my husband got on a rigorous fitness program, and he definitely looks much, much better. The problem is, he has taken to viewing our lovemaking as primarily a form of exercise. Like, for example, he wears ankle weights and Heavy Hands, which are no picnic

during foreplay. Also, I have a problem with the idea of having my sexual partner, at a very intimate moment, if you get my drift, shout his pulse rate into a tape recorder. Don't you think he's carrying this too far?

A. Absolutely. First of all, the Heavy Hands aren't doing him nearly as much good as dumbbells would, and second, I see no reason why he can't simply use a felt-tipped marker to jot his pulse rate down quietly on an exposed patch of your skin.

BEFORE   AFTER

Fitness and the Third World

Q. I'm a part of a team of CIA operatives currently operating in a fungal, lice-ridden Central American nation that I, of course, cannot reveal the name of because it's a secret. Our main mission here is to win over the local peasantry to the cause of Freedom and Democracy via a two-pronged program of (a) teaching them how to make sandwiches, and (b) shooting suspected opposition peasants in the head. What I was wondering was, do you think it would help if we also sponsored Dancercise classes?

A. Sounds like a winner! There's nothing that backward peoples enjoy quite so much as dancing, to judge from any number of comical old movies I have seen, wherein the natives are always leaping around and putting Bob Hope in a large iron pot. Be sure your peasants wear an approved style of leg warmer, which the Department of Defense will be able to procure for you at a cost of $63,400 per leg.

Postwar Fitness

Q. What preparations has the government made to insure that our top federal officials will be able to remain fit in the unfortunate event of a total thermonuclear war?

A. At the first sign of trouble, these officials will be whisked to a giant underground Strategic Fitness Facility guarded by vicious federal dogs. This facility will be staffed by a corps of female personnel who have been chosen for their knowledge of postnuclear aerobic routines as well their overall body tauntness. Also there will, of course, be a sauna and several lead-lined racquetball courts, although, as one top government planner put it, "It won't be a picnic in there. Towels will be at a premium."

Office Fitness

Q. I am employed by a large corporation, and I work in an office where my primary responsibility is to discuss "General Hospital" with Helen and Louise. As you can imagine, this does not involve a great deal of physical activity, and I have, quite frankly, developed a rear end which could serve as a bulldozer-flotation device. So I was wondering if you can suggest any kind of fitness program that a person can do at her desk.

A. Certainly. Each morning, during a quiet period, quietly slip off your shoes, push your chair away from your desk, and engage in five minutes of gentle stretching, followed by five minutes each of toe touches, dressage, the luge, and the 400-meter butterfly. Of course, some of these activities may require minor changes in your office routine, to allow for such things as feeding

HAVING A DESK JOB OFTEN LEADS TO SLIGHT WEIGHT DISTRIBUTION PROBLEMS

the horse, but I'm sure your employer will have no objection once you threaten to file a gigantic class-action suit alleging you are being discriminated against on the basis of being pear-shaped.

Index

A
"All My Children," 199
American Beet Farmer, 259
Arbor Day, 238

B
Bertha the Amazing Land
    Whale, 201–202

C
Carp, giant, 227
Clinic, Dr. Ted, 265
Communists, 188

F
Ford, Gerald, 193
Frequent Casual Motel Sex
    Diet, The, 246

G
Godzilla, 261
Gone with the Wind, 198

H
Hummocks, 226

J
Jacks, Cracker, 190

M
Manilow, Barry, 211
Mister Sphincter, 198

N
Nature, Mother, 196
Newton, Wayne, 241

O
Oyl, Olive, 214

P
Plenty, Good 'n', 240

R
Rabbits, diseased baby, 197

S
Social Democrats, 235

T
Trigger, 242

V
Viewfinder, Ernst, 246

W
Whack-a-Mole-Game-Machine
    Maintenance School, 258
Whiz, Cheez, 215

CLAW YOUR
WAY TO THE
TOP

How to
become the head
of a major corporation
in roughly a week

Contents

Introduction... page **281**

Chapter 1   **The History of Business** .... page **287**

Chapter 2   **Getting a Job** .... page **295**

Chapter 3   **How to Do Your Job, Whatever It Is**.................... page **307**

Chapter 4   **Stepping Over Your Co-Workers**........................ page **317**

Chapter 5   **Business Communications**................................. page **332**

Chapter 6   **Giving Good Lunch** .... page **345**

Chapter 7   **How to Dress Exactly Like Everybody Else**.......... page **353**

Chapter 8   **Sales**.. page **358**

Chapter 9   **How to Go Into Business For Yourself**................ page **363**

Chapter 10   **How Finance Works** .... page **368**

            Afterword .... page **372**

DEDICATION

This book is dedicated to Burton R. Legume, inventor, who in 1907 dreamed up the concept of the hold button, without which the modern industrial economy would not be possible.

INTRODUCTION

YOU AND THIS BOOK

Maybe you're a young graduate looking for his or her first job. Or maybe you're a veteran employee who'd like to advance up the corporate ladder. Or maybe you're a Labrador retriever who nosed this book off the coffee table, and it fell open to this page.

It makes no difference who you are: the important thing is, this book can show you how to ACHIEVE YOUR CAREER GOALS and WIN THE REWARDS OF SUCCESS such as CARS and HOUSES and GREAT BIG BOATS where, any time you feel like it, you press a little button and UNIFORMED SERVANTS FROM SOME DISEASE-RIDDEN FOREIGN NATION WHERE EVERYBODY IS WRETCHEDLY POOR WHICH IS WHY THEY CAME OVER HERE bring you PLATES OF LITTLE CRACKERS WITH TOASTED CHEESE ON TOP or, if you prefer, RALSTON-PURINA DOG TREATS.

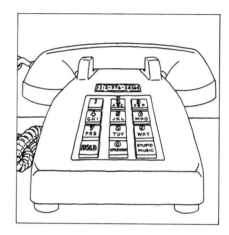

TODAY'S BUSINESS CLIMATE

Today's business climate is partly cloudy with highs in the mid-70s.

Ha ha! That is just a sampler of the kind of snappy humor you will find throughout this book, along with a lot of words printed in capital letters to keep you from falling asleep. Actually, today's business climate is perfect. It is a reaction against the violently anti-business mood that swept the nation back in the sixties, when the young people of America, except for Julie and David Eisenhower, decided to reject money as a life objective and became "hippies." They scorned the corporate world, with its sterility, its greed, its exploitation, its conformity, its Xerox machines that were forever breaking down. They embarked instead upon a quest for a transcendent universal consciousness imbued with peace and love, which they sought to achieve by saying "dude" to members of minority groups and smoking reefers the size of marine flares.

But gradually these young people realized they were paying a subtle price for their counterculture lifestyle, in the sense that they were always waking up in Volkswagen Microbuses with lice in their hair. So they decided that, hey, maybe it wouldn't be so bad to become a sterile conforming greedy exploiter after all, so they went to work for large corporations. Soon they developed children and houses and Volvos, and within a few years they had reached the point of central air-conditioning, from which there is no turning back. Most of them can no longer locate their Grateful Dead albums.

So now everybody except Ralph Nader is strongly pro-business. People who, only a few years back, would have hurled pig blood at Lee Iacocca for some symbolic protest reason or another now think he should run for president. What this means for you is: This is a GREAT TIME for you to get into business. And

1960s PERSON WAKING UP AND REALIZING IT'S TIME TO STOP BEING A HIPPIE AND START MAKING MONEY

don't worry about qualifications: ANYBODY can make it in the business world. All you really need is a little gumption, a willingness to work, some common sense, and a brother-in-law who is Vice-President in Charge of Personnel.

Ha ha! Another business-related joke! This is gonna be some fun, getting you a job, all right!

STEP ONE: SETTING YOUR GOALS

The first step toward your successful business career is to determine your Career Objectives. To do these things, you'll need a nice sharp number-two pencil and some three-by-five cards. I'll wait right here while you go get them, okay? I'll meet you underneath the asterisks on the next page! Hurry back! This is going to be exciting!

(Brief pause.)

The point of the preceding paragraph, obviously, was to get rid of the totally hopeless dweebs who actually think they need three-by-five cards to determine their Career Objectives. These are the same people who you just know are going to write down things like:

1. I would like to work with people.

Which of course is a joke, because it is a proven fact that the more you work with people, the more you hate them. Look at the clerks at any big-city Bureau of Motor Vehicles: They work with people all day long, and their basic approach to human interaction is to make you wait in line as long as possible and then tell you you're in the wrong line, in hopes that you'll have a very painful and ultimately fatal seizure, and they'll get to watch.

So you savvy persons have ruled out "working with people" as a Career Objective. What you want, from your career, is a SENSE OF FULFILLMENT AS A HUMAN BEING and MAXIMUM PERSONAL SAT-ISFACTION as measured in U.S. DOLLARS. You want a Rolex watch and numerous fast cars. You want employees so desperate for your approval that you could put your cigar out on their foreheads and they'd thank you. You want to be able to leave Supreme Court justices on "hold" for upwards of an hour. And you know that you do not get these things by diddling around with three-by-five cards.

*　　　*　　　*

Welcome back! Got your cards? Great! Now first, I'd like you to write down, on each card, a Career Objective, such as "working with people." Okay? I want you to do this until you have listed 800 Career Objectives—you might have to go get some more cards!—and then I want you to arrange them in order according to which objective contains the most vowels, okay? Great! We're on our way! Call me when you're done!

TEST YOUR BUSINESS I.Q.

1. You are the world's largest manufacturer of carbonated beverages, and you have a product that is famous worldwide, that is virtually synonymous with the term "soft drink," and that has had the same formula for 99 years. It has a very loyal following. You are making millions and millions of dollars selling it. You should:

(a) Just keep it the way it is.
(b) Change the formula.
(c) Set fire to your own hair.

CORRECT ANSWER: Either *(b)* or *(c)*.

2. You are a major defense contractor, and you are building a gun for the Army that is supposed to be able to shoot down enemy planes. So far the taxpayers have paid you nearly $2 billion for it, and all your tests indicate that the only way it would have any negative effect on an enemy plane is if you could somehow sneak into the cockpit and manually whack the pilot over the head with it. How should you deal with this problem?

(a) You should try really hard to do a better job.
(b) You should tell the Defense Department that they probably should get another contractor.
(c) You should refund at least some of the taxpayers' money.

CORRECT ANSWER: What problem?

3. You are a major automobile manufacturer. You have been losing sales to cars from other nations, particularly Japan, because their cars tend to be fuel efficient, technologically advanced, and extremely well made, whereas the most innovative concept you have come up with in the past two decades is the opera window. You should:

(a) Have Congress pass a law restricting Japanese imports, so consumers will have no choice but to buy your cars.

(b) Have Congress pass a law making it legal for you to kidnap consumers' children and not return them until the consumers buy your cars.

(c) Have Congress pass a law ordering the United States Army to barge directly into consumers' homes and take their money at gunpoint and give it to you.

(d) Remind everybody a lot about Pearl Harbor.

CORRECT ANSWER: These are all pretty good.

4. You are in charge of a large department, and you have an opening for a supervisor. The two obviously best-qualified candidates are women who have worked in the department for the same amount of time. Both are intelligent, highly competent, and respected by the other employees. In every way they seem equally qualified, although it happens that one of them is black. What decision do you make?

(a) You promote the black woman, on the theory that it will help compensate for past injustices.

(b) You promote the white woman, on the theory that if you promote the black woman, people will say it was just because she's black.

(c) You flip a coin.

CORRECT ANSWER: You promote a man.

HOW TO SCORE
Give yourself one point for each close friend you have in the Personnel Department.

Chapter One

THE HISTORY OF BUSINESS

When we look around us at the modern world, we see businesses everywhere, unless of course we happen to be, for example, in the bathroom. But even there, we see EVIDENCE of a thriving industrial economy, such as the Ty-D-Bowl automatic commode freshener. Sitting there and thinking about it, you have to marvel at the incredible creativity and diversity of the business world. Where did all of this come from? How did the human race get from the point of being primitive and stupid to the point where it could automatically, without lifting a finger, turn its toilet water blue? Let's see if we can answer some of these questions. My guess is we can't.

THE VERY FIRST BUSINESSES

Many, many years ago, there was no business on Earth. This is because the Earth was primarily molten lava, which is not a good economic climate. Office furniture would melt in a matter of seconds.

Then the Earth started to cool, and tiny one-celled animals—the amigo, the paramedic, the rotarian—began to form. Over the course of several million years, these animals learned to join together to form primitive corporations, called "jellyfish," which were capable of only the most basic business activities, such as emitting waste and eating lunch. By today's standards, these corporations were very unsophisticated: if, for example, you mentioned the phrase "Dow Jones Industrial Average" to them, they would have no idea what you were talking about. They would probably sting you.

DID DINOSAURS HAVE BUSINESSES?

Nobody can really say for sure, because the Ice Age destroyed all their records. But paleontologists now believe that, yes, dinosaurs probably did have businesses. Not the Brontosaurus, of course. That would be ridiculous. How would he hold his briefcase? But the Tyrannosaurus Rex has those funny little arms, which would have been perfect (see diagram at left). Paleontologists think he was probably in Sales.

PRIMITIVE HUMAN BUSINESSES

When primitive humans first came along, they did not engage in business as we now think of it. They engaged in squatting around in caves naked. This went on for, I would say, roughly two or three million years, when all of a sudden a primitive person, named Oog, came up with an idea. "Why not," he said, "pile thousands of humongous stones on top of each other in the desert to form great big geometric shapes?" Well, everybody thought this was an absolutely *terrific* idea, and soon they were hard at work. It wasn't until several thousand years later that they realized they had been suckered into a classic "pyramid" scheme, and of course by that time, Oog was in the Bahamas.

BUSINESS
DURING THE MIDDLE AGES

Business during the Middle Ages was slow. The main job opportunity available was serf, which involved whacking at the soil with a stick. It was not the kind of work where you had a lot of room for advancement. The best a serf could hope for, if he was really good at it, was that he would be rewarded by not having one of his arms sliced off by a passing knight.

If you wanted to be a knight you had to know somebody, and it really wasn't that much better than being a serf. You were always being sent off to try to get the Holy Land back from the Turks. This was no fun at all, because of course the Holy Land is very sunny, meaning your armor would get hot enough to fry an egg on. In fact the Turks, who dressed in light, casual, 100 percent cotton garments, would often do this. They'd sneak up behind a knight and crack an egg on his armor, then race away, laughing in Turkish, before he could turn around. So as you can imagine, knights would come back in a pretty bad mood, and often would have to slice off several serf arms before they even wanted to *talk* about it.

So the bottom line is that the Middle Ages were hardly the kind of ages where anybody wanted to make any long-term business commitments. All the really smart investors were waiting for the Renaissance.

THE RENAISSANCE

The Renaissance was caused by Leonardo da Vinci, who drew the first primitive sketches of what would eventually become the helicopter. Of course, nobody really understood the significance of this at the time. But people did realize that, whatever this new invention was, it was going to require a tremendous amount of insurance. Thus a major business was born.

This was followed by trade with the Orient. The way this worked was, Europeans would gather up some gold, and they would tromp across Asia to the Orient, where they would trade their gold for spices. They didn't really *want* spices, you understand, but the Orientals claimed that spice was all they had, and the Europeans, having tromped all that way, wanted to take home *something*.

After some years of this, the Europeans were starting to run out of gold. Also their food was so heavily spiced that it glowed in the dark. They probably would have all died of heartburn if Columbus had not discovered the New World.

THE BIRTH OF THE HELICOPTER

THE NEW WORLD

Every schoolchild is familiar with the story of how Columbus set off in three tiny ships (the *Pinto,* the *Cordoba,* and the *Coupe de Ville*), and right away his crew started getting very nauseous and asking why for God's sake he had decided on three *tiny* ships instead of one *medium* ship. Nevertheless Columbus pressed on, ignoring popular fears that he would sail off the edge of the Earth, and finally he and his hardy band made it to the New World, except for the *Pinto,* which mysteriously exploded, and the *Cordoba,* which due to a navigational error actually *did* sail off the edge of the Earth.

The New World had an extremely good business climate. For one thing, there was plenty of land, and nobody owned it, unless you counted the people who had been living there for several thousand years. For another thing, it had an abundance of the two crucial factors you need for economic development: Water Power, in the form of rivers, and Raw Materials, in the form of ore. So soon millions of Europeans flocked over to the New World to make their fortunes. They stood around all day, sunup to sundown, throwing handfuls of ore into the rivers and waiting for economic development to take place. They would have starved to death if a friendly Indian named Squanto (which is Indian for "Native American") hadn't come along and shown them how to plant corn. "You put the seeds in the ground," explained Squanto. He couldn't believe what kind of morons he was dealing with.

Soon the corn came up, and the Europeans decided to celebrate by inviting all the Indians over for a big Thanksgiving dinner, then sending them off to live on reservations in North Dakota.

THE RISE OF THE MODERN CORPORATION

At the beginning of the modern corporate era, many businesses actually made things. Typically, they'd get hold of a Raw Material, which they'd smelt and pour into a mold, where it would cool and form a product, which they'd sell for a profit, which the owner would use to buy his family a nice house on Long Island.

The problem was that when the owner died, the family members were darned if they'd come in off Long Island and engage in anything as filthy as smelting, so they'd hire a professional manager to run the business. Often, however, the professional manager was a graduate of Harvard Business School, and consequently *he* wasn't exactly dying to smelt either. So he'd dream up other corporate activities for himself to engage in, such as Marketing, Long-Range Planning, Management by Objectives, and Lunch, and he'd hire additional managers, who of course would turn right around and hire managers of their own, and so on.

This is how we arrived at the modern corporation, where at the very top you have a chief executive who spends his entire day posing for Annual Report photographs and testifying before Congress; and beneath him you have several thousand executives engaged in "middle management," which is the corporate term for "management activities in which there is no possible way for anybody to tell whether you're screwing up"; and beneath them you have tens of thousands of secretarial, clerical, and reception personnel; and beneath *them,* somewhere in a factory nobody ever goes to because there is no decent place around it where you can have lunch, you have the actual production work force, which consists of a grizzled old veteran employee named "Bud."

This modern corporate system offers something for everybody:

• THE EXECUTIVES get enormous salaries and bonuses and stock options and offices big enough to play jai alai in.

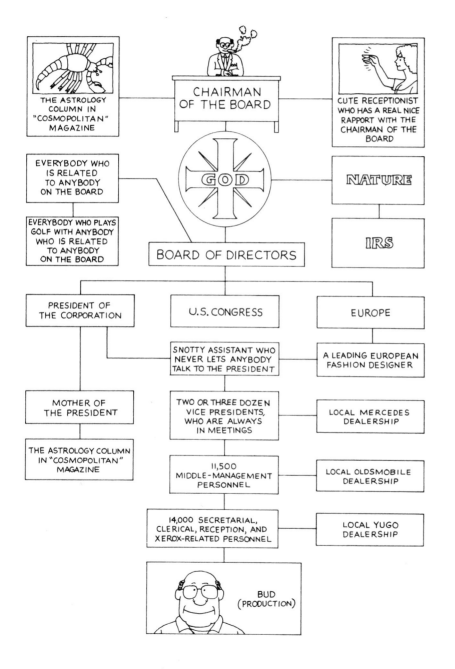

THE ASTROLOGY COLUMN IN "COSMOPOLITAN" MAGAZINE

CHAIRMAN OF THE BOARD

CUTE RECEPTIONIST WHO HAS A REAL NICE RAPPORT WITH THE CHAIRMAN OF THE BOARD

EVERYBODY WHO IS RELATED TO ANYBODY ON THE BOARD

GOD

NATURE

EVERYBODY WHO PLAYS GOLF WITH ANYBODY WHO IS RELATED TO ANYBODY ON THE BOARD

BOARD OF DIRECTORS

IRS

PRESIDENT OF THE CORPORATION

U.S. CONGRESS

EUROPE

SNOTTY ASSISTANT WHO NEVER LETS ANYBODY TALK TO THE PRESIDENT

A LEADING EUROPEAN FASHION DESIGNER

MOTHER OF THE PRESIDENT

TWO OR THREE DOZEN VICE PRESIDENTS, WHO ARE ALWAYS IN MEETINGS

LOCAL MERCEDES DEALERSHIP

THE ASTROLOGY COLUMN IN "COSMOPOLITAN" MAGAZINE

11,500 MIDDLE-MANAGEMENT PERSONNEL

LOCAL OLDSMOBILE DEALERSHIP

14,000 SECRETARIAL, CLERICAL, RECEPTION, AND XEROX-RELATED PERSONNEL

LOCAL YUGO DEALERSHIP

BUD (PRODUCTION)

- **THE SECRETARIAL, CLERICAL, AND RECEPTION PERSONNEL** get medical plans, dental plans, pension plans, savings plans, go-to-college plans, stop-smoking plans, lose-weight plans, softball plans, and bulletin boards it takes upwards of two working days to read.
- **THE STOCKHOLDERS** get regular annual reports printed on top-quality paper informing them that despite less-than-projected earnings caused by impossible-to-foresee foreign-currency fluctuations exacerbated by a short-term restructuring of the long-term capitalized debenturization of the infrastructure and the discovery that certain moths may mate for life, the future continues to look very bright inasmuch as the corporation quite frankly has the best darned management team the human mind can conceive of.
- **BUD** gets regular five-minute breaks.

AND SO . . .

. . . and so we have come to the present day, to the incredibly sophisticated world of the modern corporation—a world that YOU, thanks to this book, are about to become part of! In the next chapter, we'll talk about how you can land that all-important entry-level job, so you'll want to study it *very carefully!* Unless your dad owns the company, in which case you can head on out to the golf course.

Chapter Two

GETTING A JOB

In this chapter, we'll take you step-by-step through the job-hunting process, starting right at the beginning.

BIRTH

This is the time to start preparing for your business career. You can bet your little navel protuberance that the *other* babies are preparing, and you don't want to fall so far behind that they wind up as vice-presidents and you wind up serving them food and wearing a comical white hat in the corporate cafeteria. In fact, I'd recommend that you start preparing *before* birth, except that you'd have trouble seeing the flashcards.

The flashcard procedure is as follows: you lie on your back in your crib, and your parents lean over you and hold up cards, each of which has printed on it a basic fact that will help you succeed in business.

As your parents show you the card, they should read it out loud in a perky voice, as though they are just having the time of their lives,

295

and you should indicate comprehension by waving your arms and pooping.

You should spend as much time with the flashcards as possible. Ideally, you'll reach adolescence without ever once getting an unobstructed view of your parents' faces. As an adult, you'll carry around a little wallet card that says "7 × 9 = 63," because it will remind you of Mother.

PRESCHOOL

Look for a strong pre-business curriculum, one that emphasizes practical activities, such as blocks, over liberal-arts activities, such as gerbils.

ELEMENTARY SCHOOL

This is where you should learn to add, subtract, multiply, and divide, which are skills that are essential for filling out expense reports; you should also develop lifelong chumships with anybody whose name ends in "II," or, even better, "III." You might also consider learning to read. This is not really necessary, of course, inasmuch as you will have a secretary for this purpose, but some businesspersons like to occasionally do it themselves for amusement on long airplane trips.

HIGH SCHOOL

The point of high school is to get yourself into a good college. The way you do this is by being well rounded, which is measured by how many organizations you belong to. Many college admissions officers select students by actually slapping a ruler down on the list of accomplishments underneath each applicant's high school yearbook picture. So you should join every one of the ludicrous high school organizations available to you, such as the Future Appliance Owners Club and the National Honor Society. If they won't let you into the National Honor Society, have your parents file a lawsuit alleging discrimination on the basis of intelligence.

Another thing you need to do in high school is get good SAT scores, which are these two numbers you receive in the mail from the Educational Testing Service in Princeton, New Jersey. They have a whole warehouse filled with numbers up there. To get yours, you have to send some money off by mail to Princeton, then you have to go sit in a room full of other students with number-two pencils and answer questions like "BRAZIL is to COMPENSATE as LUST is to. . . ." Then you have to look at the various multiple choices and try to figure out what kind of mood the folks up at the Educational Testing Service were in on the day they made up that particular question.

Nobody has the vaguest idea anymore how this elaborate ritual got started, what it has to do with anything in the real world, or how the Educational Testing Service decides what numbers to send you. My personal theory is that it has to do with how much money you send them in the mail. I think the amounts they tell you to send are actually just Suggested Minimum Donations, if you get my drift.

COLLEGE

College is basically a large group of buildings, usually separated by lawns, where you go to major in business. This means you must avoid:

• Courses where you have to trace the Development of something, such as the Novel.

- Courses that involve numbers that cannot be categorized as debits or credits, such as "square roots."
- Courses involving a foreign language, such as French (this also includes courses involving funny-sounding English, like in those old plays where everybody is always saying: "Whatst? Dost thou sittest upon mine horst? Egad!" etc.).
- Any course involving maps, the Renaissance, or specific dates such as "1066."
- Any course where you sit around a classroom trying to figure out what the hell Truth is.

What you want to take are courses that have the word "Business" in them somewhere, such as Introduction to Business, Getting to Know Business a Little Better, Kissing Business Right on the Lips, etc.

GRADUATE SCHOOL

There are advantages and disadvantages to going to graduate school. The main advantage is that if you go to a really good graduate school, like Harvard, you'll have a very easy time finding a good job. At night, as you lie in your bed, your window will often be broken by stones, around which have been wrapped lucrative offers. The main disadvantage is that you couldn't get admitted to Harvard even if you held the dean's wife at gunpoint. So I think you're better off applying for a job.

ARE THERE JOBS AVAILABLE?

Heck yes! Don't you listen to those Negative Nellies who tell you there aren't any good jobs anymore, just because the steel, automobile, shoe, clothing, railroad, and agricultural industries have all collapsed! There are new career opportunities opening up all the time in today's fast-changing economy. Just to give you an idea, let's look at

LOBSTER REPAIR:
A FAST-GROWING FIELD

You know how, when you go into a seafood restaurant, they have the lobsters up front, in a tank, all trying to scuttle back out of the way and hide under each other so they won't get eaten? Well, it's inevitable that some lobsters get damaged in the process—broken claws, eye stalks falling off, that kind of thing. And then you have the problem that (a) you have damaged lobsters, which you can't serve to your customers and (b) you have these loose random eye stalks lying around the bottom of your tank, which hardly act as a Cheerful Greeting to your incoming customers. This is why there is such a tremendous demand today for people who know how, using modern adhesives, to reassemble a damaged lobster, or use the leftover parts to construct a whole *new* one, often incorporating a new and improved design ("Hey," more than one delighted restaurant patron has cried recently. "My lobster has a claw made entirely out of eye stalks!").

And this is just *one* new emerging-growth career field. Others include: Drug Overlord; Computer Geek; Televised Christian; Person Who Sells Staples to the Defense Department for What It Cost to Liberate France; Vigilante; and Pip, whose job is to stand behind Gladys Knight and go "whooo whooo" at certain points during the song, "Midnight Train to Georgia."

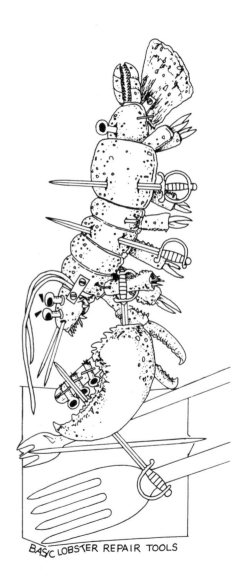

BASIC LOBSTER REPAIR TOOLS

WHERE SHOULD YOU BEGIN YOUR JOB SEARCH?

WELDER WANTED—To weld certain pieces of metal together.

ADMINISTRATIVE ASSISTANT

Young-thinking, fast-moving, forward-looking emerging-growth company with dynamic, attractive plant-filled lobby featuring modernistic, incomprehensible sculpture and old, heavily thumbed issues of *Pork Buyer Weekly* seeks eager, ambitious, personable, aggressive, can-do, confident, hard-driving, highly motivated self-starter to clean scum-encrusted office coffee-related implements.

The answer to that question is right in your local newspaper. That's right! Every day, hundreds of employers pay good money to advertise jobs in the classified ad section, apparently unaware that practically nobody reads it! So I want you to turn to the help wanted section right now and locate all the ads that look promising.

The way to do this is to count the adjectives. For example, take the ads shown at left.

The first ad contains only one adjective, and thus represents a poor career opportunity. The second ad, on the other hand, clearly offers a very exciting opportunity, based on the adjective count.

YOUR RESUME

Your resume is more than just a piece of paper: it is a piece of paper with lies written all over it. Often, a good resume can mean the difference between not getting a job and not even coming close.

In writing your resume, you should follow the format shown in the example on page 15, although you might want to modify it to suit your individual situation. For example, you may want to use your own name, instead of the word "NAME." Unless you have a name like "Dewey."

A lot of people make a really stupid mistake, namely, they send their resume to the Personnel Department. Pay close attention here: NEVER SEND ANYTHING TO THE PERSONNEL DEPARTMENT.

```
                    RESUME

NAME:    (Last name first, first name in
         the middle, middle name way off
         to the right, in a little box.
         Should sound British.)

ADDRESS: (Include clear directions as to
         how to get there, such as, "If
         you come to a Dairy Queen on your
         left, you have gone too far.")

PHONE:   (Specify whether "Princess" or
         "Standard" model; note any special
         features such as "last number re-
         dial.")

CAREER OBJECTIVE:  (This should sound like
the speeches given by Miss America contes-
tants to demonstrate that they have a Per-
sonality.  For example: "I would very much
like to utilize my skills to the greatest
of my ability in hopes of achieving a sig-
nificant degree of accomplishment."  Leave
out the part about hoping someday to work
with handicapped animals.)


SUMMARY OF CAREER ACCOMPLISHMENTS:  (The
important thing here is verbs.  Verbs verbs
verbs! You want to sound like a person with
a slightly overactive thyroid.  Be vague.
Lie.  Remember that nobody's going to read
this.)

   September, 1985 to present: ADMINISTRATOR.
   Initiate, coordinate, participate,
   and eliminate all traces of long-
```

```
and short-term mid-range interim
approaches.

1983 to 1985:  COORDINATOR.
Gathered, analyzed, and collated
a wide range of data, then kneaded
it on a floured surface and baked
it in a moderate oven until a tooth-
pick inserted in the center came
out clean.  Served six.
REASON FOR LEAVING:  Communists.

1981 to 1983:  ASSOCIATE.
Put my right hand in, took my right
hand out, did the hokey-pokey, and
shook it all about.
REASON FOR LEAVING:  Ennui.

              EDUCATION

GRADUATE SCHOOL:  Harvard and Yale University
School of Learning, Ph.D. in Business Appli-
ance Management, 1980.

COLLEGE: Fargo and Surrounding Farms College
of Arts and Sciences Such as Long Division,
B.M. in Restaurant Communications, 1978.

              REFERENCES

I should be happy to supply the names of any
number of deceased grade-school teachers upon
request.
```

The absolute last thing the people in Personnel want the company to do is hire you. They don't want the company to hire *anybody,* because it just means more work for them. As far as Personnel is concerned, every new employee is one more cretin who will never learn how to fill out his medical and dental claim forms correctly.

So if you send your resume to Personnel, they'll set fire to it immediately and send you back the following letter:

```
Dear (YOUR NAME):

Thank you so very, very much for sending us
your resume.  What a nice surprise it was!
"Look at this,"  the mail person cried as we
all gathered 'round.  "(YOUR NAME) has been
so kind as to send us his or her resume!"
What excitement there was, here in Personnel!
We danced far into the night!

Sadly, however, we do not expect to have any
positions available until approximately the
end of time.  We will, however, keep the re-
mains of your resume on file, in a tasteful
urn, and you may rest assured that nobody
will disturb it except for routine dusting.


Sincerely,

The Personnel Department

LG:pu
```

So the question becomes: what do you do with your resume? My advice is, set fire to it yourself. Nobody ever reads resumes anyway. I only told you to write one because it's an old jobseeker tradition, and we have so few traditions left.

Good! We've taken care of that! Now let's move on to the next step, which is. . .

WRITING AN EFFECTIVE LETTER THAT WILL GET YOU A JOB INTERVIEW

In an ideal world, of course, your letter would say, "Dear Sir or Madam: Give me a job interview or I will kill your spouse."

But we do not live in an ideal world. We live in a world that has strict postal regulations regarding what you can say in letters. So you're going to have to take the "soft sell" approach to getting an interview. Chances are, you've already written such a letter, and chances are it sounds something like this:

```
Dear Sirs or Madams:

As a dynamic, eager, hardworking young
person who brings an enormous quantity
of enthusiasm to every task, on account
of being so eager, I am writing to ex-
press my sincere desire to be considered
for the position of Employee within your
company.  I am confident that once we
have had a chance at some mutual and con-
venient time to meet and shake hands
firmly while making eye contact and re-
viewing all my major accomplishments
dating back to the birth canal, you will
realize how mutually beneficial it would
be for your firm and myself to seek some
means of achieving our future goals in
a way that would benefit both parties.
Mutually.  I shall contact your office
by telephone every seven or eight min-
utes, starting this morning, to determine
a time that would be mutual and dynamic
for you.


Very sincerely,
Byron B. Buffington II
Byron B. Buffington II
```

The advantage of this kind of letter is that it has a confident, positive, assertive, enthusiastic tone. The disadvantage is that it makes you sound like the biggest jerk ever to roam the planet. I mean, look at it from the perspective of the people at the company: they have to actually *work* with the people they hire, and nobody is going to want to work with a little rah-rah snotface.

What you want is a job application letter that makes you sound like a regular person, somebody who would be fun to work with:

```
Hey--

So the priest says to the rabbi, he
says, "But how do you get the snake to
wear lipstick?" Ha ha! Get it? Say,
did you get a load of the new clerk in
Accounts Receivable? Whoooo! She is so
ugly, it takes two men and a strong dog
just to look at her! Ha ha! How about
those Giants? I don't know about you,
but I say we knock off early today.


Take it easy,



Byron "The Buffer" Buffington
```

WHOM YOU SHOULD
SEND YOUR LETTER TO

A vice-president. It makes no difference which one. All vice-presidents do exactly the same thing with their mail, namely write the first name of a middle-management subordinate in the upper right-hand corner, followed by a question mark, like this: "Dan?" They do this by reflex action to everything placed in front of them, usually without reading it, then they toss it into the "OUT" basket. If an employee is hospitalized and a get-well card is passed around the company, it usually winds up with an unintelligible blot in the upper right-hand corner where all the vice-presidents wrote the names of subordinates followed by question marks.

Nobody will ever dare throw your letter away, once a vice-president has written on it. Eventually somebody is going to ask you to come in for an interview, if only to find out how the snake joke starts.

HOW TO PREPARE
FOR YOUR JOB INTERVIEW

One obvious way to remain calm and perspiration free during an interview, of course, is narcotics, but there you run into the problem of scratching yourself and trying to steal things off the interviewer's desk. So as a precaution, what most veteran employment counselors recommend is that you wear "dress shields," which, as some of you women already know, are these highly absorbent devices that you stuff into your armpits. They are available in bulk at any good employment agency. For a job interview, you should stuff three or four shields into each pit. This will cause your arms to stick out from your body at an odd angle, so to prevent your interviewer from attaching any significance to this, you want to begin the interview with a casual remark, as is illustrated by the following "model" interview dialog:

INTERVIEWER: Hello, Bob. Nice to meet you.
YOU: There's nothing odd about *my* arms!

THE INTERVIEW PROCESS

Basically, what the interviewer wants to know is how well you can "think on your feet." So what he'll try to do, with his questions, is throw you some "curve balls," which means you should come to the interview well supplied with snappy retorts. Let's go back to our "model" interview:

INTERVIEWER: Tell me, Bob, why are you interested in coming to work for us?
YOU: Who wants to know?
INTERVIEWER: Ha ha! Got me there! Bob, what specific strengths do you feel you would bring to this job?
YOU: So's your old man!
INTERVIEWER (tears of laughter streaming down his face):   Bob, you sound like the kind of quick-thinking employee we are looking for! How about a large starting salary?
YOU: You and what army?

CONGRATULATIONS

You've got the job! In the next chapter, you'll learn how to figure out what exactly the nature of this job is—specifically, whether it involves any duties, and if so, how you can get out of them.

Chapter Three

HOW TO DO YOUR JOB, WHATEVER IT IS

To really succeed in a business or organization, it is sometimes helpful to know what your job is, and whether it involves any duties. Try to find this out in your first couple of weeks by asking around among your co-workers. "Hi," you should say. "I'm Byron Buffington, a new employee! What's the name of my job?" If they answer Long-Range Planner or Lieutenant Governor, you are pretty much free to lounge around and do crossword puzzles until retirement. Most other jobs, however, will involve some work.

There are two major kinds of work in the modern corporation or organization:

1. Taking phone messages for people who are in meetings; and

2. Going to meetings.

Your ultimate career strategy will be to get to a job involving primarily number two, going to meetings, as soon as possible, because that's where the real prestige is. But most corporations and organizations like to start everybody out with a couple of years of taking messages, so we'll discuss this important basic business skill first.

TAKING A PHONE MESSAGE

When the phone rings, lift the receiver, punch whichever button is lit, and say: "Thank you for calling the Marketing Department (or whatever). Kindly hold the line." Then quickly punch the hold button.

Now you should check around briefly to make sure that everybody the caller could possibly want to talk to is in a meeting. This is also a good time to go to the bathroom. When you return, punch the hold button again, and say: "I am sorry, but whomever the person is to whom you wish to speak is in a meeting at this present time and is expected to remain there until at least the next major economic recession. Did you wish to leave a message?"

Now this is very important: the *instant* the caller starts to respond, you must say: "Will you please hold again for a moment?" and punch the hold button with a very rapid and sure motion. Now you should head on down to the Supplies Cabinet and get some handy preprinted phone message forms, in case the caller did wish to leave a message.

When you get back to the desk, push the button again and say, "I am sorry. Now, did you wish to leave a message?" And the caller will say something like, "Listen, I'm calling from France and I don't *want* Marketing, so could you ask the operator to transfer. . . ."

Now at this point, if you are an experienced message-taker, your sixth sense tells you the caller is *just about to complete a sentence,* and we certainly don't want *that* to happen! So you will have to very quickly—but politely!—ask the caller to please hold the line again for a moment, and at the same time strike the hold button the way a hungry cobra strikes a small furry mammal.

Okay, we're almost ready to take the actual message. Punch the button again, and say (in case the caller has forgotten): "Thank you for calling the Marketing Department! How may we help you?" Now at this point, there is every likelihood that the caller will have hung up. This might seem like a major obstacle, in terms of being able to take a message, but it is not, thanks to the handy preprinted phone message forms that you got from the Supplies Cabinet. Here is what they look like:

WHILE YOU WERE OUT IN A MEETING

Mr./Mrs./Miss/
Ms./Rev./Massa/ _____
(name)

Check one:

( ) Telephoned.
( ) Did not telephone.
( ) Thought about telephoning, but then changed his or her mind.
( ) Telephoned, but could not for the LIFE of him or her remember why.
( ) Telephoned, then hung right up, but I am certain it was him or her.
( ) Wants you to call and attempt to leave a message for him or her.
( ) Wants to fire you.
( ) Wants to reveal a sordid episode from his or her past involving a goat.
( ) Wants to end World Hunger in our lifetime.
( ) Wants your body.
( ) Wants for nothing.
( ) Wants to tell you the joke about the man who finds out he has only eight hours to live, so he goes home and makes love with his wife once, twice, three times, and finally they fall asleep, and at 3 A.M. he tries to wake her up, and she says, "Not AGAIN! Some of us have to get up in the morning!"
( ) Ate paste as a child.
( ) Has the clap.

So all you have to do is check the appropriate space to indicate what message you feel the caller would have left if he or she had had the time. The only hard part is deciding what name you put where it says "name." I recommend you put the name of a corporate vice-president, for two reasons:

1. It will enhance your reputation as a person who has spoken directly to a vice-president; and

2. Nobody will ever be able to prove that you're wrong. Any attempt to contact the vice-president about his "message" will result in failure, because he will of course be in a meeting.

Okay. It is all very well and good to be able to take phone messages, but you are never going to get to a position of corporate power, a position where you can cost thousands of people their jobs with a single bonehead decision, until you learn how to attend meetings.

THE CORPORATE MEETING

It might be useful to compare the modern corporate meeting to a football huddle, in which the people attending the meeting are a "team," attempting to come up with a "play" in which each team member will be assigned responsibility to "block" a specific "defender" so that a "fullback" will be able to carry the ball through a "hole" in the "line" and get into the "end zone" for a "touchdown," which will cause everybody to exchange "high-five" handshakes and slap each other on the "butt." So we can see that in fact it is not at all useful to compare a modern corporate meeting to a football huddle. It was a pretty stupid idea, and I apologize for it.

Perhaps a better analogy would be to compare the modern corporate meeting to a funeral, in the sense that you have a gathering of people who are wearing uncomfortable clothing and would rather be somewhere else. The major differences are that:

1. Usually only one or two people get to talk at a funeral; and

2. Most funerals have a definite purpose (to say nice things about a dead person) and reach a definite conclusion (this person is put in the ground), whereas meetings generally drone on until the legs of the highest-ranking person present fall asleep.

Also, nothing is ever really buried in a meeting. An idea may *look* dead, but it will always reappear at another meeting later on. If you have ever seen the movie *Night of the Living Dead,* you have a rough idea how modern corporations and organizations operate, with projects and proposals that everybody thought were killed constantly rising from their graves to stagger back into meetings and eat the brains of the living.

HOW TO ACT IN A MEETING

This depends on what kind of meeting it is. There are two major kinds:

1. MEETINGS THAT ARE HELD FOR BASICALLY THE SAME REASON THAT ARBOR DAY IS OBSERVED, namely, tradition. For example, a lot of managerial people like to meet on Monday, because it is Monday. You'll get used to it. You'd better, because this kind of meeting accounts for 83 percent of all meetings held (based on a study in which I wrote down numbers until one of them looked about right).

This kind of meeting operates the way "Show and Tell" operates in nursery school, with everybody getting to say something, the difference being that in nursery school the kids actually have something new to say. When it's your turn, you should say you're still working on whatever it is you're supposed to be working on. This may seem pretty dumb, since *obviously* you'd be working on whatever you're supposed to be working on, and even if you weren't, you'd *claim* you were, but this is the traditional thing for everybody to say. It would be a lot faster if the person running the meeting would just say, "Everybody who is still working on whatever he or she is supposed to be working on, raise your hand!" You'd all be out of there in five minutes, even allowing time for jokes. But this is not how we do it in America. My guess is, it's how they do it over in Japan.

2. MEETINGS WHERE THERE IS SOME ALLEGED PURPOSE. These are trickier, because what you do depends on what the purpose is. Sometimes the purpose is harmless, like somebody wants to show everybody slides of pie charts and give everybody a copy of a big fat report. All you have to do in this kind of meeting is sit there and have elaborate sexual fantasies, then take the report back to your office and throw it away, unless of course you're a vice-president, in which case you write the name of a subordinate in the upper right-hand corner, followed by a question mark, like this: "Norm?" Then you send it to Norm and forget all about it (although it will plague old Norm for the rest of his career).

But sometimes you go to meetings where the purpose is to get your "input" on something. This is very serious, because what it means is, they want to make sure that in case whatever it is turns out to be stupid or fatal, you'll get some of the blame. I mean, if they thought it was any good, they wouldn't want your "input," would they? So you have to somehow escape from the meeting before they get around to asking you anything. One way is to set fire to your tie. Another is to have an accomplice interrupt the meeting and announce that you have a phone call from somebody very important, such as the president of the company, or the Pope. It should be either one or the other. It would sound fishy if the accomplice said, "You have a call from the president of the company. Or the Pope."

A FUN THING TO DO IF SOMEBODY FALLS ASLEEP IN A MEETING

Have everybody leave the room, then collect a group of total strangers, from right off the street, and have them sit around the sleeping person and stare at him until he wakes up. Then have one of them say to him, in a very somber voice, "Bob, your plan is very, very risky, but you've given us no choice but to try it. I only hope, for your sake, that you know what the hell you're getting yourself into." Then they should file quietly from the room.

HOW TO TAKE
NOTES DURING A MEETING

Use a yellow legal pad. At the top, write the date and underline it twice:

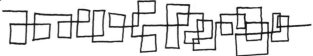

Now wait until an important person such as your boss starts talking. When he does, look at him with a look of enraptured interest, as though he is revealing the secrets of life itself. Then write interlocking rectangles, like this:

If it is an especially lengthy meeting, you can try something like this:

After a while, you will want to fill in any holes in the date:

Also, if you're sitting next to somebody you can trust, you can use your notepad to discuss various other people at the meeting:

EL DORKO

SPECIAL NOTE OF ENCOURAGEMENT TO TIMID HOUSEWIVES WHO HAVE BEEN THINKING ABOUT MAYBE TRYING TO GET INTO THE BUSINESS WORLD BUT ARE WORRIED THAT IT MIGHT BE TOO HARD AND THEY MIGHT NOT BE QUALIFIED TO DO ANYTHING EXCEPT MAKE TUNA CASSEROLE

Boy, are YOU ever in for a surprise. I mean, here you have been staying home, day after day, cooking meals and doing the laundry and praising the primitive refrigerator art your children produce and scrubbing away at the advanced fungal growths around the base of the toilet, during which time your husband has been GONE. And when he gets home, all he has the energy to do is just COLLAPSE on the Barca-Lounger and talk about what a DIFFICULT DAY he has had because the ACCOUNTS RECEIVABLE (whatever *that* is) won't "BALANCE" (whatever *that* means). So you have naturally come to believe that whatever goes on in the business world must be just DEATHLY difficult and complex, to cause a grown man such ANGUISH.

Well, just you wait until, following the program outlined in this book, you get your first actual job in business. You are going to think you died and went straight to heaven. For one thing, everybody there is a GROWNUP. They allow NO CHILDREN in business. You never have to take ANYBODY, for any reason, to the potty. Speaking of which, if a business toilet gets dirty, you just CALL MAINTENANCE ON THE PHONE, and THEY COME AND CLEAN IT! And if they don't, YOU CAN WRITE A SNOTTY MEMO-RANDUM ABOUT IT!

And the best part of it is—as you will see, once we get into how businesses work—YOU NEED NO SPECIAL SKILLS OR QUALIFICATIONS TO BE PART OF A BUSINESS. All you have to do is figure out what simple concept the other people are really talking about when they use their complex business terms. For example, when your husband says the "Accounts Receivable" won't "balance," what he means is, he has these two NUMBERS that are supposed to be the SAME, but instead they're DIFFERENT. Is that pathetic, or what? I mean, really, would you call that a PROBLEM? Especially if you compare it with, say, a situation where you're at the shopping mall Burger King and you have finally managed to get your food and your children and your packages to a table, and just as you start to bite into your Whopper Junior, your two-year-old knocks his chocolate milk onto a priest, your six-year-old commences projectile vomiting and your four-year-old wanders off, enraptured, in the company of a toothless man with needle marks and Nazi tattoos. Now THIS is what I would call a PROBLEM, and you have to deal with it ALL BY YOURSELF. Meanwhile, back at "work," your husband is drinking nice hot coffee in a nice clean vomit-free office, fretting about his two little NUMBERS with the aid of a COM-PUTER and probably three or four CO-WORKERS, all of whom will eventually go have a nice quiet lunch featuring MARGARITAS and NO CHILDREN.

So trust me, housewives. You'll do FINE in the business world. Your husband does, right? How hard can it be?

Chapter Four

STEPPING OVER YOUR CO-WORKERS

Okay. Now you can take phone messages. You can go to meetings. In short, you can do everything that can be reasonably expected of an employee. If you want, you can spend the rest of your professional life very comfortably doing these things. Ultimately, you can look forward to getting a couple of small promotions, followed by retirement, followed by death, followed by having your body eaten by insects and bacteria and then excreted in the form of basic chemicals that will serve as fertilizer for unattractive plants with names like "duckweed." Is that what you want?

I didn't think so. Because you're the kind of person who wants to be Number One. Not in the sense of being bacterial excrement, but in the sense of having POWER. We're talking about CLOUT. We're talking about having a staff so large that when you have a dental appointment, you send an aide to get *his* teeth drilled. We're talking about CLAWING YOUR WAY TO THE TOP.

GETTING PROMOTED

You can't expect to get a promotion right away, of course. You should wait two, maybe even three days before you start pushing for it. This will give you time to look around to see who your serious competitors are, to size them up, to evaluate their strengths and weaknesses, and to crush them under the freight elevator.

ATTILA AND BOB

ETHICAL QUESTION: DO YOU HAVE TO BE SCUM TO GET AHEAD?

As the famous baseball codger Leo Durocher was fond of saying before he died: "Nice guys finish last." There is some truth in this. Take the example of Attila the Hun, who was an unpleasant person but an extremely successful Hun, one of the top Huns in the business. His lesser-known brother, Bob the Hun, was a nice guy, but a failure. Bob would show up with this horde outside a medieval village and say, "Listen, would you folks mind if we raped the women and stole everything and killed everybody? You would? Oh my gosh! Sorry!" And off he'd slink, very embarrassed. His was by far the lowest-ranked horde in the league.

But that is just one isolated incident. There are plenty of examples of nice people who DID get to the top. Just look around! There's, ummmm, there's . . . ah, hmmmmm. Ha ha! I'm sure there are *lots* of examples, and for some reason I can't think of a single . . . *wait!* I've got one! Mother Theresa! That's it! Here's a very nice person who nevertheless rose to the top of her profession. So the moral is: even in this dog-eat-dog, highly competitive world, you *can* be a decent human being and still attain a career position where you kneel in the Third-World dirt trying to help the wretched and diseased. But if you want to succeed in a large modern corporation, scum is definitely the way to go.

Okay, let's talk nuts and bolts. In most corporations and organizations, a person gets promoted via a five-step procedure:

1. He works diligently and competently at his job for several years.

2. His superiors gradually start to notice him.

3. Somebody above him in the organization dies, retires, leaves, or is promoted, thus creating an opening.

4. His superiors, after carefully considering all the qualified candidates, promote him.

5. An announcement of the promotion is put up on bulletin boards throughout the building, and his co-workers gather around and pound him on the back (many of them aim for his kidneys).

This procedure is all well and good for most people, but you are not "most people." You are a highly motivated individual who wants to be on the fast track, and you cannot afford to fritter away valuable time working diligently and competently at your job. So your best bet is to skip over steps 1 through 4 and go directly to the only really essential step: the bulletin board announcement. Type it on a quality typewriter, using the format shown here.

That's it! All you have to do now is put it up on the bulletin boards and wait for the congratulations to pour in from your co-workers. Don't let them circle around behind you.

Okay, I know what some of you are thinking. You're thinking: "Dave, doesn't this particular method of career advancement carry with it a certain element of risk?"

I am very pleased to announce that (YOUR NAME) has been promoted to the position of (NAME OF POSITION YOU WOULD LIKE TO BE PROMOTED TO) and will henceforth receive a much larger salary. He will report to me, in the unlikely event he ever has anything to report.

(NAME OF RANDOM VICE-PRESIDENT)

PLEASE POST
ON
Bulletin Board

Yes, it does. For one thing, you have to be very careful about what position you promote yourself to. If you pick a position with a highly specific name such as Auditor, people might expect you to actually "audit" something. You want to pick a position involving words that could mean virtually anything, such as Coordinator and Administrator. If you promote yourself to Coordinating Administrator or Administrative Coordinator, nobody will ever be able to pin an actual job responsibility on you. You can devote full time to deciding on your next promotion.

Another possible problem is: What if your company uses the kind of bulletin boards that are covered by little locked glass doors? What you have to do here is find the person who has the key—this is going to be a low-level employee, of course—and make friends with him and explain that if he will let you use the key, you will promote him to a much, much better job than screwing around with bulletin boards. Like, if your company has a fleet of corporate jets, you could offer to make him a Senior Pilot.

HOW TO ACT LIKE AN EXECUTIVE

As you gradually work your way up through the organization over the course of, let's say, a week, you're going to have to change. You're going to have to become an executive. This means showing maturity, integrity, and leadership. It means having the foresight to know what needs to be done, and the courage to do it. It means not picking your nose in group situations. Did you ever see Lee Iacocca pick *his* nose? Or, for that matter, *anybody*'s nose? Of course not. Lee Iacocca didn't get to be one of the top executives in the history of the world by publicly engaging in personal nasal hygiene. He got there by wearing sharp clothes and smoking expensive cigars. He got there because he had executive *style*. You need to get hold of some, too.

I do not mean to suggest for a moment that all it takes to be a top executive is a custom-tailored European suit. You also need the correct shirt and tie. And for women executives, there is the whole issue of hosiery. This is why I have devoted an entire chapter later in this book to the crucial matter of your wardrobe. But for now we're going to talk about the human side of the executive's job, by which I mean the side where you use humans for various purposes.

DEALING WITH YOUR SUBORDINATES

Always remember this: your subordinates are not machines. They are human beings, with the same needs, the same wants, and the same dreams as you. Okay, maybe not *all* the same dreams. Probably they don't have the one where you're naked in a vat of Yoo-Hoo with the Soviet gymnastics team.

But they want to get ahead, just like you do. They, too, are part of the Carnival of American Capitalism. Like you, they want to reach out from the Carousel of Hard Work to grasp with Brass Ring of Success. And when, after riding 'round and 'round, they finally get their shot at realizing this dream, your job, as a caring and concerned superior, is to give them that extra shove they need to pitch forward off their horses and land headfirst among the Discarded Candied Apple Cores of Failure. Because there are only so many Brass Rings of Success, and you sure as hell don't want a bunch of subordinates barging past you and snatching them all.

So the trick, with subordinates, is to keep them happy, productive, hopeful, and—above all—subordinate. Here's how you do this:

1. MAKE THEM THINK YOU'RE THEIR FRIEND. The way you do this is by engaging in casual office banter with them to indicate that you are Just a Regular Person Who Really Cares for Them as Human Beings. Keep a little file with a three-by-five card for each subordinate, on which you've written personal details such as the subordinate's nickname, hobbies, sex, etc. Review these cards regularly, then go out and make personal remarks to your subordinates:

YOU: Hello, "Bob."
SUBORDINATE: Hello.
YOU (glancing at your three-by-five card):   So! You're still a white male with an interest in photography, eh, "Bob"?
SUBORDINATE: Yes sir.
YOU: Ha ha! Good. Let's engage in casual office banter again sometime soon, "Bob."
SUBORDINATE: Yes sir.
YOU (moving along to next subordinate):   Hello, there, "Chuck." I am very. . .
SUBORDINATE: Excuse me, sir, but my name is Mary. Chuck left last year.
YOU (testily):   Not according to this three-by-five card, he didn't!
SUBORDINATE: Yes sir.

YOU: As I was saying, "Chuck," I am very sorry your wife, Edna, died on October 3, 1981.
SUBORDINATE: Thank you, sir.

2. GET RID OF THEM IF THEY START COMING UP WITH IDEAS. Remember the old saying: "A subordinate capable of thinking up an idea is a subordinate capable of realizing that there is no particular reason why he or she should be a subordinate, especially *your* subordinate." This is why dogs are so popular as pets. You can have a dog for its whole lifetime, and it will never once come up with a good idea. It will lie around for over a decade, licking its private parts and always reacting with total wonder and amazement to *your* ideas. "What!?" says the dog, when you call it to the door. "You want me to go *outside!!?* What a *great* idea!!! I *never* would have thought of that!!!"

Cats, on the other hand, don't think you're the least bit superior. They're always watching you with that smartass cat expression and thinking, "God, what a cementhead." Cats are always coming up with their own ideas. They are not team players, and they would make terrible corporate employees. A corporate department staffed by cats would be a real disciplinary nightmare, the kind of department that would never achieve 100 percent of its "fair share" pledge quota to the United Way. Dogs, on the other hand, would go way over the quota. Of course they'd also chew up the pledge cards.

The point I'm trying to make here, as far as I can tell, is that you want subordinates who, when it comes to thinking up ideas, are more like dogs than like cats. Ideally, you should determine this before you hire people, by giving them a test, as explained in the box on page 38.

A DEPARTMENT STAFFED BY CATS WOULD BE A NIGHTMARE.

TEST TO FIND OUT IF A POTENTIAL EMPLOYEE IS THE KIND OF PERSON WHO THINKS UP IDEAS

Show the person three forms, marked A, B, and C. Tell him that part of his job would be to fill out the three forms, then throw Form B away. Stress that this is company policy. If he nods and says, "Okay," or if he asks you a question like, "How can you tell which one is Form B?" hire him. But if he says something like, "Gee, it seems kind of inefficient to fill out a form you're just going to throw away," get rid of him. This is the kind of person who will eventually, no matter how much training you give him, come up with an idea.

You should also check the person's references for telltale statements like: "Ellen comes up with a lot of good ideas." Or: "Ellen is a real innovator." What these people are trying to tell you is: "Ellen will get your job, and you'll wind up on the street licking the insides of discarded chicken gumbo soup cans."

HOW TO FIRE PEOPLE

This is the most painful part of being a supervisor, except for the part when you slam your finger in a file drawer. You never *want* to fire anybody, but sometimes you have an employee who has done something totally unacceptable, such as stealing, or drinking liquor on the job without sharing it, or coming up with an idea, and you have no choice but to let this person go.

There is no good way to fire an employee, but there are some things you can do to make it easier. You can have compassion. You can have understanding. You can have two large security guards named Bruno standing next to you and holding hot knitting needles. Call the employee in and say, "Ted, your performance has been unsatisfactory, so I'm afraid these two Brunos are going to have to poke out your eyes with hot knitting needles. I hate to do this, but the only alternative is to fire you." At this point, Ted will *beg* you to fire him. He may well confess to the Lindbergh baby kidnapping.

That about covers how you should behave around your subordinates. Now for the really important issue, which is

HOW YOU SHOULD BEHAVE AROUND OTHER EXECUTIVES

Years ago, corporation executives tended to be middle-aged white Anglo-Saxon Protestant males with as much individuality, style, and flair as generic denture adhesive. Today's corporations, however, thanks to a growing awareness of the value of diversity and of avoiding giant federal lawsuits, have opened their executive ranks to people of all races and sexes, provided they are willing to act, dress, and talk like middle-aged white Anglo-Saxon Protestant males. This is what you need to learn how to do.

LIST OF TOPICS THAT MIDDLE-AGED WHITE ANGLO-SAXON MALES TALK TO EACH OTHER ABOUT WHEN THEY'RE NOT TALKING BUSINESS

1. SPORTS.

As we can see from the above list, if you want to get along with the other executives, you have to learn how to talk about sports. This is pretty easy, if you know certain key phrases, as shown in the chart.

CHART OF KEY PHRASES TO USE WHEN TALKING ABOUT SPORTS

SPORT	SEASON	KEY PHRASE
FOOTBALL	July to February	"They got some really bad calls."
BASEBALL	March to October	"Some of those calls they got were really bad."
BASKETBALL	August to March	"I can't believe some of those calls they got."
ICE HOCKEY	Eternal	"Can you believe some of those calls they got?"

To you, these phrases may not seem to have a whole lot of meat on them, but believe me, middle-aged white Anglo-Saxon Protestant males can use them to keep a conversation going for hours.

Here's an interesting Ethical Question you might care to think about: If you go to a meeting of executives, and just by chance it happens that not a single one of you is a middle-aged white Anglo-Saxon Protestant male, do you still have to talk about sports? Or could you, in that one meeting, without telling anybody else, switch over to another topic, such as the theater? ("I can't believe some of the reviews they got!")

My personal feeling about this is, it's not worth the risk. Somebody might report you.

JOINING A CLUB

At some point, if you really want to make it to the top, you have to join a club. Actually, you have to join *two* clubs: one should be in the city, and it should be very old and have big dark drafty rooms where deceased members sit and read the paper all day. It should also have really bad food. The idea is, when you want to make a deal with an important client, you take him to your club for lunch, and eventually he realizes that unless the two of you reach an agreement, you'll take him to your club again, so he gives you whatever you want.

The other club is your country club. This is a place where during the day you can relax by putting on ugly pants and golfing with other executives, and at night you can hold social affairs where you give each other golf trophies and, if everybody is in a really funky

mood, dance the fox-trot. This is called "networking," and it is very valuable because in the business world, a golf trophy creates a lifelong bond between two people.

Of course most clubs have certain requirements regarding who they will allow to become a member. I don't mean to suggest here that they don't admit minority groups. Ha ha! Don't be ridiculous! After all, these are the eighties! Today's clubs are more than happy to admit any minority person whatsoever, provided this person is also a member of the U.S. Supreme Court. But even if you don't fall into this category, you should apply for membership. What's the worst they can do? Laugh at you? Blow their noses on your application? Foreclose your mortgage? Have you fired and see to it that you'll never again get a job, anywhere in the country, better than Urinal Cake Replacer? Don't be intimidated! Go before the Membership Committee and explain to them that you really, sincerely want to join, and that you will work hard to be the best darned member they have ever had, and that you have photographs of them entering and leaving rooms at the Out-O'-Town Motor Lodge and Motel in various interesting groups of up to six people and two mature female caribou. They'll welcome you with open arms. Don't let them kiss you on the lips.

COMPUTERS IN BUSINESS

You won't last long in the modern business world if you're not comfortable with computers. Computers are involved in every aspect of business from doing the payroll to running the elevators, and if they don't like you, they can make your elevator drop like a stone for 20 floors, then yank it up and drop it again until your skeletal system looks like oatmeal. So you damn well better read this chapter and get comfortable with them and become their friend.

GLOSSARY OF STANDARD
COMPUTER TERMS

BUG. A cute little humorous term used to explain why the computer had your Shipping Department send 150 highly sophisticated jet-fighter servo motors, worth over $26,000 apiece, to fishermen in the Ryuku Islands, who are using them as anchors.

DATA BASE. The information you lose when your memory crashes.

GRAPHICS. The ability to make pie charts and bar graphs, which are the universal business method for making abstract concepts, such as "three," comprehensible to morons like your boss (see page 44).

HARDWARE. Where the people in your company's software section will tell you the problem is.

SOFTWARE. Where the people in your company's hardware section will tell you the problem is.

SPREADSHEET. A kind of program that lets you sit at your desk and ask all kinds of neat "what if ?" questions and generate thousands of numbers instead of actually working.

USER. The word that computer professionals use when they mean "idiot."

HOW COMPUTERS WORK

The first computers were big clumsy machines that used vacuum tubes. By today's standards, they were extremely primitive. For example, they believed the sun was carried across the sky on the back of a giant turtle. But the modern computer is much more sophisticated, and far smaller, thanks to a device called the "micro-chip," which, although it is less than one-thousandth the size of a moderate zit, is capable of answering, in a matter of seconds, mathematical questions that would take millions of years for a human being to answer (even longer if he stopped for lunch).

How does the computer do this? Simple. It makes everything up. It knows full well you're not going to waste millions of years checking up on it. So you should never use computers for anything really impor-tant, such as balancing your personal checkbook. But they're fine for corporate use.

HOW TO USE COMPUTER-GENERATED PIE CHARTS AND BAR GRAPHS TO MAKE ABSTRACT CONCEPTS UNDERSTANDABLE TO MORONS LIKE YOUR BOSS

Let's say you have to write a Safety Report. The old-fashioned, pre-computer way to do this would be something like this:

```
In March, we had two people who
got sick because they forgot and
drank coffee from the vending ma-
chine.  Also, Ed Sparge set fire
to his desk again.  Ed has prom-
ised that from now on he will put
his cigar out before he dozes off.
```

But now, using the graphics capability on your computer, you can produce a visually arresting and easy-to-understand report like this:

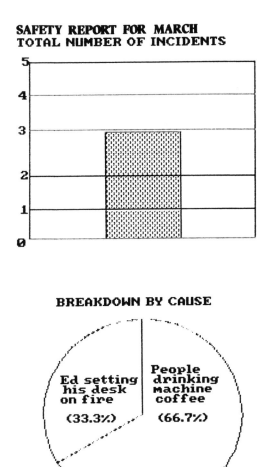

SAFETY REPORT FOR MARCH
TOTAL NUMBER OF INCIDENTS

BREAKDOWN BY CAUSE

Ed setting his desk on fire (33.3%)

People drinking machine coffee (66.7%)

Chapter Five

BUSINESS COMMUNICATIONS

No modern corporation can survive unless its employees communicate with each other. For example, let's say that Stan, who works in Building Administration, notices that the safety valve on the main steam boiler is broken. If he doesn't communicate this information to Arnie, over in Maintenance, you are going to have little bits and pieces of the corporation spread out over three, maybe four area codes. So communication is very, very important. It should not, however, be confused with memos.

WHAT MAKES
A GOOD BUSINESS MEMO

Ask any business school professor, and he'll tell you a good memo is clear, concise, and well organized. Now ask him what his annual salary is. It's probably less than most top executives spend in a month on shoe maintenance. What you can learn from this is that in your business correspondence, you should avoid being clear, concise, and well organized. Remember the Cardinal Rule of Business Writing (invented by Cardinal Anthony Rule, 1898–1957): "The primary function of almost all corporate correspondence is to enable the writer to avoid personal responsibility for the many major bonehead blunders that constantly occur when you have a bunch of people sitting around all day drinking coffee and wearing uncomfortable clothing."

There are big balloons of blame in every corporation, drifting gently from person to person. The purpose of your memos is to keep these balloons aloft, to bat them gently on their way. This requires soft, meaningless phrases, such as "less than optimal." If you write a direct memo, a memo that uses sharp words such as "bad" to make an actual point, you could burst a balloon and wind up with blame all over your cubicle.

STANDARD FORMAT
FOR THE BUSINESS MEMO

1. ALWAYS START BY SAYING THAT YOU HAVE RECEIVED SOMETHING, AND ARE ENCLOSING SOMETHING. These can be the same thing. For example, you could say: "I have received your memo of the 14th, and am enclosing it." Or they can be two different things: "I have received a letter from my mother, and am enclosing a photograph of the largest-known domestically grown sugar beet." As you can see, these things need have nothing to do with each other, or with the point of the memorandum. They are in your memo solely to honor an ancient business tradition, the

Tradition of Receiving and Enclosing, which would be a shame to lose.

2. STATE THAT SOMETHING HAS BEEN BROUGHT TO YOUR ATTENTION. Never state who brought it. It can be virtually any random fact whatsoever. For example, you might say: "It has been brought to my attention that on the 17th of February, Accounts Receivable notified Collections of a prior past-due balance of $5,878.23 in the account of Whelk, Stoat, and Mandible, Inc." Ideally, your reader will have nothing to do with any of this, but he will think he *should,* or else why would you go to all this trouble to tell him? Also, he will get the feeling you must be a fairly plugged-in individual, to have this kind of thing brought to your attention.

3. STATE THAT SOMETHING IS YOUR UNDERSTANDING. This statement should be firm, vaguely disapproving, and virtually impossible to understand. A good standard one is: "It is my understanding that this was to be ascertained in advance of any further action, pending review."

4. END WITH A STRONG CLOSING LINE. It should leave the reader with the definite feeling that he or she is expected to take some kind of action. For example: "Unless we receive a specific and detailed proposal from you by the 14th, we intend to go ahead and implant the device in Meredith."

The beauty of this basic memo format is that it can even be adapted for sending personalized communications to your subordinates ("It has come to my attention that your wife, Edna, is dead.").

In addition to writing memos, every month or so you should generate a lengthy report. This is strictly so you can cover yourself in case something bad happens.

STANDARD FORMAT TO USE FOR LENGTHY REPORTS TO INSURE THAT NOBODY READS THEM

I. SUBJECT: This is entirely up to you. If you follow the format, it will have virtually no impact on the rest of the report.

II. INTRODUCTION: This should be a fairly long paragraph in which you state that in this report, you intend to explore all the ramifications of the subject, no matter how many it turns out there are.

III. STATEMENT OF PURPOSE: This is a restatement of the Introduction, only the sentences are in reverse order.

IV. OBJECTIVES: This is a restatement of the Statement of Purpose, only you put the sentences in a little numbered list.

V. INTRODUCTION: By now, nobody will remember that you already had this.

VI. BACKGROUND: Start at the dawn of recorded time.

VII. DISCUSSION: This can be taken at random from the *Encyclopedia Britannica,* because the only people still reading at this point have been able to continue only by virtue of ingesting powerful stimulants and will remember nothing in the morning.

VIII. CONCLUSIONS: You should conclude that your findings tend to support the hypothesis that there are indeed a great many ramifications, all right.

IX. INTRODUCTION: Trust me. Nobody will notice.

X. RECOMMENDATIONS: Recommend that the course of action outlined in the Discussion section (Ha ha! Let them try to find it!) should be seriously considered.

HOW TO WRITE LETTERS

There are various types of letters you write in business, each requiring a different tone.

LETTERS TO CUSTOMERS
OR POTENTIAL CUSTOMERS

The basic idea here is to grovel around like a slug writhing in its own slime. For example:

```
Dear Mr. Herckle:

   It certainly was an extremely great
pleasure to fly out to your office in
Butte last week, and even though I didn't
have the enormous gigantic emotional
pleasure of meeting with you in person to
discuss our new product line, I was
certainly extremely pleased and grateful
for the opportunity to squat on your door-
step, and I certainly do want to apologize
for any inconvenience or bloodstains I
may have caused when your extremely impres-
sive dog, Bart, perforated my leg.


Your humble servant,

Byron B. Buffington

Byron B. Buffington
BBB:bbb
```

LETTERS TO COMPANIES
THAT OWE YOUR COMPANY MONEY

In these cases, you want to set a tone that is polite, yet firm:

Dear Mr. Hodpecker:

In going over our records, I note that you have not responded to our invoice of January 12, nor to our reminders of February 9, March 6, April 11, May 4, and June 6; and when we sent Miss Bleemer around to discuss this matter with you personally, you locked her in a conference room with a snake.

Mr. Hodpecker, we of course value your business, and we very much want to keep you as a customer. At least that is what I am trying to tell my two top collection assistants, the Bulemia brothers, Victor and Anthony. They, on the other hand, would prefer to keep you as a pet. They even bought one of those little cages that airlines transport animals in. To me, it looks just barely big enough for a cocker spaniel, but Victor and Anthony believe they can make you fit.

Expecting to hear from you very, very soon in regards to this matter, I remain

Sincerely yours,

Byron B. Buffington

Byron B. Buffington

BBB:ip

P.S. Victor has a complete set of auto-body tools.

LETTERS OF RECOMMENDATION

You have to be thoughtful here. See, *anybody* can get a nice letter of recommendation written about him ("Mr. Hitler always kept his uniform very clean"). So most prospective employers tend to discount what such letters say. This means that to make any kind of impression at all, you must exaggerate violently.

Let's say, for example, you're writing a letter of recommendation for a good employee named Bob, and you tell the simple truth:

"Bob Tucker is by far the best foreman we ever had. He never missed a day of work, got along well with his subordinates, and increased our productivity by 47 percent."

If a prospective employer saw such a ho-hum letter of recommendation, he would naturally assume that Bob was an arsonist child molester. You should spice up the letter with statements such as: "Working on his own time during lunch hour, Bob developed a cure for heart disease." Or: "On at least three separate occasions, Bob sacrificed his life so that others might live."

THE BASIC RULES
OF BUSINESS GRAMMAR

1. USE THE WORD "TRANSPIRE" A LOT.
Wrong: The dog barked.
Right: What transpired was, the dog barked.
Even better: A barking of the dog transpired.

2. *ALSO USE "PARAMETER."*
    Wrong: Employees should not throw paper towels into the toilet.
    Right: Employees should not throw paper towels into the parameters of the toilet.

3. *ALWAYS FOLLOW THE PHRASE "TED AND" WITH THE WORD "MYSELF."*
    Wrong: Ted and I think the pump broke.
    Right: Ted and myself think the pump broke.
    Even better: It is the opinion of Ted and myself that a breakage of the pump transpired.

4. *IF SOMETHING IS FOLLOWING SOMETHING ELSE, ALWAYS LET THE READER KNOW IN ADVANCE VIA THE WORDS: "THE FOLLOWING."*
    Wrong: We opened up the pump and found a dead bat.
    Right: We opened up the pump and found the following: a dead bat.

5. *ALWAYS STRESS THAT WHEN YOU TOLD SOMEBODY SOMETHING, YOU DID IT VERBALLY.*
    Wrong: I told him.
    Right: I told him verbally.

6. *NEVER SPLIT AN INFINITIVE.* An infinitive is a phrase that has a "to" at the beginning, such as "Today, I am going to start my diet." You should not split such a phrase with another word, as in "Today, I am definitely going to start my diet," because it makes you sound insecure about it. It sounds like you know darned well you'll be hitting the pecan fudge before sundown.

7. *NEVER END A SENTENCE WITH A PREPOSI-TION.* Prepositions are words like "with," "into," "on," "off," "exacerbate," etc. The reason you should never end a sentence with one is that you would be violating a rule of grammar.

> *Wrong:* Youse better be there with the ransom money, on account of we don't want to have to hack nobody's limbs off.
>
> *Right:* . . . on account of we don't want to have to hack off nobody's limbs.
>
> *Even better:* . . . on account of we don't want to have to hack off nobody's limbs with a chain saw.

8. *AVOID DANGLING PARTICIPLES.* A participle is the letters "ing" at the ends of words like "extenuating." You want to avoid having it "dangle" down and disrupt the sentence underneath:

There appear to be some extenuatin_g circumstances. Ted and myself feel that these ^{g} Hey! Get that participle out of here!!

COMMON GRAMMAR QUESTIONS

Q. When's it okay to say "between you and I"?

A. It is correct in the following instance: "Well, just between you and I, the cosmetic surgeon took enough cellulite out of her upper arms to raft down the Colorado River on."

Q. What is the purpose of the apostrophe?

A. The apostrophe is used mainly in hand-lettered signs to alert the reader that an "S" is coming up at the end of a word, as in: WE DO NOT EXCEPT PERSONAL CHECK'S or: NOT RESPONSIBLE FOR ANY ITEM'S. Another important grammar concept to bear in mind when creating hand-lettered signs is that you should put quotation marks around random words for decoration, as in "TRY" OUR HOT DOG'S or even TRY "OUR" HOT DOG'S.

Q. When do you say "who" and when do you say "whom"?

A. You say "who" when you want to find out something, like for example if a friend of yours comes up and says, "You will never guess which of your immediate family members just lost a key limb in a freak Skee-Ball accident," you would reply: "Who?" You say "whom" when you are in Great Britain or you are angry (as in: "And just *whom* do you think is going to clean up after these elk?").

Q. Like many writers, I often get confused about when to use the word "affect" and when to use "infect." Can you help me out?

A. Here is a simple pneumatic device for telling these two similar-sounding words (or "gramophones") apart: Just remember that "infect" begins with "in," which is also how "insect" begins, while "affect" begins with "af," which is an abbreviation for "Air Force."

Q. I have a question concerning the expression: "As far as Fred." I would like to know whether it is preferable to say: "As far as Fred, he always gets the hives from that spicy food"; or, "As far as Fred, that spicy food always gives him the hives."

A. They are both preferable.

Q. What do they mean on the TV weather forecast when they say we are going to have "thunder-shower activity"?

A. They mean we are not going to have an actual thundershower, per se, but we are going to have thundershower activity, which looks very similar to the untrained eye.

Q. I think my wife is having an affair.

A. I wouldn't doubt it.

MAKING SPEECHES AND ORAL PRESENTATIONS

Most people, no matter how competent they are, break into a cold sweat when they have to speak in public. This is perfectly natural, like being afraid to touch eels. But once you learn a few of the "tricks of the trade" used by professionals, you find it's surprisingly easy, and can even be fun! I'm talking here about eel-touching. Public speaking will always be awful. There are, however, some standard techniques you should be aware of:

1. ACT VERY NERVOUS. A lot of inexperienced speakers try to act cool and confident, which is a big mistake because if your audience thinks you're in control, they'll relax and fall asleep. So you want to keep them on their toes. Have a great big stain under each armpit. Speak in a barely audible monotone. From time to time, stop in mid-sentence and stare in horror at the water pitcher for a full 30 seconds. Try to create the impression in your audience that at any moment they may have to wrestle you to the conference table and force a half dozen Valiums down your throat. After a while, they'll start to feel really sorry for you. They'll help you finish your sentences. At the end, if you ask for questions, the room will be as silent as a tomb. If anybody even starts to ask a question, the others will kick him so hard he may never walk again.

2. *ALWAYS START WITH A JOKE.* Probably the most famous example of a good opening joke is the one Abraham Lincoln used to start the Gettysburg Address. "Four score and seven years ago," he said, and the crowd went nuts. "What the hell is a score?" they asked each other, tears of laughter streaming down their faces.

3. *USE QUOTATIONS FROM FAMOUS DEAD PEOPLE.* You can obtain these in bulk from *Bartlett's Familiar Quotations,* a book of quotations nobody is familiar with.

4. *USE A PIE CHART.* This is pretty much a federal requirement for making a business presentation. It has to have the words "market share."

5. *IF YOU HAVE TO SCRATCH SOMEPLACE LIKE YOUR CROTCH, DRAW THE AUDIENCE'S ATTENTION AWAY FROM YOURSELF VIA A CLEVER RUSE.* Like, you could suddenly point at the window and say, "Hey! What the heck is *that!!??*"

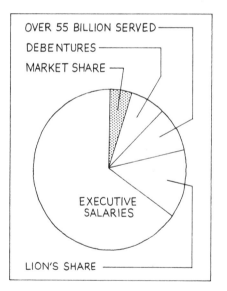

Now let's see how you'd put all these elements together. Suppose you've been called upon to make a presentation to top management from all over the country to explain how come a new product, Armpit Magic Deodorant Soap, is not selling well. Here's what you'd say:

"Good afternoon. A priest and a rabbi are playing golf. The priest hits an incredible shot, and . . .

(30-second pause)

"Staring at this water pitcher, I am reminded of the Bartlett's familiar quotation by the ancient dead Chinese painter, Ku K'ai-Chih, who said: 'Of all kinds of painting, figure painting is the most difficult; then comes landscape painting, and next dogs and horses.'

"But as this pie chart shows . . . *Hey!* What's that over there, away from my crotch!!??

"Ha ha! My mistake. But as this pie chart shows, our 'market share' for Armpit Magic Deodorant Soap is not going to improve in a day, or even two days. It's not going to improve until we figure out some way to make it stop causing the consumer's skin to develop oozing craters the size of Susan B. Anthony dollars. Thank you, and you've been a wonderful audience."

Chapter Six

GIVING GOOD LUNCH

When you're trying to get a prospective client to sign a big contract, it's a good idea to get him away from the formality of the office and into a relaxed dining environment that is more conducive to getting liquored up. But you must select the restaurant carefully: it could destroy the whole effect if his entrée were to arrive in a colorful box festooned with scenes from *Return of the Jedi*. No, you must select a classy restaurant, the kind with valet parking and dozens of apparently superfluous personnel lounging around in tuxedos. You can tell this kind of restaurant by its name.

EXAMPLES OF CLASSY RESTAURANT NAMES	EXAMPLES OF NON-CLASSY RESTAURANT NAMES
Eduardo's	Booger's
La Pleuve en Voiture	The Chew 'n' Swallow
Ye Reallie Olde Countrie Manour Downes Inne	Commander Taco

When you arrive at the restaurant, turn your car over to the youthful narcotics offender in charge of valet parking and promise him a large tip if he doesn't drive it over any preschool children. Now go inside, where you'll be approached by the *maître d'hôtel* (literally, "man who run de hotel"). He will ask: "May I help you?" They're always making this kind of snotty remark.

"NAME-THE-WAITER QUIZ"

WHICH WAITER IS "ERMA MAY"?
WHICH IS "SPUDS"? WHICH IS "THAD"?

This is where you get to show your prospective client that you have a great deal of *savoir faire* ("five-dollar bills"). Hand the *maître d'* some money. Make sure the prospective client sees this; you might have to snatch it back and hand it over again several times, just to be on the safe side. Then say: "A table for two, my good man." Wink at the prospective client when you say this, so he will realize that you are "slipping" the *maître d'* "a little something" to "grease his palm."

At this point, the *maître d'* may say something like: "But sir, it's 11 A.M. and we don't open for lunch until noon." He is indicating here that he would like several more five-dollar bills. This kind of thing goes on all the time in classy restaurants. Give your prospective client a knowing elbow in his rib cage, then stuff several additional bills into the *maître d's* breast pocket and say: "Oh, I'm sure you can find a table for *us.*" Don't quit until he gives you one.

When you are seated, your waiter will arrive with the menus and make the following three statements, all of which are required under the Federal Waitperson Control Act:

1. His name is Thad.

2. It will be His Pleasure to serve you.

3. Would either of you care for a cocktail.

(By the way, this is an ideal opportunity for you to make a witty remark, such as: "What, exactly, is involved in 'caring for' a cocktail? Do they need special food?" This will cause Thad to roar with approving laughter. Tip him $5.)

Now as regards cocktails: the days of the "three-martini lunch" are long gone. In today's high-pressure, brutally competitive business environment, you want a minimum of four martinis, and you want them before the salad comes. Order the same for your prospective client. If he balks, stress that you're paying for them, but that he should not feel obligated because of this.

Now it's time to examine the menu. This requires a great deal of concentration, because you no longer see the simple American menus you knew as a child, which said:

MEAT . . . . $ 5.95
"Fish" or Chicken . . . . . . $ 4.95
Spageti . . . . $ 3.95

In those days, you'd mull over the menu for a while, then you'd say, "I'll have the chicken or fish," and the waiter would say, "Excellent choice," and that would be that.

But the modern restaurant menu is much, much more complex, consisting of two or three dozen totally unintelligible items like this:

Les Arbitrages en Console

(Broached Strumpets in Harrow Sauce)
$26.95

Don't panic. Examine your menu carefully, trying not to let on to the prospective client that the only word on it you understand is "Menu" and wait for Thad to return with your drinks. Here's what he'll say:

"Today we are out of everything on the menu, but we do have some very nice specials. For our appetizer, we have an excellent Tête de Chou au Sucre Flambé, which is a head of cabbage covered with sugar and set on fire; we also have a very nice Poisson Sacre Bleu, which is a Norwegian fluke that has been minced into tiny little pieces, then defiled in lemon sauce and stirred until dawn with attractive utensils; we have a superb Coquille St. Jacques au Lanterne, which is a pumpkin stuffed with live writhing scallops; we have a traditional Merde aux Tuilles, which is of course a beef which has been chipped, served with a white sauce on bread which has been toasted; we have a very popular Papier du Oiseau dans la Cage, which is. . . ."

And so on. Thad will keep this up for maybe ten minutes, after which you should tip him $5 and tell him, "I'll have the chicken, and my prospective client here will have whichever menu selection is the most expensive." Stress to the prospective client that this will cost him nothing, as you are paying for it. In fact, it would be a good idea to reassure him on this point several more times during the meal, with such phrases as, "It's on me" and "I'm paying for your food."

After you've ordered from Thad, the wine steward will come around and give you the wine list. The correct wine to select, of course, depends on the kind of entrée you order, as shown in this handy chart:

ENTRÉE	CORRECT WINE
Meat	The appropriate wine here would cost at least $45 a bottle
Fish	With fish you want a bottle of wine costing a minimum of $45
Poultry	You should spend $45 or more for this bottle of wine

If you have trouble remembering all this information, don't worry. Your wine steward will be more than happy to help you make your wine selection:

YOU: How is this wine that costs $12 a bottle?
WINE STEWARD: We use that primarily as a disinfectant.
YOU: I see. Then we'll have something much more expensive.
WINE STEWARD: Excellent choice.

When the steward brings you the wine, he'll show you the label; you should examine it closely for spelling and punctuation errors (see pages 52 to 54, The Basic Rules of Business Grammar). He will then pour a little into your glass. Taste it, and if necessary, have him add a couple of packets of Sweet 'n Low.

At the end of the meal, be sure to make a lighthearted remark about the size of the check, such as: "My God! This check is so large that unless I sign a big contract with a prospective client soon, I'll never be able to afford the operation that will restore the precious gift of sight to my three-year-old daughter, Little Meg, ha ha!" This is your humorous signal to the prospective client that it's time to "talk turkey."

"Ed," you should say (if his name is Ed), "this meal has been a tremendously tax-deductible pleasure for me personally, but let's get down to brass tacks. Looking at this thing objectively, I think it would be a big mistake for you not to sign this contract, especially if you want a ride home." Now give him some time to think it over. Maybe even sprint for the door a couple of times, as if you're running off without him. Better yet, offer to stay there until night falls and buy him dinner. He'll come around.

ENTERTAINING AT HOME

The first question, of course, is: whose home? I think we can rule out *your* home, since, let's be honest here, nobody in your home has ever made a really sincere effort to clean the toilets, and it's far too late to start now. A much better bet would be the client's home. Call him up and explore this possibility with him:

YOU: Ed, Denise and I are wondering if you and Trudy would be free to have dinner with us at your home Friday night.
CLIENT: What?
YOU: How are your toilets?
CLIENT: What?
YOU: Cleaner than ours, I bet!
CLIENT: You want to have dinner at *our home?*
YOU: Sounds good to me! Eight o'clock Friday it is!

You should arrive a bit early, say fiveish, to rummage around and make sure there's plenty of pre-dinner liquor on hand. When Ed and Trudy come out of their bedroom, your first responsibility is to make them feel at ease. I suggest you get a copy of the *Complete Book of Games and Stunts* published in MCMLVI by Bonanza Books and authored by Darwin A. Hindman, Ph.D., professor of physical education at the University of Missouri. This is an actual book, available at garage sales everywhere. I especially recommend the "Funnel Trick" described in chapter 4 ("Snares"), wherein you have the victim lean his head back and place a penny on his forehead, then you tell him that the object of the trick is to tilt his head forward so the penny drops into a funnel stuck into his belt.

However—get this—while he's got his head tilted back, you pour a pitcher of water into the funnel and get his pants soaking wet! Ha ha! Be sure to follow this with a lighthearted remark ("You look like a cretin, Ed!") and offer everybody a swig from the liquor bottle.

Now that everybody is loosened up, drop a hint ("God I'm hungry! Any food around here?") that it's time to move to the dinner table. Your goal at dinner, of course, is to somehow cause the prospective client to get a wad of food caught in his throat and start choking, so you can leap up and dislodge the food by means of the "Heimlich maneuver," thus causing the client to be indebted to you for the rest of his life. This means you have to startle him just as the food is going down his throat. The most reliable way to do this is to have a pistol hidden under the table, and fire it off just as he starts to swallow. You should of course use blanks, as bullets would be irresponsible.

THE HEIMLICH MANEUVER

Stand behind the victim and put your arms around him. Make a fist with one hand and grab it with the other, then yank your hands sharply into the victim's abdomen, thus causing the wad of food to be expelled.

HEIMLICH-MANEUVER HOCKEY

Have two opposing players, each holding a victim, stand about six feet apart. Each player tries to expel his victim's food wad into the other victim's mouth.

WHAT TO DO IF A CLIENT OR BUSINESS ASSOCIATE DIES

INAPPROPRIATE

APPROPRIATE

Send a flower arrangement that does *not* have little pink or blue rattles in it. Wear black clothes to the funeral. If you don't have black clothes, wear the darkest clothes you have. Tiptoe up to the next of kin during the service and explain this fact to them. "These are the darkest clothes I have," you should say, taking care to whisper. Next you should tell them how awful you feel. "God!" you should say. "I feel terrible! Just horrible!"

Next you should go up and examine the deceased, then go back and inform the next of kin how good he looks. "Ed looks great!" you should say. "You can hardly even tell he's dead!" Unless Ed is in an urn.

Chapter Seven

HOW TO DRESS EXACTLY LIKE EVERYBODY ELSE

Take a moment to consider the way the world's truly successful people dress. They dress like mental patients. Your prime example is Prince Charles. Here is one of the world's top princes, if not *the* top prince, yet he is constantly showing up in public wearing ludicrous Sergeant Pepper-style outfits featuring hats with enormous feathers. Or you'll see a picture of him visiting some remote fungal nation and cheerfully wearing ritual native vegetation around his neck. There are plenty of other examples of highly successful people who dress absurdly: Mick Jagger, the Joint Chiefs of Staff, and Ronald McDonald, to name just three. And of course you can't find a really successful world religious leader who doesn't wear a comical outfit.

So what does this tell you about how you should dress if you want to succeed in American business? Nothing. Because the way we dress in American business is not based on the way the world's truly successful people dress. It is based on the way John T. Molloy says we should dress. Molloy is the author of the best-selling books *Dress for Success, The Woman's Dress for Success Book, Live for Success,* and *Success in the Afterlife.* He openly admits to practicing a science called "wardrobe engineering." He has done extensive wardrobe research, wherein he tested the reactions of thousands of groups of people to the way different individuals were dressed. What he found, after years and years of study, was that the groups always liked it best when the individuals were naked. So he pretty much gave up the research and decided instead to author best-selling books containing incredibly detailed instructions on how to dress and what accessories to carry, instructions that were so slavishly followed by the business community that they briefly resulted in a worldwide shortage of Cross pens.

The bottom line is, if you truly want to present a business wardrobe image that makes the all-important fashion statement: "I look exactly like everybody else in American business," you damn well better dress the way John T. Molloy says you should. So listen up.

HOW MEN SHOULD DRESS

Basically, the American businessman should dress as though he recently lost his entire family in a tragic boat explosion. We are talking about a subdued look here. This doesn't mean that you have no choice in what you wear. Au contraire.* For example, you may wear two completely different colors of woolen suit: you may wear a dark gray woolen suit, or, if you want to get really crazy, you may wear a dark blue woolen suit.

You may *not* wear a brown, green, or (God forbid) plaid polyester suit, because everybody will think you just tromped into town from rural Louisiana to attend the Live Bait Show. Men wearing these colors are very likely to be passed over for promotion, as is shown by this actual simulation of a scene that for all we know probably occurs every day in major corporations:

(We are in the office of the president, who is meeting with a vice-president to decide whom to promote to director of the Research Department.)

*"Ah, that country air."

VICE-PRESIDENT: Well, there's Barkley, of course. He's the one who came up with the way to turn discarded wads of Kleenex into gold using only common household ingredients.

PRESIDENT: What color suit does he wear?

VICE-PRESIDENT: Brown.

PRESIDENT: Well forget *him*.

SHIRTS

Your shirt should be white, and it should not have the name "Earl" embroidered anywhere on it.

TIES

The purpose of your tie is to suggest that you attended an Ivy League university, so the key is to select the right pattern, as shown here.

HOW TO TIE A TIE

Face southwest, with the long end of the tie hanging down casually from your right hand (the audience's left hand). Now bring the short end of the tie around the back of your neck and let it hang down your front, so that it just touches the scar you got ironing shirts naked. Now take the "wide" (or "long") end of the tie and pass it three times around the "short" (or "long") end, then up through the loop. (What do you mean, "What loop?" Check again!) Now pull everything snug, unless you have forgotten to put on a shirt, in which case you had best remove the tie, by force if necessary.

SHOES

These are a "must" in most business situations. If you use "Odor Eaters," they should be beige or navy blue.

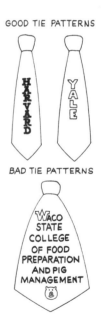

GOOD TIE PATTERNS

HARVARD YALE

BAD TIE PATTERNS

WACO STATE COLLEGE OF FOOD PREPARATION AND PIG MANAGEMENT

POWER UNDERWEAR PATTERNS

STRONG   VERY STRONG

LEE IACOCCA'S PERSONAL
UNDERWEAR PATTERN

FIGURE I   FIGURE 2

UNDERWEAR

No area of the male business wardrobe is as important as his underwear. Next time you're in a room with a group of successful executives, take a few moments to examine their underwear, and you'll find they're all wearing underwear with proven "power patterns" that have been shown in scientific tests to create a feeling of awe and respect in others.

In situations where you really need to enhance your power image, you should wear your power underwear *outside* your pants (figure 1). In extreme situations, such as you are arguing before the U.S. Supreme Court, you will want to wear them in an even more visible location, such as on your head (figure 2).

HOW WOMEN SHOULD DRESS

In deciding how to dress for business, women must understand certain basic facts, the foremost being that all men are scum. If a woman, no matter how competent, gives off the slightest hint that she has any feelings that could be remotely construed as sexual, this is all that the men in her corporation will ever think about. That's not just my opinion: it is a scientific finding based on years of extensively hanging around with guys and talking.

What does this mean, in terms of your business wardrobe? It means you want to adopt a fashion look that has become the standard for the woman on the corporate fast track, a look that can best be described as: Modified Nun. As you can see from the illustration on page 71, all we've really done to the basic nun look is remove the headpiece. This conveys to the men in your corporation that you are not a sex object, but an authority figure who must be taken seriously because at any moment you might strike them on the hands with a ruler.

HOSIERY

This is mandatory. I realize you women hate to be constantly shelling out money for a product manufactured by an industry that pays its scientists huge bonuses if they can develop fibers even weaker than the ones they currently use. I realize you go around saying: "If we can land a man on the moon, why can't we develop pantyhose that will last longer than a small vanilla cone on a hot day?" Well I'm sorry, but rules are rules. Also, we haven't landed a man on the moon for a very long time now, and we probably never will again unless something urgent comes up, such as the Defense Department suspects there are Cuban troops up there.

MAKEUP

A good rule of thumb is: if you can stick a pin more than a quarter inch into your face and still not feel anything, you're wearing too much makeup for the business environment. Or else you have a medical problem.

SHOES

The ideal shoe for the career woman is the basic pump with a "sensible" heel, by which I mean a heel that will just fit through the holes in a standard street grate.

NUN   BUSINESSWOMAN

Chapter Eight

SALES

What makes a good salesperson? In an effort to answer that question, I asked my research associates to interview the top 100 salespeople, based on dollar volume, in the nation. Naturally, my associates refused to do this. I wouldn't have done it either. Life is hard enough without voluntarily subjecting yourself to top salespeople.

What we can learn from this research is that if you want to become a top salesperson, you must develop drive, determination, and persistence such that people do not wish to be within thousands of yards of you. How can you become this kind of person? By BELIEVING IN YOURSELF. You must develop a FAITH IN YOUR OWN ABILITIES so strong that YOU DON'T FEEL THE LEAST BIT EMBARRASSED ABOUT ACTING LIKE A SCUZZBAG. You don't get this kind of confidence from other people; it has to COME FROM WITHIN, from having a comprehensive, meaningful, and deep-rooted PHILOSOPHY OF LIFE based on TIMELESS TRUTHS, which you get from MOTIVATIONAL BOOKS THAT ARE ALSO AVAILABLE ON CASSETTE TAPES COSTING $49.95 PER SET.

Without question, the number-one cassette thinker in the world today is Dr. Lance M. Canker, the man whose famous motivational tape "Dare to Be a Jerk" is believed to be the single biggest factor in the historic decision by Coca-Cola executives to change the

Coke formula so it tasted more like children's cough syrup. Dr. Canker, who has had a lifelong interest in motivational thinking ever since 1963, when he had his name legally changed from "Lance Canker" to "Dr. Lance Canker," has written a number of self-help books, including the hugely popular *God, Are You Fat!* But his greatest contribution to the business world is his classic how-to-sell book *Buy This Book or You'll Starve to Death,* which is filled with true-life inspirational anecdotes such as these:

> Not long ago, I gave a dinner party attended by every major Western head of state and a young man I'll call "Jon." Although he is attractive, intelligent, and talented, "Jon" was a very unhappy person, and he was thinking of killing himself. So I took him aside. " 'Jon,' " I said. "Lighten up." Today, he is the president of General Motors.

> Not long after that, I got a telephone call from a major world religious leader, whom I'll call "the Pope." Although he is attractive, intelligent, and talented, he was feeling tremendous anxiety about the fate of mankind. "Hey," I advised him. "Forget it." And today he, too, is the president of General Motors.

Using proven techniques such as these, Dr. Canker shows in *Buy This Book or You'll Starve to Death* how any member of the vertebrate family can develop powerful selling skills. In this chapter, we shall draw extensively on the information contained in Dr. Canker's book, and by the time Dr. Canker finds out about this, we shall be long gone.

RULE #1: MAINTAIN EYE CONTACT WITH THE PROSPECT AT ALL TIMES NO MATTER WHAT

This is extremely important. If the prospect tries to glance out the window, you must race over and stand in front of the window. If you hand him a document and he attempts to read it, you must place your head between the document and his eyes. If he goes to the bathroom, you must maintain eye contact as best you can from the adjacent stall or urinal. This may make you uncomfortable, especially if you and the prospect happen to belong to differing sexes, but if you don't do it, you'll give the impression that you're not being totally honest and you don't truly believe in your product, whatever the hell it is.

COMMON QUESTION #1: What if the prospect is blind?

ANSWER: Then you must maintain *knee* contact.

COMMON QUESTION #2: Well, what if the prospect is blind *and* has a wooden leg?

ANSWER: Well, then you would . . .

COMMON QUESTION #3: Also he's in a coma.

ANSWER: Hey! *These* aren't common questions!

RULE #2: CALL THE PROSPECT BY HIS FIRST NAME A LOT, BECAUSE HE MIGHT FORGET YOU'RE TALKING TO HIM

WRONG: "Bob, have you ever given any thought as to who would provide for the financial security of your wife and children if, God forbid, you were to be killed by falling cement?"

RIGHT: "Bob, have you, Bob, ever given any thought as to who would provide for the financial security of your, Bob's, wife and children if you, Bob, were to be killed by falling cement, Bob? Huh? Bob?"

RULE #3: LEARN TO READ THE PROSPECT'S "BODY LANGUAGE"

If you've ever driven on the Long Island Expressway, you know that people often communicate to each other "nonverbally," which means rather than using words, they use fingers, arm gestures, facial expressions, teeth, knives, etc. As a smart salesperson, you must learn to "read" the prospect's body language so you can take appropriate action, such as shielding your face.

RULE #4: GET THE PROSPECT INTO A "YES" FRAME OF MIND

The way you do this is by making a series of statements that the prospect cannot help but agree with. Let's listen in to this actual transcript of a top salesperson applying this technique:

SALESPERSON: Hi, Bob! Great to see you! Bob, I want to thank you for giving me an appointment. Bob.
PROSPECT: I didn't give you an appointment. You got in here by sedating my receptionist with chloroform.
SALESPERSON: Ha ha! Bob, Bob, Bob. I can't put anything over on you, can I? But seriously, Bob, wouldn't you agree that Adolf Hitler was a bad person?
PROSPECT: Well, yes, but I . . .
SALESPERSON: And don't you feel, Bob, that child abuse is wrong?
PROSPECT: Of course. Sure. I mean . . .

BODY LANGUAGE POSITIONS

PROSPECT IS SAD

PROSPECT HAS AN AXE

PROSPECT IS SURROUNDED BY GIANT BIRDS, SOME OF WHICH HAVE TEETH

PROSPECT HAS JUMPED OUT THE WINDOW

SALESPERSON (swinging a watch back and forth rhythmically on a chain):   And would it not be correct to state, Bob, that in a right triangle, the square of the hypotenuse equals the sum of the squares of the other two sides?

PROSPECT (getting drowsy):   Whatever you say.

At this point, if you have the prospect in a positive enough mood, you may be able to simply take his wallet. Otherwise you should go on to Rule #5.

RULE #5: ASK FOR THE SALE

Be direct. Something like: "Bob, how about a large order for whatever it is I'm selling?"

Usually the prospect will balk, offering any one of a number of standard excuses, such as:

- "I want to think about it."
- "I want to talk to my husband or wife about it, depending on what sex I am."
- "Get out of my sight before I kill you and feed your pancreas to rats."

This is normal sales resistance, and you must not let it faze you. Go back and repeat your presentation, very slowly, starting with "Hi, Bob! Great to see you, Bob!" Try to get the prospect to voice specific objections so you can overcome them ("Are you saying, Bob, that you think Adolf Hitler was *not* a bad person?"). Do this as many times as necessary, until Bob comes around. Remind him that if he doesn't, you may have to take him to Lunch (see chapter 6).

Chapter Nine

HOW TO GO INTO BUSINESS FOR YOURSELF

The story of America is the story of individuals—the Henry Fords, the John DeLoreans, the Speedy Alka-Seltzers, the Don Corleones—who started out alone, with little more than a dream and a willingness to work toward it, and ended up running large organizations and eventually either dying or getting indicted. Chances are that you, too, have an idea for a business percolating inside you, an idea you're sure would work, if only you gave it a chance.

Well, why not? What, really, are you getting from your company job, aside from a steady paycheck, regular raises, job security, extensive medical benefits, and a comfortable pension? Hey, if *that's* all they think you're worth, well, in the words of the popular country-and-western song: "Take This Job and Let Me Hold onto It while I Start My Own Little Business on the Side."

Step one is to find out what legal requirements you have to meet to register yourself as a small business. In most states, this is a two-part process:

1. You have several boxes of cheap business cards printed up with the wrong phone number.

2. You go around and pin your card onto those bulletin boards you see in supermarkets and low-rent restaurants, the ones with 10,000 other business cards that look like the one shown here.

Stuart A. Caliper
Accounting and Light Masonry
"Since April 3, 1986, at about 4:30"

TAX IMPLICATIONS OF GOING INTO BUSINESS FOR YOURSELF

The tax implications are that you can deduct every nickel you ever spend for the rest of your life, including on bowling accessories (see chapter 10, How Finance Works).

THREE SUREFIRE BUSINESS CONCEPTS

Over the years, I have thought up several business concepts that are so obviously brilliant that the only way they could conceivably fail would be if somebody actually tried them. This is where you fit in. Pick any one of the concepts below and invest your life savings in it. If you are not completely satisfied that the concept was not all that I said it was, if not more, then you do not owe me a cent. Sound too good to be true? Well just wait until you see these concepts!

CONCEPT #1: THE ELECTRIC APPLIANCE SUICIDE MODULE

This concept is based on the known fact that it is impossible to get electronic devices repaired. Let's say you have purchased a videocassette recorder, and after a while, because of normal wear and tear such as your nephew Dwight stuck a Polish sausage into the slot and pushed the fast forward button, it stops working.

Now you have two options. One is to take it back to the store where you got it, which will send it back to the "Factory Service Center." Here's what I have to say about this option: Hahahahahahaha. Because the "Factory Service Center" is in fact a giant warehouse containing hundreds of thousands of broken electronic devices, including 1952 Philco television sets. The staff consists of two elderly men, named Roscoe and Lester, who will poke around inside your VCR with cheap cigars and go, "Lookit all them *wires* in there!"

Your other choice is to take it to a local "repair shop," which will consist of a sullen person standing behind a counter with an insulting sign like the one shown here.

Obviously, neither of these is an acceptable option. So the logical thing to do, when an electronic device breaks, is to just throw it away and get another one, right? But you can't bring yourself to do this. You paid $700 for it, and you'd feel guilty. So you put yourself in the hands of incompetents and thieves.

This is where the Electric Appliance Suicide Module would come in. It would be a device costing $29.95 and consisting of a small, powerful explosive charge, coupled to a tiny electronic "brain," which the consumer would implant inside his VCR or television set via a simple procedure requiring only a screwdriver and three beers. They way the Suicide Module would work is, as soon as the brain sensed that the appliance was no longer working properly, it would set off the charge. For safety reasons, this would occur in the middle of the night, when the consumers were asleep. The consumer would be awakened by a large BLAM!! in his living room, and he'd come rushing out, and there, where his television set used to be, he'd see a grayish cloud of vaporized plastic, and he'd say: "Huh! Time to get a new TV!" Besides eliminating a lot of consumer guilt, the Suicide Module would probably provide a very powerful incentive for appliances to perform well. They would work their little diodes to the bone, for fear that otherwise the Suicide Module might think they were starting to come down with something.

CONCEPT #2: THE "MISTER MEDIOCRE" FAST-FOOD RESTAURANT FRANCHISE

I have studied American eating preferences for years, and believe me, this is what people want. They don't want to go into an unfamiliar restaurant, because they don't know whether the food will be very bad, or very good, or what. They want to go into a restaurant that advertises on national television, where they *know* the food will be mediocre. This is the heart of the Mister Mediocre concept.

The basic menu item, in fact the only menu item, would be a food unit called the "patty," consisting of—this would be guaranteed in writing—"100 percent animal matter of some kind." All patties would be heated up and then cooled back down in electronic devices immediately before serving. The Breakfast Patty would be a patty on a bun with lettuce, tomato, onion, egg, Ba-Ko-Bits, Cheez Whiz, a Special Sauce made by pouring ketchup out of a bottle, and a little slip of paper stating: "Inspected by Number 12." The Lunch or Dinner Patty would be any Breakfast Patties that didn't get sold in the morning. The Seafood Lover's Patty would be any patties that were starting to emit a serious aroma. Patties that were too rank even to be Seafood Lover's Patties would be compressed into wads and sold as "Nuggets." Any nuggets that had not been sold as of the end of the month would be used to make bricks for new Mister Mediocre restaurants.

CONCEPT #3: THE "BINGO THE LEECH" LICENSED CHARACTER

If you have young children, you know how they tend to develop powerful attachments, similar to cocaine addiction only more expensive, to the toy industry's many lovable and imaginative licensed characters such as (for girls) Rainbow Brite, Strawberry Shortcake, Wee Whiny Winkie, The Dweebs, and The Simper Sisters; and (for boys) He-Man, The Limb Whackers, The Eye Eaters, Sergeant Bicep, and Testosterone Bob's Hurt Patrol. Once a child gets one of these characters, he or she suddenly just *has* to have all the others in the set, plus the accessories, all of which are—believe me when I tell you this—Sold Separately.

BINGO THE LEECH

So I have come up with this concept for a truly irresistible licensed character named Bingo the Leech. Bingo would be an adorable little stuffed leech with big loving eyes and a tube of industrial quick-drying epoxy concealed in his lips. When a child picked up Bingo at the store and squeezed him, Bingo would emit some epoxy and become permanently bonded to the child's skin, and the parent would have to buy him so as to avoid shoplifting charges. Then the parent would have to buy all the other members of the Bingo family, because only by combining their lip secretions would you obtain the antidote chemical required to get Bingo off the child before it was time to go to college.

Chapter Ten

HOW FINANCE WORKS

WHO SHOULD READ THIS CHAPTER

At some point in your rise to the top, you may find yourself appointed to a job where you have to know something about finances, such as as Controller or Treasurer or Chairman of the Federal Reserve Board. If this happens, you should read this chapter. But I warn you: this stuff is deadly dull, as is illustrated by accountants. You never hear people say: "Let's have some *fun* tonight! Let's go find some *accountants!*" So unless you have no choice, you should skip this chapter. I myself am going to require powerful illegal stimulants to write it.

HOW CORPORATE FINANCES WORK

You look at a big corporation, with giant expensive buildings filled with tasteful carpets and big desks and rental plants and well-paid employees making Xerox-brand copies of the crossword puzzle, and you wonder, "How on earth do they make any money?"

The answer is, they don't. They lose money hand over fist. Read the business section of any newspaper, and just about every day you'll see a story like the one reproduced at left.

The reason these executives can afford to be so cavalier is that they know they can always get more money—any amount, any time—by means of a process so simple you are going to laugh when I tell you about

DETROIT—The General Motors Corporation reported today that it lost $64.6 million in the first fiscal quarter. "We have no idea what happened to the money," said top GM officials, in unison. "One moment it was lying on the dresser, and the next moment it was gone! We could just kick ourselves! Ha ha!"

it, unless you have already fallen asleep at this point. All they have to do is print up some "stock." A stock is basically a piece of high-quality paper, similar to what certificates of appreciation from bowling leagues are printed on, except it has a nice border and a statement such as the following printed on it in an attractive and historic type style:

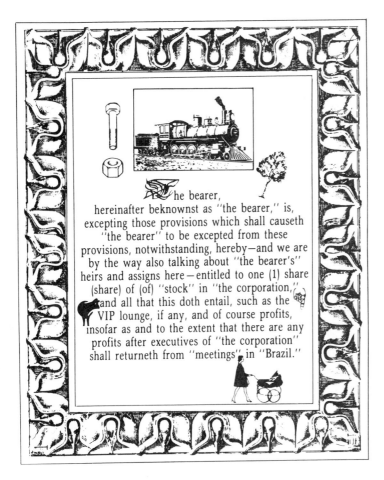

Now you're thinking: "Yes, but who would be so stupid as to exchange money for this piece of paper?" Well, I realize it makes very little sense to a person of normal intelligence, but it turns out there is a major financial institution devoted to this very purpose.

THE STOCK MARKET

The Stock Market is what they are talking about on television when they tell you the "Dow Jones Industrial Average" is "up" in "active trading." Sometimes they show you a picture of it: you see a lot of men with bad armpit stains yelling and waving their arms. These men are ordering lunch. The actual trading of stocks is done by computers:

```
FIRST COMPUTER: HOW MUCH YOU WANT
FOR THOSE 20 SHARES OF STOCK

SECOND COMPUTER: THESE ARE VERY
NICE SHARES AND BECAUSE WE ARE
FRIENDS I MAKE FOR YOU A SPECIAL
DEAL $600

FIRST COMPUTER: YOU CALL ME A
FRIEND AND HERE YOU ARE STAB-
BING ME IN THE BACK THESE SHARES
I WOULD NOT FEED TO A GOAT $400
IS THE BEST I CAN DO

SECOND COMPUTER: $550 IS THE
LOWEST I CAN GO MAY GOD STRIKE
ME DEAD IF I AM LYING
```

Of course all this takes less than a billionth of a second. At the end of the day, the computers divide the total prices of all stocks sold by the number of stocks, then they take the numbers of the horses that won the first three races, and. . . . No, wait a minute. That's the "Trifecta" I'm thinking of. Well, somehow, they figure out the Dow Jones Industrial Average, and they tell the television news people about it.

COMMON FINANCIAL QUESTIONS

Q. What makes one corporation's stock more valuable than another one?
A. The most important factor is what kind of hors d'oeuvre the corporation serves at its Annual Stockholders Meeting, which is when all the stockholders get invited to a hotel ballroom to hear highly paid executives attempt to explain how come the corporation is making less of a profit than it would if it had just sold all of its factories and machines and put the money in Christmas Clubs. If the corporation serves a cheap hors d'oeuvre, such as crackers and cheese, its stock will drop; if it switches over to, say, shrimp, the stock will rise. Of course the people on Wall Street don't want to admit this, which is why they're always making up preposterous explanations as to why stock prices rise and fall, such as "tension in the Middle East," when of course there is *always* tension in the Middle East. When we finally have a nuclear war and there is no life left on Earth except cockroaches, the cockroaches in the Middle East will be tense.

Q. Who is "Dow Jones"?
A. A dead person.

Q. What is the "options" market?
A. This is a special market for people who are too stupid even to buy stocks. The way it works is, let's

say a farmer or somebody realizes he has 500 pork bellies. Now I think we can all agree that no sane person would want to have even *one* pork belly, let alone 500 of them, so what this farmer does is look around for the stupidest person he can find, and he sells him a pork-belly "future," which means that the stupid person gives the farmer some money and agrees to take delivery of the pork bellies at a later date. I know you think I'm making this up, but believe me, people actually do this.

When the stupid person realizes what he has done, he of course tries to find an even stupider person to buy the "future," and this person sells it to an even stupider person, and so on until the big day arrives and a person with no discernible brain whatsoever has 500 pork bellies dumped on his lawn and is immediately arrested by the Board of Health.

AFTERWORD

And so, here you are. Just a dozen or so chapters ago, you were a recent graduate or some other kind of low-life scum, and now, thanks to this book, look what you have become! A highly paid corporate executive! Or a convicted felon!

I do not ask for your gratitude. I seek no reward. No, for me it is enough simply to know that I have, in some small way, helped to make you the kind of executive who can provide much-needed leadership as the corporation of today faces the challenges of tomorrow; the kind of executive who will not be afraid to meet these challenges head-on by means of innovative and far-reaching new management techniques such as bringing me in as a consultant for $2,000 per day plus lunch money. I'll be calling you real soon.